JEFFERSON AND MADISON

JEFFERSON

AND

MADISON

The Great Collaboration

BY

Adrienne Koch

KONECKY&KONECKY

Konecky & Konecky
72 Ayers Point Road
Old Saybrook, CT 06475

ISBN: 1-56852-501-X

Manufactured in the United States of America

To

ELSA AND McNEIL LOWRY

PREFACE

Long study of the philosophy of Thomas Jefferson convinced me of the need for further research into the development of Jefferson's thought. And this became impossible without a systematic study of the friendship of Jefferson and Madison in working out a comprehensive ideology of democracy. Here were two men who had been joined in an intimate and congenial partnership for a period of almost fifty years. Their philosophic principles and political pursuits could not be isolated from the larger setting of their friendly collaboration and it was thus that *Jefferson and Madison* developed.

A study, then, in the history of ideas, the book explores more fully than before the political theory that Jefferson and Madison jointly professed, and indicates their characteristic differences as well as their basic agreement about political values. Their massive writings have often been consulted separately to throw light on one or the other man. Now the correspondence has been studied for the interplay of ideas between the two greatest philosopher statesmen of the American Enlightenment. The spotlight is on ideas and the interrelations of two minds. The inescapable conclusion of this investigation is that the political philosophy known simply as "Jeffersonian" is actually an amalgam of ideas, which owes very much to James Madison.

Jefferson and Madison must inevitably cut across neat

academic boundaries in its effort to illuminate the philosophy of democracy in a significant historical context. It in no way substitutes for conscientious and full-length biographies of Jefferson and Madison, nor they for it. The present generation will be given two rounded and detailed biographies, one of Jefferson by Dumas Malone and one of Madison by Irving Brant. But their work is clearly different from a study of the unique relationship of Jefferson and Madison in formulating the principles of democracy and in attempting to realize their ideals.

The material for this interpretation of Jefferson and Madison comes largely from research in the primary sources. The great historical undertaking now in progress at Princeton, the editing of *The Papers of Thomas Jefferson*, will in time make it obvious that close investigation of a vast body of manuscripts is essential for any genuine study of the philosophy and career of Jefferson, not in the interest of a cult of antiquarianism or out of some special pose of historic purism, but for a more authentic presentation of the American political tradition. It was necessary, even for the limited purposes of this study, to delve deeply into the manuscript collections of Jefferson and Madison in the Library of Congress, and to fill in important gaps by consulting photostats at Princeton of other manuscripts.

It was natural that this extensive research into unpublished primary sources should yield significant new facts. Some of the new information provides missing links in otherwise imperfectly known episodes. My account of "The Virginia and Kentucky Resolutions," for example, embodies several discoveries that permit a more accurate version of the crucial roles played by Jefferson and Madison. Another example is the account of their detailed collaboration on the University of Virginia—a relationship that has not previously been properly assessed. Other new facts clarify hitherto obscure or supposedly disconnected elements in the development of their thought. This is illustrated by the chapters on "The Constitution and the Bill of Rights" and "The Earth Belongs to the Living," which show the give and take between the two statesmen on fundamental issues of democratic theory.

The most important result, however, is the reappraisal of democratic theory in the American tradition. In this respect, the study would have failed had it not used the manuscript sources in order to avoid accepted, but often inaccurate, clichés about the political theory of the founding fathers. By a quirk in the American liberal psychology, it has often been assumed that we started the American political tradition in a heady and pure idealism and betrayed it by corroding concessions—wrung by political bosses and robber barons. Although Jefferson conceived democratic society to be fundamentally different from a society based on force or fraud, and repeatedly affirmed his unshakable faith in intelligence, popular consent, and the moral objects of democratic society, he recognized that such a society would have to trim its ideals in order to keep afloat. And Madison affirmed that that government is best which is least imperfect, an affirmation that has not been sufficiently understood by doctrinaire American liberals. These two philosophical statesmen brought their generous and humanistic political theories to the test of action, and action, as ever, necessitated compromise. But the reality of political compromise in their case never defeated their political ideals. They recognized the requirements of power in order to realize more fully the root ideal of political freedom. This, in sum, is their faith in an "empire for liberty."

Any new insight into Jefferson and Madison should

prove useful to those who care about democracy today. For no other two men in the American past had a more pervasive philosophy of democracy, a firmer faith in human intelligence, or a more progressive view of the American experiment as a "workshop of liberty." The problems they posed and solved over a half-century of combined efforts can hardly fail to grip those who live in a world where the conditions of democracy are more fateful than ever before.

ACKNOWLEDGMENTS

THIS STUDY was made possible by a number of institutions whose generous aid I am happy to acknowledge: the Guggenheim Foundation, for two fellowships that permitted the major research for this book to be done; the Rockefeller Foundation, for a grant that made possible its completion; Tulane University, for a faculty grant from its Graduate Council on Research; and the Institute for Advanced Study at Princeton, for the benefits of working there at the beginning of this study.

Further, it is a great personal pleasure to thank the people whose encouragement or assistance helped me on my way. Unfortunately, there are many more than can be mentioned here. But I wish particularly to thank my husband, Lawrence R. Kegan, for his invaluable criticism, which constituted a genuine revaluation of the whole study; Dumas Malone, for his careful reading of the entire manuscript and his perceptive criticism of it; Julian Boyd and Lyman Butterfield, editors of *The Papers of Thomas Jefferson*, now in preparation at Princeton, for making available to me the most extensive Jefferson files in existence, and for calling my attention to several significant items; Harry Ammon, for permission to adapt material from our joint article on the Virginia and Kentucky Resolutions; Dr. Luther Evans, Librarian of Congress, for his interest in this study and his readiness to give me access to the varied resources at his command; and Helen Bullock and the staff of the Manuscripts Division at the Library of Congress for their general assistance and good will in the long period of my research there. I also wish to acknowledge Mrs. Bullock's expert assistance in compiling the index.

NOTES

IN GENERAL, citations are given to Jefferson's and Madison's published works wherever possible to facilitate the reader's own investigations. I have worked largely, however, from manuscript collections of Jefferson and Madison papers, and related collections, at the Library of Congress. These manuscript sources have been cited not only for unpublished letters and items, but for letters that have been printed in the standard collected works in a materially abridged or inaccurate form. It was naturally not possible to check every manuscript item against every printed version; but all letters of importance for this study were so checked, and when there were important errors, relevant omissions or deletions, references have been given to the appropriate manuscript collection.

Fortunately, the inadequate editions of Jefferson's writings that now exist are soon to be remedied by the publication of a comprehensive edition of *The Papers of Thomas Jefferson*, now in progress at the Princeton Library under the editorship of Julian Boyd. It is regrettable that no similar undertaking exists for editing Madison's papers.

The standard collected works most frequently referred to in the footnotes are:

The Writings of Thomas Jefferson, edited by Paul Leicester Ford (10 vols. New York: G. P. Putnam's Sons; 1892–9). Referred to as "Ford."

The Writings of Thomas Jefferson, edited by Andrew A. Lipscomb and Albert Ellery Bergh (20 vols. Washington, D. C.: The Thomas Jefferson Memorial Association; 1905). Referred to as "Memorial."

The Writings of James Madison, edited by Gaillard Hunt (9 vols. New York: G. P. Putnam's Sons; 1900–10). Referred to as "Hunt."

The Writings of James Madison, published by order of Congress (4 vols. Philadelphia: J. B. Lippincott & Co.; 1865). Referred to as "Congress."

CONTENTS

JEFFERSON AND MADISON

"... we should have such an empire for liberty as she [the world] has never surveyed since the creation; and I am persuaded no constitution was ever before so well calculated as ours for extensive empire and self-government."

—JEFFERSON TO MADISON, April 27, 1809

"The free system of government we have established is so congenial with reason, with common sense, and with a universal feeling, that it must produce approbation and a desire of imitation. . . . Our country, if it does justice to itself, will be the officina-Libertatio, to the Civilized World, and do more than any other for the uncivilized."

—MADISON TO DE PONCEAU, January 23, 1826

"Mr. Madison was the intimate, confidential, and devoted friend of Mr. Jefferson, and the mutual influence of these two mighty minds upon each other, is a phenomenon, like the invisible and mysterious movements of the magnet in the physical world, and in which the sagacity of the future historian may discover the solution of much of our national history not otherwise easily accountable."

—JOHN QUINCY ADAMS: The Jubilee of the Constitution. A Discourse . . . , 1839

Chapter One

THE CAUSE OF LIBERTY

"If justice, good faith, honor, gratitude and all the other qualities which ennoble the character of a nation & fulfill the ends of government, be the fruits of our establishments, the cause of liberty will acquire a dignity and lustre, which it has never yet enjoyed, and an example will be set, which cannot but have the most favorable influence on the rights of Mankind."

—MADISON: "Address to the States," April 1783

JEFFERSON AND MADISON appear to have met in 1776 as fellow members of the Virginia House of Delegates. They became friendlier during the early months of Jefferson's governorship, in the summer of 1779, when Madison, as a member of the Virginia Council of State, had the opportunity to confer with Jefferson daily. The latter was then thirty-six years of age, eight years Madison's senior. Madison, who had been the product of a "Northern" education at Princeton College, was a scholarly, promising, but shy Southerner. Jefferson, who had studied at the College of William and Mary in Williamsburg, where Governor Fauquier's soirees were the envy of the town, was already a successful lawyer, a distinguished legislator, and the famous author of the Declaration of Independence.

The first evidence in writing of Madison's friendly regard for Jefferson occurs when the latter had already ended his troubled regime as Governor of Virginia. A resolution

3

introduced into the Virginia Assembly by young George Nicholas, after Jefferson had resigned his office, called for an inquiry into "the conduct of the Executive of this State for the last twelve months." [1] It implied that Jefferson had failed to provide proper leadership and adequate defense during the British invasion. Aghast, Jefferson wrote Nicholas demanding what "particular instance or instances of ill conduct" had been the occasion of the motion. "I suppose," he added, "it could not be intended first, to stab a reputation by a general suggestion under a bare expectation that facts might be afterward hunted up to bolster it." [2] And in retirement at Monticello he reflected unhappily on the lot of citizens who serve the public. For himself, he wrote to Lafayette, he hoped that private life "under the protection of republican laws" would yield "that happiness from which no slave is so remote as the minister of a commonwealth." [3]

Madison sympathized with Jefferson in the unwarranted assault upon his reputation and defended him from malicious gossip. He was determined, moreover, to work for Jefferson's re-entry into politics. In December 1781 he expressed to a friend of both his "great pleasure" at the formal apology the Virginia legislature had tendered to Jefferson. In view of the honorable acquittal, he added, Jefferson might change his decision to stay in retirement. "We are impatient to know whether he will undertake the new service to which he is called," [4] the new service being Jefferson's election by the Virginia Assembly to represent the com-

[1] See Dumas Malone: *Jefferson the Virginian* (Boston: Little, Brown & Company; 1948), Chapters xxii–xxv, pp. 301–52.

[2] Jefferson to George Nicholas, Monticello, July 28, 1781. Jefferson Papers, Library of Congress (hereafter "L.C.").

[3] Jefferson to Lafayette, Monticello, August 4, 1781. *Writings* (Ford), III, 49.

[4] Madison to Edmund Pendleton, Philadelphia, December 25, 1781. *Writings* (Hunt), I, 167.

monwealth in Congress. But Jefferson refused this appointment, just as earlier in the year he had refused to consider a congressional appointment to the peace commission in Europe.

Madison, however, was not easily discouraged. When the question of Virginia's claims to the Western territory was under investigation by a congressional committee, Madison appealed to Jefferson to submit "such information as your researches have yielded, with the observations which you have made in the course of them." [5] Jefferson proceeded to study the history of the claims. He proved that Madison had been right in suspecting that the request could not have been directed "with equal prospect of advantage elsewhere." [6]

In the spring of 1782 Jefferson refused the place in the Virginia legislature to which he had been recently elected, and Madison's impatience with his attitude was marked. He shared the view of Edmund Randolph, who reported to him on a letter from Jefferson to Monroe "in which he assigns reasons for refusing his seat in the house of delegates. The pathos of the composition is really great; and the wound, which his spirit received by the late impeachment, is, as he says, to be cured only by the all-healing grave. His triumph might certainly be an illustrious one over his former enemies, were he to resume the legislative character: for in the constant division between the two leaders, Henry and Lee, he might incline the scale to whichsoever side he would. . . ." [7]

Madison replied to Randolph: "Great as my partiality is to Mr. Jefferson, the mode in which he seems determined

[5] Madison to Jefferson, Philadelphia, January 15, 1782. Ibid., I, 173.
[6] Madison to Jefferson, Philadelphia, April 16, 1782. Ibid., I, 186.
[7] [Edmund Randolph] to James Madison, Richmond, June 1, 1782. Madison Papers, L.C.

to revenge the wrong received from his country does not appear to me to be dictated either by philosophy or patriotism. It argues, indeed, a keen sensibility and strong consciousness of rectitude. But his sensibility ought to be as great toward the relentings as the misdoings of the Legislature, not to mention the injustice of visiting the faults of this body on their innocent constituents." [8]

There is a final note of triumph, however. Under date line of November 12, 1782 Madison made the following entry in his notes on the debates in Congress: "The reappointment of Mr. Jefferson as Minister Plenipo: for negotiating peace was agreed to unanimously and without a single adverse remark. The act took place in consequence of its being suggested that the death of Mrs. J. had probably changed the sentiments of Mr. J. with regard to public life, & that all the reasons which led to his original appointment still existed and indeed, had acquired additional force from the improbability that Mr. Laurens would actually assist in the negotiation." [9] Rushing to get the news to Jefferson, Madison asked Edmund Randolph to inform him "as quickly as secrecy will admit." Two days later Madison wrote to Randolph: "I confide in his [Jefferson's] acceptance and flatter myself with the pleasure of soon seeing him in Philada." [10]

In truth, the ties that had bound Jefferson to Monticello had been sharply cut by the death of his wife. Within two weeks of Madison's note Jefferson wrote to Robert R. Livingston, then Secretary of Foreign Affairs, accepting the

[8] Madison to Edmund Randolph, Philadelphia, June 11, 1782. *Writings* (Hunt), I, 207–8.

[9] Madison's notes on "Debates in the Congress of the Confederation from November 4th, 1782, to February 13th, 1783." Ibid., I, 259–60.

[10] Madison to Edmund Randolph, November 12, 1782; and Madison to Randolph, November 14, 1782. Ibid., I, 259, n.1.

appointment to join the peace commission in Europe which Congress had for the second time tendered him. He was ready, he said, to employ "the best of my poor talents" in his arduous charge.[11]

2

It is from this period that the warm personal friendship, fortified by close political collaboration, between Jefferson and Madison developed. Congress had scarcely acted when Jefferson wrote to Madison announcing an early arrival in Philadelphia. "Some days," he explained, "I must certainly pass there; as I could not propose to jump into the midst of a negotiation without a single article of previous information." [12] Jefferson arrived in Philadelphia on December 27. He stayed a month, examining the papers in the office of the Secretary of Foreign Affairs [13] and spending many hours daily in Madison's company. In letters written shortly after leaving Philadelphia, Jefferson referred to the pleasant society of "the good ladies & gentlemen of your fireside."

While waiting to sail to Europe from Baltimore, Jefferson wrote Madison "some reflections . . . which can only be hazarded to the ear of friendship." Since peace rumors had come to his attention, he requested Madison to find out what Congress wished him to do about his departure.[14] Madison replied post-haste that Jefferson had better

[11] Jefferson to Robert R. Livingston, Chesterfield, November 26, 1782. *Writings* (Ford), III, 62.

[12] Jefferson to Madison, Ampthill in Chesterfield, November 26, 1782. Ibid., III, 66.

[13] Henry S. Randall: *The Life of Thomas Jefferson* (3 vols. New York, 1858), I, 386.

[14] Jefferson to Madison, Baltimore, February 7, and added note, February 8, 1783. *Writings* (Ford), III, 300–4.

sit tight and patiently await further word.[15] The disagreeable waiting was over in a few weeks. Early in April, Madison wrote to Edmund Randolph that "the mission of Mr. Jefferson has been entirely superseded by the last advices. . . . As his services are not required, at least for the present, in Europe, it is to be most devoutly wished that they could be engaged at the present crisis at home." [16]

Free to worry about the "crisis at home," Jefferson and Madison were soon collaborating on ways and means to strengthen the power of the Continental Congress against the selfish policies of individual states. Madison, with Hamilton, led the group in Congress that promoted a strong federal union. Toward this end Madison presented resolutions in March 1783, which were a firm endorsement of the federal impost duties previously approved by Congress but obstructed by the several states. In his "Address to the States," accompanying the resolutions, Madison reminded the states that:

it has ever been the pride and boast of America, that the rights for which she contended were the rights of human nature . . . the citizens of the United States are responsible for the greatest trust ever confided to a political society. If justice, good faith, honor, gratitude and all the other qualities which ennoble the character of a nation & fulfill the ends of government, be the fruits of our establishments, the cause of liberty will acquire a dignity and lustre, which it has never yet enjoyed, and an example will be set, which cannot but have the most favorable influence on the rights of Mankind. If on the other side, our governments should be unfortunately blotted with the reverse of these cardinal and essential virtues, the great cause which we have engaged to vindicate, will be dishonored and betrayed; the

[15] Madison to Jefferson, Philadelphia, February 11, 1783. *Writings* (Congress), I, 62.
[16] Madison to Edmund Randolph, Philadelphia, April 8, 1783. Madison Papers, L.C.

last and fairest experiment in favor of the rights of human nature will be turned against them. . . .[17]

Madison had dramatically proved the strength of his own adherence to the welfare of the Confederacy by breaking free of his instructions in supporting the impost program. In commenting to Jefferson on the resolutions, he confessed that he had not been able to devise any "bait" for Virginia to entice its support. Yet he knew that Jefferson, who would promote their acceptance by the Virginia legislature, would agree with him that " a respect for justice, good faith and national honor" [18] was more important than territorial concessions for Virginia, or advantageous revenues.

Jefferson conceded the general position, recognizing that strong federal revenue measures were necessary to avert the bankruptcy of the new nation. He even hailed Madison's proposal to convert state debts as at least "one palatable ingredient . . . in the pill we were to swallow." [19] He had faithfully "waited a fortnight in the neighborhood of Richmond" to converse with as many members as he could; and finally, he indicated the line-up of leaders who would resist everything that might give influence to Congress (especially Patrick Henry), and the more enlightened legislators who could be counted on to defend Madison's position.

Only men of virtue and ability would, he thought, support the measures Madison recommended for liquidating United States debts in a fashion that would bring honor to the Confederacy. Madison proceeded, therefore, to make

[17] Madison's "Address to the States," agreed to by Congress, April 24, 1783. *Writings* (Hunt), I, 459–60, n.

[18] Madison to Jefferson, Philadelphia, April 22, 1783. Madison Papers, L.C.

[19] Jefferson to Madison, Tuckahoe, May 7, 1783. *Writings* (Ford), III, 317–19.

a private appeal to his Virginia friends to support only such men for the general or state governments. He was particularly interested that Jefferson's abilities be employed, preferably in Congress, where "temperate and experienced" men were desperately needed to assure "those catholic arrangements on which the harmony and stability of the Union must greatly depend. . . ." [20]

These hopes were realized a few days later when Jefferson was elected to the Continental Congress on June 6, 1783. Jefferson entered upon his term of duty in November, following on Madison's departure, and carried forward Madison's program to strengthen the United States and thereby the cause of liberty. There ensued a brief period of service on Jefferson's part, with prodigious committee activity, resulting in a number of major legislative proposals. Among these were Jefferson's recommendations on a sound coinage system and a draft for temporary government of the Western territories. This draft foreshadowed the Northwest Ordinance of 1787 by stressing the principle of equality between the original and the new states and by excluding slavery from all the territories after 1800.

Now the tables were turned; Jefferson, in Congress, called on Madison, in Virginia, to promote measures influencing Virginia's recognition of the needs of the Union above narrow state interests. Young men of ability and virtue should be appointed to Congress. "They see the affairs of the Confederacy from a high ground; they learn the importance of the Union & befriend federal measures when they return. Those who never come here, see our affairs insulated, pursue a system of jealousy & self interest, and distract the Union as much as they can." Congress's

[20] Madison to Edmund Randolph, May 27, 1783. *Writings* (Hunt), I, 474, n.

tax requisitions were naturally of the first order of importance in this strategy. Jefferson, therefore, enjoined Madison's help:

The produce of our slave tax being nearly equal to the Continental requisitions, can you not get it appropriated to that
purpose, and have it all paid in money? Virginia must do something more than she had done to maintain any degree of respect
in the Union and to make it bearable to any man of feeling to
represent her in Congress. The public necessities call distress-
ingly for aid, and very ruinous circumstances proceed from the
inattention of the states to furnish supplies in money. S. Carolina is the foremost state in supplies notwithstanding her dis-
tresses. Whence does this proceed? From a difference of spirit
solely; from a pride of character; from a rejection of the unmanly
supineness which permits personal inconveniences to absorb
every other sentiment.[21]

To do his share, Madison soon re-entered the Virginia
legislature, primarily interested in promoting new grants of
power to Congress to "rescue . . . the Union and the
blessings of liberty staked on it from an impending catas-
trophe." [22]

3

Just before his election to Congress, Jefferson drew up
a new constitution for Virginia. He had been a severe critic
of the existing state constitution and virtually from the
time of its adoption in 1776 had tried to obtain a convention to form a better one. Now a convention seemed likely
and Jefferson lost no time in putting his suggestions on

[21] Jefferson to Madison, Annapolis, May 8, 1784. W. C. Rives Papers,
L.C.
[22] See Irving Brant: *James Madison: The Nationalist* (Indianapolis:
Bobbs-Merrill Company; 1948), p. 316.

paper. The convention never materialized. Nevertheless, Jefferson valued his work on the constitution. Three years later, while in Paris, he thought well enough of it to have it printed in pamphlet form and afterward included it as an appendix to his *Notes on Virginia*.

In Jefferson's constitution a tripartite separation of powers showed the kind of limited government he was proposing. The number of delegates for the two branches of the legislature was proportioned to the number of qualified electors in each county, but the total number of delegates was not to exceed three hundred or be less than one hundred. Jefferson considered this important, as his later comments on the gigantic French National Convention show. He believed that more than three hundred would prove to be an excitable mob rather than a body of deliberative legislators, and less than one hundred might become a laggard and disorganized group.

Jealous of government's tendency to presume powers over the people, Jefferson carefully provided a broad principle of suffrage and limits to government power. "All free male citizens" with one year's residence in the state should have the right to vote. The general assembly was denied the power to "infringe this constitution"; but specific provision was made (by a two-thirds vote of two branches of government) for issuing a call for a convention to alter the constitution, the new convention "to have equal powers with this present convention." He reasserted other principles of civil liberties, true to his work on the earlier revisal of the laws of Virginia—a revisal by which his native state was transformed from a relatively feudal political entity into a modern one. The benefits of the writ of habeas corpus were to be extended to all. The military was specifically made subordinate to the civil power. Printing presses were to be subject to no other restraint than "liableness to legal prosecution for false facts printed and published." [23]

Jefferson's cherished defense of religious freedom, which he had eloquently expressed in the "Bill for Establishing Religious Freedom," not yet become law, was recalled now in a clause that denied the general assembly the right to abridge the civil rights of anyone on account of his religious belief. Nor could the general assembly restrain anyone from "professing and supporting that belief, or . . . compel him to contributions."

At least one feature of Jefferson's constitution would have produced a head-on clash had it ever been actually debated by Virginia legislators. With foresight and humanity Jefferson had forbidden the introduction of "any more slaves to reside in this State, or the continuance of slavery beyond the generation which shall be living on the thirty-first day of December, one thousand eight hundred; all persons born after that day being hereby declared free." As already indicated in connection with Jefferson's work in Congress, he attempted to extend this provision to the Western territories. One can speculate on the consequences to American history had the enlightened legislation of the liberal Jefferson been adopted, but such speculation is resisted here on the condition that Jefferson's intention be noted by all who remember him as a "slave holding Virginia planter."

Jefferson forwarded a copy of his constitution to Madison in June 1783, explaining the circumstances of its birth. He asked his friend to use his opportunities in Philadelphia to consult with members from other states on its "new" parts, either to obtain criticism or possibly to encourage its

[23] Jefferson's "Proposed Constitution for Virginia" [June 1783]. *Writings* (Ford), III, 320–33.

use by other states. He requested that Madison withhold it from "any one of my own country," since he anticipated that other Virginians would be deeply prejudiced against it. Then, in a flash of clairvoyance or happy compliment, he confided it to Madison's future use, predicting that Madison might lend his aid to the making of constitutions in "some future situation." [24]

To these ties of a ripening friendship Jefferson added a loan of the notes he had taken on the debates in the Continental Congress concerning independence.[25] Madison, as he himself observed years later, considered this set of notes of great value "from its perfect authenticity . . . from the certainty that this is the first disclosure to the world of those Debates; and from the probability or rather certainty that a like knowledge of them is not to be expected from any other source." [26]

Jefferson added one gift of unique value to the loan of his notes: a copy of the original of the Declaration of Independence "at full length distinguishing the alterations it underwent." [27] The transfer of Jefferson's copy of the Declaration and his draft of the Virginia constitution to Madison symbolizes the deep friendship that the two statesmen had already achieved.

[24] Jefferson to Madison, Monticello, June 17, 1783. Ibid., III, 334.
[25] Jefferson to Madison, Monticello, June 1, 1783. Ibid., III, 320.
[26] Madison's "preface or prospectus for the 'Memoir' " [August 1826?]. Madison Papers, L.C.
[27] Jefferson to Madison, Monticello, June 1, 1783. *Writings* (Ford), III, 320.

Chapter Two

BY FRENCH PACKET

WITH A HALF-YEAR of distinguished congressional service behind him, Jefferson's European star rose once again. A hitherto unpublished letter from Jefferson to Madison of May 8, 1784 announced the happy event of a new mission to France: "Congress yesterday adjoined me to Mr. Adams and Dr. Franklin on the foreign commercial negotiations." With a maiden voyage ahead, Jefferson was elated that he was leaving "the justlings of states . . . to repair to a field where the divisions will be fewer but on a larger scale." [1]

Preparing for an extended absence, Jefferson made sure to arrange a frequent correspondence with Madison, and requested his friend to report, at the close of every session of the assembly, the general measures introduced and the positions of the different parties and personalities. On his part, Jefferson promised to "certainly maintain the correspondence" and to serve his friend gladly "by the execution of any particular commission" he might name. One advance promise Jefferson magnificently fulfilled: "In the purchase of books, pamphlets, etc. old and curious, or new and useful I shall ever keep you in my eye."

There was a substantial favor that Jefferson wanted Madison to do for him—to take charge of the schooling of

[1] Jefferson to Madison, Annapolis, May 8, 1784. W. C. Rives Papers, L.C.

15

his nephews, especially his favorite nephew, Peter Carr, the most gifted of his protégés.[2] Jefferson stated that he had thought to entrust Peter to William Short, but since the latter would probably accompany him to Europe as his secretary, "I have nobody . . . but you to whose direction I could consign him with unlimited confidence." Madison, of course, faithfully and devotedly carried out this charge.

This same letter (of which the final section is lost) inaugurated a fateful new friendship for Madison. Colonel Monroe, Jefferson wrote, wished a correspondence with Madison (no doubt at Jefferson's suggestion). The last words of this fragmentary letter apparently began a recommendation of Monroe, mentioning the "scrupulousness of his honor"—but here the extant original ends. Whatever followed this observation, however, it was a forerunner not only of a voluminous correspondence but of a close friendship between Madison and Monroe. Thus the historically important three-cornered friendship of Jefferson, Madison, and Monroe was conceived and deliberately arranged by Jefferson's own prudent hand.

As soon as Jefferson arrived in the most civilized capital of Europe, sparkling exchanges began to flow to his best friend on his impressions and discoveries of the "transatlantic world." Jefferson thus made it possible for Madison to share his experience of France. Madison, on the other hand, made it easy for Jefferson to know the true complexion of political developments in America.

Madison at once took up his role of safeguarding the

[2] See H. S. Randall's description of Jefferson's regard for his boyhood friend Dabney Carr, who later married Jefferson's sister Martha, and who died at the early age of thirty. Jefferson had him buried under their favorite oak at Monticello and took Carr's entire family into his home. *Life of Thomas Jefferson* (3 vols. Philadelphia: J. B. Lippincott & Company; 1871), I, 83–4.

interests of his vulnerable—because absent—friend. The first letter that Madison sent to Jefferson in Paris[3] informed him that a rumor was circulating to the effect that Jefferson was an active party to some land speculation in Kentucky. Grateful for Madison's protective intervention, Jefferson replied conscientiously. He had on two earlier occasions joined with friends to obtain Western lands, but "in the winter of 1782 and 1783, while I was in expectation of going to Europe, and . . . the title to western lands might possibly come under the discussion of the ministers, I withdrew myself from this company. . . . I can with truth therefore declare to you, and wish you to repeat it on every proper occasion, that no person on earth is authorized to place my name in any adventure for lands on the western waters. . . ."[4]

2

A philosopher like Thomas Jefferson was not likely to restrict an official visit to Europe to a narrow preoccupation with official duties. From a book-starved young country he had been introduced into the greatest center of intellectual life on the European continent. In a delirium of scholarly joy, Jefferson spent several hours every afternoon of his European sojourn, when he was not prevented by heavy work, browsing among the books in French, Spanish, Italian, Greek, and Latin that cluttered the bookshops and

[3] Jefferson departed for France from Boston on July 5, 1784. Madison's first letter to Jefferson, quoted here, is printed in Hunt's edition of Madison's *Writings* (II, 75), but the section under consideration is printed with many inaccuracies. I have therefore used the wording of the manuscript version, in the Madison Papers, L.C.

[4] Jefferson to Madison, Paris, November 11, 1784. *Writings* (Ford), IV, 3.

stalls.[5] Now he could touch and inspect the books he had longed to know when he had been confined at home to the cold and insufficient lists of book-dealers across "the broad Atlantic."

The constant shipment of books and curiosities is ample evidence that although Jefferson frequently discussed new inventions and new ideas with a goodly circle of friends, it was Madison who was uppermost in his thoughts. His correspondence and account books show that American friends like James Monroe, Edmund Randolph, Francis Hopkinson, Benjamin Franklin, and several others were frequent recipients of his favors. But it was Madison with whom he shared a similarity of interests and an eagerness to master the philosophy and knowledge of Europe in the "improving spirit of the age." This gave Jefferson perfect confidence in choosing volumes to suit Madison's congenial requirements and tastes. Madison specifically requested Jefferson to purchase for him "Treatises on the ancient or modern Federal Republics, on the law of Nations, and the History, natural and political, of the new World," adding to these subjects "such of the Greek and Roman authors, where they will be got very cheap, as are worth having, and are not on the common list of school classics." [6] And hardly had Jefferson arrived in Paris when he made his first purchase for his friend, a modest group including Voltaire's memoirs, a book on Frederick the Great, and a "Testament Politique d'Angleterre." [7] From this small beginning grew

[5] Jefferson to Samuel H. Smith, Monticello, September 21, 1814. Ibid., IX, 486.

[6] Madison to Jefferson, Orange, April 27, 1785. *Writings* (Congress), I, 146.

[7] Jefferson's account, "J. Madison to Th. J., Dr.," September 1, 1784. Courtesy of the *Jefferson Papers*, Princeton. Original in the Massachusetts Historical Society.

the hundreds of volumes that Jefferson, in his five charmed years abroad, procured for Madison.

Jefferson's thoughtful provision of books for Madison, including some thirty-seven volumes of the coveted *Encyclopédie méthodique*, which Madison called "a complete scientific library," [8] treatises on morality, and histories of European countries, surely made Madison the most cosmopolitan statesman never to have quit American shores. Indeed, it was often remarked a few years later that Madison was probably the best-read and best-informed member of the Constitutional Convention. Certainly his reading in the history of political theory, including the law of nature and nations, could hardly have been so comprehensive without the contents of the treasured boxes Jefferson shipped to him from France.

One glance at the other gifts and purchases is irresistible. It was a strange two-way traffic, mostly by the French packet that plowed across the Atlantic in the years of Jefferson's residence in France, from 1784 to 1789. Jefferson was enthusiastically sending "curious" objects to Madison— geegaws, works of mechanical art, the latest inventions of "useful" science such as the Continent abounded with in the innovating last years of the eighteenth century. *Objets d'art* and any object whatever of superior quality seem to have been fit game for Jefferson to capture for his friend. He ordered a very fine Swiss watch, giving exact specifications to the workman, and testing it for accuracy before sending it to Virginia. Madison's scientific hobbies made him desire a pocket telescope and a pedometer (a "step counter" Jefferson called it). Jefferson proudly produced both objects from the apparently inexhaustible supplies of

[8] Madison to ———, April 15, 1783. Madison Papers, L.C.

Paris. A portable copying machine, a chemical box, an umbrella, all found their way to a scholarly Virginian who also eagerly awaited professional aids like the *Code de l'humanité*, and journals like the *Mercure de France* and the *Leyden Gazette*.

An amusing story in this chapter of friendly purchases concerned an object more modest perhaps but infinitely more useful than an elaborate walking-stick. A forerunner of the humble but indispensable match was the object about which Jefferson elaborately wrote Madison: [9]

If the bearer . . . can take charge of a pamphlet on Animal magnetism, another giving an account of Robert's last voyage thro' the air, and of some Phosphoretic matches, I will send them to you. These matches consist of a small wax taper, one end of which has been dipped in Phosphorus, and the whole is inclosed in a glass tube hermetically sealed. There is a little ring on the tube to shew where it is to be broken. First warm the phosphorized end . . . by holding it two or three seconds in your mouth, then snap it at or near the ring and draw the phosphorized end out of the tube. It blazes in the instant of it's extraction. It will be well always to decline the tube at an angle of about 45° (the phosphorized end lowest) in order that it may kindle thoroughly. Otherwise though it blazes in the first instant it is apt to go out if held erect. These cost about 30 sous the dozen. By having them at your bedside with a candle, the latter may be lighted at any moment of the night without getting out of bed. By keeping them on your writing table, you may seal three or four letters with one of them, or light a candle if you want to seal more which in the summer is convenient. In the woods they supply the want of steel, flint and punk.

[9] The passage does not appear in the printed version of Jefferson's letter to Madison of November 11, 1784, printed in Ford's edition of Jefferson's *Writings*, IV, 368–70. The Memorial Edition does not print this letter. Therefore the portions about to be quoted can be found in the original only in the Madison Papers, L.C.

But never would Jefferson let loose the phosphoric match on his quiet friend without warning honestly about its inconveniences!

Great care must be taken in extracting the taper that none of the phosphorus drips on your hand, because it is inextinguishable and will therefore burn to the bone if there be matter enough. It is said that urine will extinguish it.

When Jefferson was not actually ordering or buying for Madison, he was sending out feelers to see whether a prospective addition to his growing stock of acquisitions would be welcome. "I have been almost tempted to buy for you one of the little clocks made here on marble columns. They strike, go with a pendulum, a spring instead of a weight, are extremely elegant and can be had for 10 guineas. But I shall wait your orders." [10]

Madison, on his part, sent whatever Jefferson desired, either to prove the charms or to display the wonders of America to skeptical Europeans of distinction. Once there was a complicated transaction involving a box of pecan nuts. Jefferson announced the arrival of a box from Madison with only thirteen nuts in it, "which I mention because I suspect it had been pillaged." Madison made good that unhappy loss and dutifully filled Jefferson's requests for pippin apples, cranberries, and grafts of different American fruit trees, not packed between layers of moss as Jefferson had suggested, but enclosed in bags of earth, a better method, Madison punctiliously informed his friend.[11] He was disappointed that he could not secure (from New

[10] Jefferson to Madison, Paris, September 17, 1787. Madison Papers, L.C.

[11] Madison to Jefferson, New York, December 9, 1787. *Writings* (Hunt), V, 62.

York) the Virginia redbirds and the opossums that Jefferson thought would be "great presents," the first for "the ladies," the second for French naturalists. To such gifts of the earth Madison added, at intervals, pamphlets, newspaper clippings, and legislative papers that he considered would help to keep Jefferson *au courant* of American events.

By these thoughtful tokens of friendship Jefferson made Madison a vital part of his French experience. Jefferson had gone further and had written an affectingly cordial letter urging Madison to come and spend the approaching summer in France, taking "room, bed, and plate" at Jefferson's commodious abode, where he would "become of the family." Agreeable society, Jefferson reminded Madison, is the first essential for happiness and value in life. Some day, he confided, he looked forward to a friendly community—Madison, Monroe, and Short settling in the neighborhood of his own Monticello, where they would form a unique "inestimable society." But first things first. At least Madison should avail himself of the opportunity to spend several months in Europe, at little more cost than his own passage money. So could he purchase cheaply "the knowledge of another world," wrote Jefferson.[12] But Madison could not trust his supposedly "inferior health," and he contented himself with the vicarious knowledge afforded by the discriminating reports, purchases, and gifts of his indefatigable and loyal friend.

Madison gradually became even more of a Francophile than he had been for reasons such as appreciation of France's aid to America in the Revolution. Jefferson's cordial attachment to France is well known, while Madison's is often forgotten. Shortly after Jefferson's arrival in Paris,

[12] Jefferson to Madison, Paris, December 8, 1784. *Writings* (Ford), IV, 17–19.

Madison wrote to Jefferson about the visit of the dashing young Marquis de Lafayette, who would soon champion Jefferson in the most "closed" diplomatic and aristocratic circles of Paris. The warm ovations that greeted the Marquis in New York must have pleased him, for he was vain; but they overjoyed Madison. Later, Madison journeyed with the Marquis to Fort Schuyler, and reported enthusiastically that "Besides the personal homage he [Lafayette] receives, his presence has furnished occasion for fresh manifestation of those sentiments towards France which have been so well merited by her but which her enemies pretended would soon give way to returning affection for Great Britain." [13] Scorning this change of sentiment in favor of a still monarchic, monopolistic, and mercantile England, Madison suggested that Jefferson arrange to republish in Paris the accounts of the ovations given to Lafayette printed in American gazettes. The republication "may be of advantage to us. They will at least give a pleasure to the friends of the Marquis." Madison shared Jefferson's friendliness to Lafayette and his sentiment that, after America, France would be every rational man's choice for his adopted country. Momentous consequences were to proceed from this belief in the coming years of party politics.

3

The trust that Jefferson placed in Madison's judgment and sure intelligence in this early period is best revealed by Jefferson's appeal to Madison for advice on his highly controversial work, the *Notes on Virginia*, the only book Jefferson ever wrote. The book had been the product of Jeffer-

[13] Madison to Jefferson, New York, September 15, 1784. *Writings* (Congress), I, 101.

son's temporary retirement to his farm and family in the summer of 1781 after resigning the governorship of Virginia. Utilizing his own bundles of notes on the natural history, climate, flora, fauna, laws, and customs of Virginia, Jefferson replied to the twenty-three comprehensive questions raised by the secretary of the French Legation in Philadelphia, the Marquis François de Barbé-Marbois.[14] Although the book that issued from this inquiry was scanned by some for its natural-science statistics on the size of American animals and other such factual questions, Jefferson understood perfectly that the heart of his controversial essay concerned experimental philosophy and free government. Religious freedom, separation of church and state, and the ideals of representative government versus those of monarchy and despotism were discussed brilliantly. Separate passages, in defense of the agricultural way of life and freedom of religion, were destined to be the target of attack for many years.

Jefferson's book was published in Paris in 1785 and had an enthusiastic reception. But Jefferson felt that this was due to the fact that the French philosophers would naturally be more broad-minded about controversial subjects like religious freedom and other democratic reforms —especially since the reforms were recommended for a country thousands of miles away—than the citizens of Virginia, who were being advised in the *Notes* to emancipate their slaves and settle their constitution on a firmer, more permanent, and more liberal basis.[15]

[14] See Marie Kimball's chapter on the *Notes on Virginia* in *Jefferson: War and Peace* (New York: Coward-McCann; 1947), pp. 259–305, for an account of the composition and content of this important publication of Jefferson's.

[15] Jefferson to the Marquis de Chastellux, May (?) 1784. Jefferson Papers, L.C.

Accordingly, Jefferson wrote to sound out Madison on how best to handle the distribution of his *Notes*. He requested his friend to read the book carefully "because I ask your advice on it and ask nobody's else. I wish to put it into the hands of the young men at the college, as well on account of the political as physical parts. But there are sentiments on some subjects which I apprehend might be displeasing to the country, perhaps to the Assembly or some who lead it. . . ." Jefferson's idea was that Madison should consult with sound friends of his own choice to help decide whether the book "will give no offense." In the event of a favorable judgment Jefferson intended to supply a copy of the *Notes* to every student at the College of William and Mary, as well as to selected friends. "Otherwise," Jefferson reluctantly concluded, "I shall only send over a very few copies to particular friends in confidence and burn the rest." [16]

Madison lost little time in dutifully reporting to Jefferson that after having looked over the *Notes* carefully himself, he had "consulted several judicious friends in confidence." In his opinion, the danger implicit in "the freedom of your strictures on some particular measures and opinions" would not outweigh "the utility of your plan." George Wythe had suggested, however, that it would be unguarded to distribute the *Notes* to students at William and Mary. "It might be better to put the number you may allot to the University into the library, rather than to distribute them among the students. In the latter case the stock will be immediately exhausted. In the former the discretion of the professors will make it serve the students as they successively come. Perhaps too an *indiscrimi-*

[16] Jefferson to Madison, Paris, May 11, 1785. *Writings* (Ford), **IV**, 46–7.

nate gift might offend some narrow minded parents." [17] The praise that every author covets intensely, even though he promises to burn most of the copies of his book, Madison reserved for one earnest sentence: "We think both the facts and remarks which you have assembled too valuable not to be made known, at least to those for whom you destine them, and speak of them to one another in terms which I must not repeat to you."

4

Madison's service to his friend during this period was most noteworthy on another of Jefferson's earlier enterprises. In 1779, while Jefferson was a member of the General Assembly of Virginia, he had worked with George Wythe and Edmund Pendleton on the modernization or "revisal" of the laws of Virginia. The report submitted to the assembly contained one hundred and twenty-six bills. The revisal involved fundamental political questions to which Jefferson had given considerable space in his *Notes on Virginia*, where he presented the philosophical justification for the more radical and fundamental measures. The report, however, had been deferred and awaited action while Jefferson was busy on the European scene. It was in support of these measures that Madison showed how ably he could supplement the work of his friend.

For the three successive sessions of the General Assembly of Virginia in 1784 and 1785 Madison, who was then a leading member in the House of Delegates, waged an adroit and successful campaign that made almost half of the proposed bills into laws. Expert handling of a poten-

[17] Madison to Jefferson, November 15, 1785 *Writings* (Congress), I, 202–3.

tially explosive and permanently evil situation was most evident in the steps Madison took to promote the passage of the Bill for Religious Freedom, which Jefferson had written and finally introduced in the Virginia Assembly in 1779, but which the conservatives had prevented from becoming law.

Madison himself many years later recounted to his old friend Lafayette the events leading to the passage of the celebrated bill. His neutral description commendably understates the perfection of his own performance, and it demonstrates the high degree of teamwork that became routine between Jefferson and Madison from the time of Jefferson's mission to Europe until the end of his life. Madison recalled:

The Anglican hierarchy existing in Virginia prior to the Revolution was abolished by an early act of the Independent Legislature. In the year 1785, a bill was introduced under the auspices of Mr. Henry, imposing a general tax for the support of "Teachers of the Christian Religion." It made a progress threatening a majority in its favor. As an expedient to defeat it, we proposed that it should be postponed to another session, and printed in the mean time for public consideration. Such an appeal in a case so important and so unforeseen could not be resisted. With a view to arouse the people, it was thought proper that a memorial should be drawn up, the task being assigned to me, to be printed and circulated through the State for a general signature. The experiment succeeded. The memorial was so extensively signed by the various religious sects, including a considerable portion of the old hierarchy, that the projected innovation was crushed, and under the influence of the popular sentiment thus called forth, the well-known Bill prepared by Mr. Jefferson, for "Establishing Religious freedom," passed into a law, as it now stands in our code of statutes.[18]

[18] Madison to General Lafayette, Montpellier, November [24], 1826. Ibid., III, 543.

27

Madison's modest reference to the memorial opposing the general tax for the "Teachers of the Christian Religion" includes no comment on the quality of the petition he composed. Actually it was so ably written, so firm in its battery of arguments, that its triumph could hardly have surprised the author. Essentially, the skill of Madison's petition was in the variety of arguments adduced against the proposed bill, each new argument trapping a different sector of the Virginia public in its decisive logic.

Religion, Madison stated, is exempt from the authority of society, and even more so from the authority of a particular legislative body, whose jurisdiction is both derivative and limited.[19] Therefore it was wise to "take alarm at the first experiment on our liberties," "prudent jealousy" being a prime duty of free men and "one of the noblest characteristics of the late Revolution." Equality in "the free exercise of Religion according to the dictates of conscience" the Virginia Declaration of Rights had affirmed; yet the proposed establishment would deny that freedom, implying that the civil magistrate is a competent judge of religious truth—an implication, Madison comments, "falsified by the contradictory opinions of rulers in all ages."

Madison also scored the lack of faith in the Christian religion on the part of those who considered "establishment" a requisite for its support. Experience conclusively proved that during the almost fifteen centuries of the *legal establishment* of Christianity, there had developed "more or less, in all places, pride and indolence in the Clergy; ignorance and servility in the laity; in both, superstition, bigotry, and persecution." Conversely, the time of Christianity's "greatest lustre" was prior to its incorporation with civil policy.

[19] Madison's "A Memorial and Remonstrance." Ibid., I, 163.

The true principle, Madison exhorted his fellow Virginians, was not to erect a spiritual tyranny, but to defend a just government that neither invades the equal rights of any sect nor permits any sect to invade those of another. In the long run, he warned, the "generous policy" that had glorified colonial America—the offer of asylum to the persecuted and oppressed of every nation and religion—might be degraded. "Distant as it [the proposed establishment] may be in its present form from the Inquisition, it differs from it only in degree. The one is the first step, the other the last, in the career of intolerance." [20] "Either we must say, that they [the legislature] may control the freedom of the press, may abolish the trial by jury, may swallow up the Executive and Judiciary powers of the State; nay, that they may despoil us of our very right of suffrage, and erect themselves into an independent and hereditary Assembly; or we must say, that they have no authority to enact into a law the Bill under consideration." [21]

With Madison's help the establishment was defeated and Jefferson's Bill for Religious Freedom, with a few deletions in the preamble but no alteration in the enacting clauses, was given to Virginia and to history. The act opened with Jefferson's hard-hitting defense of complete religious freedom, and not simply the halfway "toleration" on the English pattern. The inspired preamble, in Jefferson's language, provided that:

Almighty God hath created the mind free; that all attempts to influence it by temporal punishments or burthens, or by civil incapacitations, tend only to beget habits of hypocrisy and meanness . . . that our civil rights have no dependence on our religious opinions, any more than our opinions in physics or

[20] Ibid., I, 166.
[21] Ibid., I, 169.

geometry; that therefore the proscribing any citizen as unworthy the public confidence by laying upon him an incapacity of being called to offices of trust and emolument, unless he profess or renounce this or that religious opinion, is depriving him injuriously of those privileges and advantages to which in common with his fellow-citizens he has a natural right . . . and finally, that truth is great and will prevail if left to herself, that she is the proper and sufficient antagonist to error. . . ."[22]

Excited over his strategic victory, Madison hastened to write Jefferson the good news that the bill had now become law. He proudly reflected that it had "in this country [Virginia], extinguished forever the ambitious hope of making laws for the human mind." [23] To the immediate good effects of this law must be added the broader permanent advantage of Madison's later incorporation of its substance into the first amendment to the federal Constitution.

This enlightened act did much to win Jefferson a place among the liberal philosophers and statesmen of Europe. Jefferson himself described the European reaction to it with a glow of pride: "The Virginia Act for religious freedom has been received with infinite approbation in Europe and propagated with enthusiasm. I do not mean by the governments, but by the individuals which compose them. It has been translated into French and Italian, has been sent to most of the courts of Europe, and has been the best evidence of the falsehood of those reports which stated us to be in anarchy. It is inserted in the new Encyclopedie and is appearing in most of the publications respecting America." [24]

[22] Koch and Peden: *The Life and Selected Writings of Thomas Jefferson* (New York: Modern Library; 1944), pp. 311–13.
[23] Madison to Jefferson, Richmond, January 22, 1786. Writings (Congress), I, 213–14.
[24] Jefferson to Madison, Paris, December 16, 1786. Writings (Ford), IV, 334.

The Bill for Religious Freedom was one of the three acts for which Jefferson wished to be remembered, ranking with the Declaration of Independence and the creation of the University of Virginia. Thus a trilogy of related causes —independence, freedom of conscience and conviction, and education—can be interpreted as the symbolic definition of Jefferson's career. After Jefferson's death Madison, in preparing a descriptive introduction for the publication of some of his friend's works, recalled the stellar place the efforts for religious freedom had always held in Jefferson's estimate of his own achievements. "This act," Madison wrote, ". . . was always held by Mr. Jefferson to be one of his best efforts in the Cause of Liberty to which he was devoted. And it is certainly the strongest legal barrier that could be erected against the connection of church and State so fatal to the liberty of both." [25]

5

Across the broad Atlantic, the two friends had helped each other to grow in stature as philosopher statesmen. While Madison developed the techniques of effective statesmanship that guaranteed liberal policies for his "country," Virginia, and matured his plans for a firmer national union, Jefferson was engaged in brilliantly propagating the "holy Republican gospel" [26] to the advanced thinkers and politicians of France and all Europe.

Jefferson, while endearing himself to the intelligentsia of the leading salons in France, never forgot to spread word

[25] Madison's draft of a "preface or prospectus for the 'Memoir' " when that alone was intended for immediate publication [August 1826?]. Madison Papers, L.C.

[26] Jefferson to John Langdon [Monticello], May 17, 1814. W. C. Rives Papers, L.C.

about the excellent qualities of his inestimable friend, the modest Mr. Madison of Virginia. By the spring of 1787, when Jefferson was in Italy, William Short, his enthusiastic young secretary, wrote to Madison, telling him of the high reputation Madison now enjoyed in France. He reported unhappily the European complaints of America's failure to pay her debt to France. But he was consoled by the better record of individual states and "of no state more than Virginia." He praised Madison feelingly for his "liberal conduct" and for the great contributions he had made in the legislature and attributed to them the fame Virginia had acquired in "every part of Europe." The Bill for Religious Freedom and the firm stand on public credit particularly had acquired Virginia "a degree of éclat and of honor of which it is difficult to form an idea." Continuing he said: "The *philosophical legislation* of Virginia is in the mouths of all the learned of this place, and quoted by all the advocates of the lumières de la Philosophie." [27]

Short's unrestrained letter permits us to see more than Jefferson's sophisticated modesty allowed to come through in his own correspondence. But there can be no question about the essential fact: Jefferson, thanks to Madison, had not lost influence at home by being absent and Madison had clearly gained a firm European reputation in addition to having profited personally from a wider intellectual perspective. "Purchasing the knowledge of another world" had paid off handsomely for both friends.

[27] William Short to Madison, Paris, May 7, 1787. Madison Papers, L.C.

Chapter Three

THE CONSTITUTION AND THE BILL OF RIGHTS

In the months that followed, while a delegate to the Constitutional Convention in Philadelphia, Madison reached the height of his career as a philospher statesman. He displayed a range of statecraft and theoretical insight that not even his closest friends could have foretold, and for which historians have almost unanimously dubbed him "the father of the Constitution." [1]

Madison took the floor to debate on every important issue and gained a fabulous reputation for scholarship. Scholarly preparation had been made possible by the books that Jefferson sent him from abroad, and Madison made deliberate effort, as soon as he was appointed deputy to the Convention, to investigate constitutional history in all its "sources ancient & modern." [2] Madison's political astuteness was evident on the floor of the Convention, but even more so in his tireless and adroit work in committees. Credit must also go to Madison for realizing so fully the value of making accurate and comprehensive notes on the debates, both as a record for the American people "to trace

[1] For a few contemporary appreciations, see J. B. Scott: *James Madison's Notes and a Society of Nations* (New York: Oxford University Press; 1918), Chapter i, "The Collosal Task," pp. 1–12; Douglass Adair: "James Madison, Philosopher and Father of the Constitution," in *The Lives of Eighteen from Princeton,* edited by Willard Thorp (Princeton University Press, 1946).

[2] Madison's "Autobiography," edited by Douglass Adair. *William and Mary Quarterly,* April 1945, pp. 201–2.

the origin and progress of their political institutions" and as a source of light on "the Science of Government." [3] Jefferson himself never ceased to admire Madison's performance and considered Madison's notes "the ablest work of this kind ever yet executed. . . . The whole of everything said and done there was taken down by Mr. Madison, with a labor and exactness beyond comprehension." [4]

Amidst the unrelenting duties of the Convention, Madison had little time for detailed reporting even to his best friend. Had he had the time, however, Madison once wrote to Jefferson, he was bound, as all members were, to perfect secrecy.[5] Yet Madison in the same letter could report other news: that Jefferson's nephews Carr were progressing nicely; that John Adams's book on the constitutions of the United States would "become a powerful engine in forming the public opinion," although the unfriendly remarks it contained about the history of republicanism might become dangerous; that General Washington's attendance and the names of the members from every state proved the seriousness with which they all took the Convention, and "The whole community is big with expectation."

But just before Madison set out for the Convention, he wrote to Jefferson revealing the leading ideas he expected to present. The best way to overcome the "mortal diseases of the existing Constitution," Madison then contended, was to arm "the federal head with a negative *in all cases whatsoever* on the local Legislatures." [6] This whole-

[3] Madison to Thomas Ritchie, Orange, September 15, 1821 (confidential). *Writings* (Hunt), IX, 71, n.1.

[4] Jefferson to John Adams, August 10, 1815. *Writings* (Ford), IX, 528.

[5] Madison to Jefferson, Philadelphia, June 6, 1787. *Writings* (Congress), I, 332.

[6] Madison to Jefferson, New York, March 19, 1787. Ibid., I, 285.

sale grant of power to the federal government Madison judged to be necessary because he had witnessed the continual bafflement of federal powers under the Articles of Confederation by "the Legislative sovereignties of the States." He hoped that such a grant would achieve stable national policy, greater order and harmony in the relationships of the several states, and more "righteous" legislation from the states on the contested question of paper money, as well as other questions where majority interests might "oppress" minority rights. The time had come for demanding "from the votaries of liberty every concession in favor of stable Government not infringing fundamental principles as the only security against an opposite extreme of our present situation."

In thus formulating the problem, Madison used a hypothesis—that compromise was the only method of averting the failings of the government under the Articles of Confederation without sacrificing the fundamental principles of republicanism. This hypothesis could hardly have been objectionable to Jefferson, who knew the weaknesses of the Confederacy. But Madison's notion of compromise gave more to "stable Government" than Jefferson believed "votaries of liberty" should concede—especially in the dangerous supreme veto of the "general" government "*in all cases whatsoever* on the local Legislatures."

Jefferson's reply to Madison in June, when the Convention was already under way, granted that he himself had thought of the device of separating the executive business of the Confederacy from Congress, somewhat "as the Judiciary is already in some degree." But he asserted he had never thought of giving the "proposed negative"—that, in truth, this was the first time it had been suggested to his mind. Jefferson's reaction to it was unequivocal: "*Prima*

35

facie I do not like it. It fails in an essential character that the hole & the patch should be commensurate." Since he estimated that not more than one out of every hundred state acts concern the Confederacy, the suggested veto would give Congress ninety-nine per cent more power than it required. As an alternative Jefferson recommended an appeal from state courts to a federal court in all cases where the Act of Confederation controlled the question. "It will be said that this court may encroach on the jurisdiction of the state courts. It may. But there will be a power, to wit, Congress, to watch & restrain them. But place the same authority in Congress itself, and there will be no power above them to perform the same office. They will restrain within due bounds a jurisdiction exercised by others much more rigorously than if exercised by themselves." [7]

Shortly after the Convention had closed, Madison redeemed his promise to Jefferson to communicate real news. Jefferson had strongly disapproved of the adoption of the rule of secrecy. He had written to John Adams: "I am sorry the Federal Convention began their deliberations by so abominable a precedent as that of tying up the tongues of their members. Nothing can justify this example but the innocence of their intentions; and ignorance of the value of public discussions." [8] Madison had thought the rule unavoidable, but was glad when the time came that he could talk freely to his friend. No better brief summary is available of the major principles considered by the delegates to the Convention than Madison's first long letter to Jefferson about one month after its work was done. Madison's letter, moreover, is a highly trustworthy report of his own gen-

[7] Jefferson to Madison, Paris, June 20, 1787. *Writings* (Ford), IV, 390–1.

[8] Jefferson to John Adams, Paris, August 6, 1787. *Writings* (Memorial Edition), VI, 289.

eral philosophy and intentions during the historic Convention.

Madison formulated the basic problem that confronted the framers of the Constitution: how to supersede a system that had been founded on the principle of a confederation of "Sovereign States." This basic problem, he asserted, had now been resolved by the alternative of instituting a government which, "instead of operating on the States, should operate without their intervention on the individuals composing them." [9] Once this groundwork was laid, Madison reported that the *great* objects then debated were the following four: "1. To unite a proper energy in the Executive, and a proper stability in the Legislative departments, with the essential character of Republican Government. 2. To draw a line of demarkation which would give to the General Government every power requisite for general purposes, and leave to the States every power which might be most beneficially administered by them. 3. To provide for the different interests of different parts of the Union. 4. To adjust the clashing pretensions of the large and small States." Dryly, Madison characterized each of these objects as "pregnant with difficulties." In the light of them, the concord that ultimately prevailed at the close of the Convention he found impossible to consider as "less than a miracle."

The crux of Madison's letter, however, is an "immoderate digression" on the dynamite-laden question of the division of power between the state and general governments. Madison first established the theory that republican government, "in order to effect its purposes, must operate not within a small but an extensive sphere." [10] A small re-

[9] Madison to Jefferson, New York, October 24, 1787. Writings (Congress), I, 344.
[10] Ibid., I, 350.

public, he maintained, is essentially what the ancient Greeks called "pure" democracy—a democracy where the citizens directly voice their vote and are directly governed by it. Such small republics are constitutionally unsuited to rise above local passions and inevitably conflicting interests. Large republics, on the other hand, are essentially "representative" governments, where citizens surrender their voice to the delegates, whom they control by allowing a stipulated term of office and whom they can refuse to re-elect. Only these extensive republics can develop the interplay of opposed passions, interests, or factions to a point where it is salutary, resulting in policies such as a disinterested and dispassionate umpire could typically achieve. Triumphantly Madison concluded that " 'Divide et impera,' the reprobated axiom of tyranny, is, under certain qualifications, the only policy by which a republic can be administered on just principles." [11]

Madison then proceeded to apply this theory to the relationship between the states and the general government. The splits that inevitably occur in every society—between the rich and the poor, the agrarian and the manufacturing interests, the debtors and the creditors (to mention only a few)—show up easily and unashamedly on the level of the state legislatures. On the level of general government it is otherwise. Changes tend to become less violent under the impact of the multiple groups and interests of many states. Striving to formulate the general principle, Madison wrote: "The great desideratum in Government is so to modify the sovereignty as that it may be sufficiently neutral between different parts of the society to control one part from invading the rights of another, and at the same time sufficiently controlled itself from setting up an interest adverse

[11] Ibid., I, 353.

to that of the entire society." [12] For the United States, this desideratum implies an even balance between the general government and the state governments, which serve the "particular parties" that are inevitably present in every small unit of government. Therefore, Madison concluded, in the general government broad jurisdiction is needed to offset the heated legislation by popular majorities that might emanate from the states. Only by such a brake on interested state majorities could a more genuine representation of popular interest for the aggregate of individuals in the nation be achieved.

2

The Constitution, as a document that had emerged from so many compromises of interest, was the subject of careful study by Jefferson in Paris. At least three great men in the Convention are known to have rushed copies of it to him: Benjamin Franklin, then America's chief elder statesman, for whom Jefferson always maintained the greatest affection and admiration; General Washington, who was at this period on the friendliest terms with Madison and who had been in cordial correspondence with Jefferson since the period of his governorship; and Madison himself. Jefferson, as he pondered the worth of the document, weighed Madison's reasoning in his letters against the differing views of George Mason, who had written of the "precipitate and intemperate not to say indecent conduct of the majority in the Convention" when he raised objections in the closing days. Mason's judgment, as well as Madison's, carried great weight with Jefferson. And Mason's belief that the Constitution was setting up, at best,

[12] Ibid.

"a moderate aristocracy," which, at its worst, might devolve into monarchy or "corrupt, tyrannical aristocracy," and that it badly needed a bill of rights,[18] unquestionably impressed Jefferson.

By the end of 1787 Jefferson was ready with his first penetrating survey of the merits and shortcomings of the newly proposed American Constitution. He assured Madison that he liked very much "the general idea of framing a government which should go on of itself peaceably, without needing continual recurrence to the state legislatures." Having put himself behind the plan for a general government, Jefferson further indicated his approval of its organization in three major branches, on the principle of checks and balances; its assignment of the power to levy taxes to the "greater house" (since this preserves inviolate "the fundamental principle that the people are not to be taxed but by representatives chosen immediately by themselves"); and its "captivating" compromise of the conflicting claims between the great and little states. He also commended the substitution of the method of voting by persons instead of by states, and the executive's veto "with a third of either house" over legislation—although he added that the judiciary should have been associated in this with the executive in some fashion—a feature that Madison had repeatedly but unsuccessfully urged in the Convention.

The things that Jefferson did not like, however, raise questions that are timelessly interesting in political theory, for they go much deeper than devices and details of structure. His major objections reduce to two. First, the omission of a bill of rights "providing clearly and without the aid of sophisms for freedom of religion, freedom of the

[18] Carl Van Doren: *The Great Rehearsal* (New York: Viking Press; 1948), pp. 165–6.

press, protection against standing armies, restriction against monopolies, the eternal and unremitting force of the habeas corpus laws, and trials by jury in all matters of fact triable by the laws of the land and not by the law of nations." [14]

Jefferson's spirited assertion of the need for a bill of rights forcibly recalls the charges he pointed at the British King in the Declaration of Independence. It is an interesting demonstration that Jefferson had neither formulated the precepts of the Declaration for the sake of expediency alone, nor abandoned the philosophy of the Declaration in the more conservative period of founding the Republic. He completed his defense by insisting that "a bill of rights is what the people are entitled to against every government on earth, general or particular, and what no just government should refuse, or rest on inferences." [15]

Jefferson's second criticism was directed against the abandonment of the principle of rotation in office, particularly in the case of the president. Re-election for lifetime would almost be assured the chief executive, Jefferson pointed out, unless the Constitution expressly prohibited it. Long tenure of power in the chief executive would tend to be an open invitation to interested foreign powers to interfere in American affairs with money and with arms. The only effective remedy, therefore, would be a constitutional stipulation that the executive be ineligible for re-election. Whether Jefferson knew it or not at the time, Hamilton had unabashedly defended lifetime tenure for the powerful executive that he was eager to see commanding the United States. Jefferson, who would live to accept two terms as President himself, was voicing the spirit that prompted him to refuse a third.

[14] Jefferson to Madison, Paris, December 20, 1787. *Writings* (Ford), IV, 476.

[15] Ibid., IV, 477.

How to preserve the good features in the Constitution while incorporating these suggested changes, Jefferson could not, at this juncture, advise. Maybe the Constitution should be "duly weighed and canvassed by the people" so that a revised document would benefit by popular suggestion and approval. Perhaps it should be adopted outright "in hopes of future amendment." In any case, Jefferson was sensitive to the fact that Madison's on-the-scene knowledge of detailed issues was superior to his own.

Jefferson was unshaken, however, in his devotion to democratic fundamentals. He could not refrain from reiterating his philosophy of the difference between despotic and democratic governments, and adverting again to his theme that occasional rebellions are only a moderate price to pay for democratic liberties. "I own I am not a friend to a very energetic government. It is always oppressive. The late rebellion in Massachusetts has given more alarm than I think it should have done. Calculate that one rebellion in 13 states in the course of 11 years, is but one for each state in a century and a half. No country should be so long without one. Nor will any degree of power in the hands of government prevent insurrections." [16] Citing France, "with all its despotism," Turkey, and England, "where the hand of power is lighter than here, but heavier than with us," Jefferson showed that American rebellions had been rather orderly and self-extinguishing affairs compared with the ferocious depredations of insurgent bands in other countries. Behind these judgments was Jefferson's characteristic political ideal: "After all, it is my principle that the will of the majority should always prevail." [17]

[16] Ibid., IV, 479.
[17] Ibid., IV, 479–80.

3

The correspondence between Madison and Jefferson on the Constitution illuminates the theoretical political beliefs of the two friends. Both men were probing the root meaning of what they called "Republican theory." Both were seeking to implement the principle that ultimate power, decision, and control should belong to the aggregate of the people. Private rights, the so-called "natural" and civil rights, including property, they both agreed should be protected to the fullest possible extent. But, as the correspondence establishes, there was no total unanimity on the methods or specific proposals for attaining their common ideals. Their differences signify more than the personal equations of two genuinely different temperaments. They demonstrate ponderable differences in their definition of the ideology of democracy.

The Jeffersonian view placed greater confidence than the Madisonian in the people themselves. Indeed, it was a specifically Jeffersonian tenet that democracy would work only to the extent that it activized the great mass of the people. One must remember Jefferson's later theory of the tiny "ward" (based on the supposed Anglo-Saxon unit of the "hundred") as the root from which a society builds up democracy. In his view, even smaller units of government than the ordinary county would help to make each person in the small neighborhood of the ward a participant in government. He distrusted the grant of large powers to a governing group at the top of the hierarchy, because the people would then never have the chance to learn to correct errors through their own experiences in local political bodies, such as the ward meeting, the county council, or the state legislature. For this reason he had unfailing admiration for New England's town meetings. If the people— ordinary citizens—could not learn to check abuses, all the more reason to fear sweeping powers in the governing "experts," who could use those powers to enslave the blundering populace.

In short, Jefferson located the center of tyrannical infection in centralized power. Madison, on the contrary, located the center of tyrannical infection in the undisciplined and overbearing impulses of local majorities to trample on the private rights (and property rights) of minorities. Jefferson envisaged the continuing importance and dignity of local, state, and general government authorities; Madison saw lurking beneath these local and general governments the fractured universe of people split into factions and disposed to conduct political warfare as special-interest groups. Madison formulated this belief most sharply in 1788 when he rose in the Virginia ratifying Convention to observe that the hatred and strife caused by majority tyranny over the rights of minorities had been the great destroyer of past republics.[18]

Interestingly enough, this cleavage in political beliefs was correlated, to some extent, with the separate experiences that the two friendly philosopher statesmen had just undergone. Madison had witnessed the inflationary measures of the state legislatures and other "symptoms of a levelling spirit" that violated contracts, overthrew treaties, and breathed heretical fire at established property "rights." He thereupon fled to the high ground of stable and effective "general" government. Jefferson, on the other hand,

[18] *The Debates, Resolutions and Other Proceedings, in Conventions, on the Adoption of the Federal Constitution, as Recommended by the General Convention at Philadelphia, on the 17th of September, 1787* (4 vols. Washington: Gales & Seaton; 1838), edited by Jonathan Elliott, II, 90.

was fired by the ruthlessness of European compared with American society. In Europe he had observed that nations are divided "into two classes, wolves and sheep." He enthusiastically cheered "the people," banked his faith in liberated society, and urged his friends to cherish the spirit of the people. "Do not be too severe upon their errors, but reclaim them by enlightening them. If once they become inattentive to the public affairs, you and I, and Congress and Assemblies, judges and governors shall all become wolves." [19]

An earlier token that some theoretical disagreement between the two friends might arise had been the opposite view they took of Shays' Rebellion. Madison's reaction to this armed uprising of hard-pressed Massachusetts debtors was, like John Adams's, close to horror at the overthrow of law and order. Jefferson, having weighed democratic turbulence against the oppressions of monarchy, stoutly maintained that "it becomes nothing." He even hoped such events might be productive of good in focusing attention on public affairs. He was actually moved to his (now classic) defense of rebellions, displaying his cheerful acceptance of the necessary inconveniences attending republican government. "I hold it that a little rebellion now and then is a good thing, and as necessary in the political world as storms in the physical," Jefferson confided urbanely to Madison, whose alarm he considered undue. "Unsuccessful rebellions indeed generally establish the encroachments on the rights of people which have produced them. An observation of this truth," he warned, "should render honest republican governors so mild in their punishment of rebellions, as not to discourage them too much." [20]

[19] Jefferson to Edward Carrington, Paris, January 16, 1787. *Writings* (Ford), IV, 360.
[20] Jefferson to Madison, Paris, January 30, 1787. Ibid., IV, 362–3.

This disagreement between Jefferson and Madison must be recognized. It makes us aware of permanent personal qualities often discernible in their intellectual approach to problems, and it allows us to see that the closer harmony of their fighting years as they forged the Republican Party and then led it in power was a synthesis of previously distinct elements. The final partnership of Jefferson and Madison, which has so often been taken as bland expediency or a heaven-sent unanimity based on guileless democratic faith, is visibly a working compromise, a powerful amalgam of two distinct minds striving to approximate the political good.

4

Mutual trust and courtesy are everywhere visible in the Jefferson-Madison correspondence, and were doubtless even more graciously embodied in the friendly intercourse of real life. On the few occasions in a half-century when they seriously disagreed, it was their habit to air the differences with each other, tactfully, but without material concealment. Only in the debate on the Constitution is there evidence of unusual strain in this habitual behavior—an instance that is especially interesting because it is an exception to the even tenor of their friendship.

Almost a year after the close of the Constitutional Convention, Madison sat down to write to his best friend a letter that is strange in only a single detail, his announcement that Jefferson will soon receive a volume, *The Federalist*. "I believe," Madison comments in an offhand manner, "I never have yet mentioned to you that publication. It was undertaken last fall by Jay, Hamilton, and myself. The proposal came from the two former. The execution was thrown, by the sickness of Jay, mostly on the two others. Though carried on in concert, the writers are not mutually answerable for all the ideas of each other, there being seldom time for even a perusal of the pieces by any but the writer before they were wanted at the press, and sometimes hardly by the writer himself." [21] This is an exceedingly puzzling and disturbing passage. To interpret it is difficult, but important, and therefore relevant facts are worth examination.

Madison first mentions his co-authorship and the publication of these extremely influential political papers to his closest friend as late as August 1788. The composition of the newspaper articles that later were collected as *The Federalist* began in October 1787, shortly after the close of the Constitutional Convention. Madison and Hamilton wrote at white heat until March 1788, when Madison returned to Virginia to help secure ratification for the Constitution in his state legislature. Hamilton then dashed off the final papers (with the exception of one article by Jay) in an almost incredible final spurt of twenty articles in the space of roughly eight weeks. By March 1788, before the newspaper series had been completed, the first volume of these papers in defense of the new Constitution had been collected and rushed through publication in book form by a New York publisher. Even before the closing papers of the series had been published in the newspapers, Hamilton sent them on to his publisher, so that the second and final volume of *The Federalist* was off the press by the end of May 1788. By the first week in June the complete work was in circulation in New York and en route to Virginia and other states.

[21] Madison to Jefferson, New York, August 10, 1788. *Writings* (Congress), I, 408.

Thus it appears that during the entire six months when Madison was composing his share of the papers, he had not mentioned his engrossing activity to Jefferson; and it was not until two months after the complete two-volume work had been widely circulated in the United States that the occasion finally arose for Madison to mention "that publication" to his best friend.[22] Like any one of the eternal tribe of writers in the grip of imperative journalistic deadlines, Madison could hardly have "forgotten" the work that absorbed the lion's share of his time in the period from October 1787 to March 1788 and beyond that another five months until, in mid-August, he finally wrote of it to Jefferson.

To be sure, the authorship of these papers was supposedly a secret, each newspaper article appearing under the pseudonymous signature "Publius." Since Jefferson and Madison used a cipher to discuss the gravest political secrets, Madison's tight-lipped behavior about *The Federalist* cannot readily be attributed to his fear that the secret would be discovered. Furthermore, Madison had not really tried to keep the secret for as long as an entire month after the project started. In the middle of November he had written to General Washington, enclosing the first seven numbers of *The Federalist*. Remarking that in Virginia they might not be "superfluous antidotes" to combat the views of "a party" (the opposition party, led by Patrick Henry and George Mason), Madison prompted Washington: "perhaps the papers may be put into the hands of

[22] The authorship of *The Federalist* was so largely the work of Hamilton and Madison that Jay's contribution of eight numbers, none of them first-rate, hardly justifies giving him a full share in the collaboration. The dispute of over a century on which papers to attribute to Hamilton and which to Madison is brilliantly decided in an article by Douglass Adair: "The Authorship of the Disputed Federalist Papers," *William and Mary Quarterly*, April 1944, pp. 97–122.

some of your confidential correspondents at Richmond, who would have them reprinted there." [23] With the stimulus of this practical reason for breaking the secret, Madison then admitted his authorship, although with absurd indirection: "I will not conceal from you that I am likely to have such a *degree* of connection with the publication here as to afford a restraint of delicacy from interesting myself directly in the republication elsewhere."

Oddly enough, Madison wrote several letters to Jefferson in the period between October 1787 and March 1788. In them considerable space is given to "the proposed federal Constitution" and how it fared in the different states, and there is no diminution of cordiality or skimping of friendly interchanges between Jefferson and Madison in this period. The only important topic deliberately avoided by Madison appears to be the political essays he and Hamilton were writing.[24] Late in April, just when Madison was awaiting the last papers in *The Federalist* series from Hamilton's pen, he added to his round-up of news on the campaign to secure adoption of the Constitution a brief paragraph saying that he would send Jefferson "the Debates of the Conventions in Pennsylvania and Massachusetts, and any other publications worth your reading"—but still no mention of *The Federalist*.[25]

Madison again wrote to Jefferson late in July (when the two-volume work had been out for some weeks), not mentioning *The Federalist*, but discussing the final questions debated by the Virginia Convention prior to its rati-

[23] Madison to General Washington, New York, November 18, 1787. *Writings* (Congress), I, 360–1.

[24] See Madison to Jefferson, New York, February 19, 1788. Madison Papers, L.C.

[25] Madison to Jefferson, Orange, April 22, 1788. *Writings* (Hunt), V, 123.

fication of the Constitution on June 25. Among the "variety of expedients" employed by the opposition to the Constitution, Madison reported, was the introduction by Patrick Henry and George Mason of Jefferson's opinions "expressed in a letter from you to a correspondent, (Mr. Donald or Skipwith, I believe,) and endeavored to turn the influence of your name even against parts of which I knew you approved." Concealing his own feelings, Madison continued: "In this situation I thought it due to truth, as well as that it would be most agreeable to yourself, and accordingly took the liberty to state some of your opinions on the favorable side. I am informed that copies of extracts of a letter from you were handed about at the Maryland Convention, with a like view of impeding the ratification." [26]

Madison's information was correct. Jefferson had written to numerous correspondents in Europe and America expressing his strong objections to various aspects of the Constitution, but particularly to its omission of a bill of rights.[27] These critical letters began in mid-November, after he had received the first news of the Constitution, and continued till the end of December, when in a letter to a sympathetic correspondent he finally admitted his differences with Madison and gave permission to the recipient to make use of his views but not his name.[28]

Jefferson withheld his name because he was genuinely concerned that it might exert excessive influence in support of views that, he confessed, were formed so distant from

[26] Madison to Jefferson, New York, July 24, 1788. *Writings* (Congress), I, 405.
[27] To cite only a few: Jefferson to Colonel W. S. Smith, Paris, November 13, 1787, *Writings* (Ford), IV, 465–7; to John Adams, Paris, November 13, 1787, *Writings* (Memorial) VI, 368; and, reviewing his major objections most systematically, to W. Carmichael, Paris, December 15, 1787, *Writings* (Ford), IV, 468–72.
[28] Jefferson to Colonel Uriah Forrest (spelled with one "r" by Ford), Paris, December 31, 1787. *Writings* (Ford), IV, 484–5.

the scene that he was diffident "to detail them lengthily and publicly." [29] He credited the "framers" of the Constitution with much honesty "and a presumption that all succeeding rulers would be as honest as themselves." In brief, Jefferson had no quarrel with the will to compromise and get on with the work of founding the new government. He appreciated Madison's anxiety to secure at least that indispensable beginning. But he could not suppress his own concern for the time when the fundamental charter of the United States might be made the basis for the assumption of undemocratic powers by unscrupulous rulers.

Obviously, Madison could not help being embarrassed by the opposition's use of his best friend's name on their side. Yet he carefully refrained from charging that Jefferson's views had impeded ratification in Virginia, in Maryland, and perhaps in other states too. He could say honestly that Jefferson was favorable to certain parts of the new Constitution, but he could hardly be free from disappointment that Jefferson had at this critical time expressed unfavorable opinions on other parts. Jefferson had correctly described the sum of his reactions: "I find myself nearly a neutral." [30] But he was tenacious and uncompromising about the bill of rights—so much so that Madison reintroduced the subject in the same letter in which he at last revealed his co-authorship of *The Federalist*.

Now that the New York Convention had ratified the new government, Madison observed, the greatest remaining danger concerned amendments. For "if another Convention should be soon assembled it would terminate in discord, or in alterations of the federal system, which would

[29] Ibid., IV, 484.
[30] Jefferson to Edward Carrington, Paris, December 21, 1787. Ibid., IV, 481.

throw back *essential* powers into the State Legislatures. The delay of a few years will assuage the jealousies which have been artificially created by designing men, and will at the same time point out the faults which really call for amendment. At present, the public mind is neither sufficiently cool nor sufficiently informed for so delicate an operation." [31] Madison's ground had shifted: only experience would prove the real shortcomings of the Constitution, and guarantees of fundamental civil liberties would be better formulated after several years' trial of the Constitution, and after the antipathy to federal powers exemplified in the constitutional debates in the state legislatures would have died down.

Thus it would appear that there was a temporary breach in the political unity of Jefferson and Madison from the time Madison learned Jefferson's reactions to the Constitution throughout the winter and spring of 1787–8. The strain was eased when Madison saw the triumph of the Constitution after its ratification by the key states, Virginia and New York. By the late summer of 1788 he was to talk freely on the issues that had been troubling him.

What was Madison's motive in keeping silent on his share in *The Federalist*? He had stated his views openly and responsibly to Jefferson on many occasions. There was, of course, their disagreement on the Constitution. Could Madison also have felt uneasy about telling Jefferson of his collaboration with Hamilton? To be sure, Jefferson and Hamilton had not yet been pitted against each other; but Madison knew the tenor of Hamilton's contempt for democracy and democratic republicanism.

Hamilton, in the Convention, attacked the Virginia

[31] Madison to Jefferson, New York, August 10, 1788. *Writings* (Congress), I, 407.

and New Jersey plans, castigating "the people" as turbulent and changing: "they seldom judge or determine right." [32] Rather than trust them, Hamilton had advised, give to the rich "a distinct, permanent share in the government." Only men of property and wealth could check the unsteadiness of the people, and "Nothing but a permanent body can check the imprudence of democracy"—that permanent body to be composed of the patricians not the plebeians. [33] While these terms had been abolished by the "Tribunitial power" of Rome, Hamilton contended that they returned under the everlasting distinction of the rich and the poor.

Madison himself, being the keenest of political theorists, certainly did not misjudge the hostility to republicanism in Hamilton's attack. Nor could he assume that Jefferson would have been kept in ignorance of this startling turn in the constitutional debate. But if he disliked having to confess his partnership with Hamilton to Jefferson, his fellow worker in "the cause of liberty," how could he have found it agreeable to associate his own views with those of the patrician-loving New Yorker?

Madison himself may have had considerable difficulty in his collaboration with Hamilton if the internal evidence of the text of *The Federalist* is added to the facts already recited. As an acute critic of American political thought has already pointed out, there are essentially two different political philosophies present in *The Federalist*—the Madisonian and the Hamiltonian. [34] The Madisonian view was that a limited and balanced government was to be recom-

[32] Alexander Hamilton: *Works* (Henry Cabot Lodge, ed.; New York, 1904), I, 401.
[33] *Journal of the Constitutional Convention*. Madison: *Writings* (Hunt), III, 289.
[34] Herbert W. Schneider: *A History of American Philosophy* (New York: Columbia University Press; 1946), pp. 89–99.

mended above all, devoted mainly to effecting justice and equality; and that ultimate popular sovereignty is the only defensible ground of good government. The Hamiltonian view was predominantly an early system of economic nationalism. Its chief concern was to achieve energetic administration, and according to this view the central function of government was the active promotion of the "general interests" of the people, interpreted not through their own presumably "unreasonable" eyes, but through the "sounder" judgment of the country's financial and industrial leaders—the managerial élite of a system of economic enterprise and government administration. In view of such different political philosophies, Madison may have hesitated to confide in Jefferson, whose own philosophy was even more democratic than his own.

In any case, Jefferson's handling of the curious episode of *The Federalist* was suave, gracious, and wise. He thanked Madison, after a time, for *The Federalist*, lightly remarking that he had already received a copy from a friend of both his and Madison's and that the three authors had previously been named to him. He complimented Madison without stint on his contributions, which he wrongly judged to be the most numerous in the book. "I read it with care, pleasure and improvement, and was satisfied there was nothing in it by one of those hands, and not a great deal by a second. It does the highest honor to the third, as being, in my opinion, the best commentary on the principles of government which ever was written." [35] However, Jefferson politely recognized that in certain sections the author meant only to do his best for opinions in which he did not "concur." And as for the bill of rights, however much *The*

[35] Jefferson to Madison, Paris, November 18, 1788. *Writings* (Ford), V, 52–3.

Federalist had corrected certain views, Jefferson held firm. He still thought it should be added.

5

On June 8, 1789 Madison rose on the floor of the First Congress to recommend the adoption of the Bill of Rights. He altered the severity of his original stand in order to accommodate the new government to the wishes of those leaders and that part of the public who had opposed the Constitution principally because it lacked a bill of rights. This group included, not only Jefferson, but important opposition elements throughout the country and in key states like Virginia, New York, Massachusetts. The last had ratified only on the condition that a bill of rights be submitted to the state conventions shortly after ratification. The group also included other Virginia friends, whose unswerving republicanism Madison knew well, especially James Monroe and Governor Edmund Randolph.[36]

In recognizing the criticism of these friends and sections of the American public, Madison departed from the stated view of his former collaborator, Hamilton, who had insisted in *The Federalist* that the movement for a bill of rights was unnecessary: "the constitution is itself . . . A BILL OF RIGHTS," he had announced.[37]

When Madison presented his proposed amendments to Congress, he struck a new note. He conceded publicly:

[36] Randolph had refused to sign the Constitution in the Convention, but was, with difficulty, brought back by Madison to support the federalist cause in the close debate preceding ratification in the Virginia legislature. It has been asserted that Randolph's aid to Madison and federalism in this crucial debate turned the vote in favor of ratification. Samuel Eliot Morison and Henry Steele Commager: *The Growth of the American Republic* (New York: Oxford University Press; 1930), pp. 164–5.

[37] *The Federalist*, No. 84. Everyman Edition, p. 440.

"I do conceive that the Constitution may be amended; that is to say, if all power is subject to abuse, that then it is possible the abuse of the powers of the General Government may be guarded against in a more secure manner than is now done. . . . We have in this way something to gain, and if we proceed with caution, nothing to lose." This significant act of welcoming a set of liberal amendments to the Constitution was not to be taken as an invitation to re-think the entire document. Madison emphatically stated that he was unwilling to "see a door opened for a reconsideration of the whole structure of the Government—for a reconsideration of the principles and the substance of the powers given." [38] The substance of his concession about amendments, however, was probably in principle a victory born in part of lengthy arguments with Jefferson.

On this occasion it was with considerable dispatch that Madison wrote to his friend in Paris that he had sponsored amendments to the Constitution of exactly the type Jefferson had advocated months earlier. He was persuaded that the amendments would "be satisfactory to a majority of those who have opposed the Constitution" and, mindful of men like George Mason and James Monroe—men whom Jefferson respected—"to a majority of that description in Virginia." [39]

A week later Madison predicted that it would take Congress some time to get to a real discussion of the amendments and pointed out, almost apologetically, that "Every thing of a controvertible nature that might endanger the concurrence of two-thirds of each House and three-

[38] Madison's Speeches in the First Congress, First Session. June 8, 1787. *Writings* (Hunt), V, 375.

[39] Madison to Jefferson, New York, June 13, 1789. Madison Papers, L.C.

fourths of the States was studiously avoided. This will account for the omission of several amendments which occur as proper." [40] At the same time he was pleased to report a gratifying bit of personal news for Jefferson: that finally the American Minister to France had been granted permission to make a visit to America, an expressed wish of Jefferson's since half a year earlier [41] when he had written to Madison to help get action on his formal request to visit his native country.

In the "form and extent" Madison originally proposed, the amendments were designed to be worked into the text of the Constitution at appropriate places—not blocked off in splendid isolation as they now are in the Bill of Rights. He was worried that the amendments, set apart, might be treated as a second basic document, interpreted as a philosophy different from that of the Constitution, and made to become the fulcrum of silent or overt warfare against the original document. [42]

Madison supported his conciliatory amendments, however, in a fashion acceptable to two thirds of both houses. He argued that a declaration of the rights of the people would restrain potential abuses of power by the legislative and executive branches of the government. [43] Recognizing that he had not always been sympathetic to demands for a bill of rights, Madison carefully reminded his audience that he had never opposed the ideas motivating these demands. Now that the new government was under way, a bill of

[40] Madison to Jefferson, New York, June 30, 1789. *Writings* (Congress), I, 485.

[41] Jefferson to Madison, Paris, November 18, 1788. *Writings* (Ford), V, 54–6.

[42] Madison to Alexander White, New York, August 24, 1789. *Writings* (Hunt), V, 418, n.–419n.

[43] Madison's speech in Congress, June 8, 1789. Ibid., V, 385.

rights was "neither improper nor altogether useless." [44] Explicit guards for the "great rights" of liberty of conscience, freedom of the press, and trial by jury—which Madison called the "choicest liberties of the people"—would certainly reassure the citizenry. Moreover, safeguarding these liberties would conform to the most enlightened of the states' bills of rights, and to the republican principle that the powers of government should be limited by specifying areas where the government must not transgress, or where it can act only in "a particular mode." [45]

Although Madison recommended his amendments cautiously, the introductory statements in his proposed first amendment were quite as bold as Jefferson would have wished. They were, in truth, a restatement of the underlying philosophy of the Virginia Declaration of Rights, written by George Mason, and of Jefferson's Declaration of Independence. Had Madison's first amendment passed the Congress, there would have been even less basis than there now is for the frequent criticism that the basic philosophy of "natural rights" of the American Declaration of Independence is incompatible with the federal Constitution. Madison was apparently of the opinion that he could integrate with the text of the Constitution the following statements, repeating almost verbatim Mason's language in his second paragraph of the Virginia Declaration of Rights:

First. That there be prefixed to the Constitution a declaration, that all power is originally vested in, and consequently derived from, the people.

That Government is instituted and ought to be exercised for the benefit of the people; which consists in the enjoyment

[44] Ibid., V, 380.
[45] Ibid., V, 381.

of life and liberty, with the right of acquiring and using property, and generally of pursuing and obtaining happiness and safety.

That the people have an indubitable, unalienable, and indefeasable right to reform or change their Government, whenever it be found adverse or inadequate to the purposes of its institution.[46]

The tangled confusion of the First Congress in the newly established Republic worked against Madison's plan to declare the original principles of freedom and to incorporate the amendments in the main text of the Constitution. Madison knew what he was up against and he described the new Congress pithily to Jefferson as "a wilderness without a single footstep to guide us." [47] Accordingly, he was resigned when confronted with the committee's changed version of his proposed amendments. The best he could say for the changes was that some of them were perhaps for the better, others for the worse. But at least something "will be effected," he wrote to Jefferson.[48]

Madison's confidence was not misplaced. His wish to please the American people by declaring "the great rights of mankind secured under this Constitution" was, in effect, honored by Congress, and later by the state legislatures that ratified the amendments.[49] The general declaration of principles that Madison had included in his first amendment,

[46] Ibid., V, 376.

[47] Madison to Jefferson, New York, June 30, 1789. *Writings* (Congress), I, 480.

[48] Madison to Jefferson, New York, August 2, 1789. From the collection of the Pierpont Morgan Library. Taken from photostat, by courtesy of the editors of *Jefferson Papers*, Princeton.

[49] The twelve amendments submitted to the states by Congress were reduced to ten, the third of the original list becoming the official first amendment. The two rejected concerned adjusted proportions for congressional representation, and a limiting condition on changing the compensation for senators and representatives.

however, was eliminated in the committee. Prominent in the final list were those declaring religious freedom, the freedom of speech and press, freedom from unreasonable searches and seizures, freedom of the people to assemble peaceably and to "petition the Government for a redress of grievances." But, as we have seen, Madison had wished to guarantee more than the right of the people to "petition the Government for a redress of grievances"; he had spoken directly and democratically of the right of the people "to reform or change their government." Other changes in Madison's proposals were in the same more conservative direction. Madison had provided for a "well-regulated militia," the right of the people to keep and bear arms, and the exemption of conscientious objectors from military service. This last privilege disappeared in the revised list. Nevertheless, the liberal provisions in the fifth, sixth, seventh, and eighth amendments stood firm. These concerned the conduct of criminal cases, trial by jury for suits at common law, prohibition of excessive bail or fines or cruel punishments. The ninth and tenth amendments of the final list, which later became the battleground of the strict and the broad constructions of the Constitution, are substantially similar to Madison's version—although the crucial tenth amendment, reserving powers not delegated to the United States by the Constitution, nor prohibited by it "to the States respectively, or to the people," revised Madison's more explicit directive that the powers delegated by the Constitution should not be so construed as to enlarge them or to diminish other rights retained by the people.[50]

Jefferson's only direct comments on Madison's list of amendments were unfortunately confined to a letter packed

[50] Madison's amendments to the Constitution, *Writings* (Hunt), **V**, 376–80.

with the exciting details of the most recent development in his own tumultuous world: Revolutionary France. Accordingly, the emotional tone of these comments is noticeably reduced. Also, Jefferson had been deeply immersed in preparations to sail from Havre with his two daughters in October. He made it clear, however, that his doubts about the Constitution had been relieved. The Bill of Rights, he commented, "I like . . . as far as it goes; but I should have been for going further." [51]

[51] Jefferson to Madison, Paris, August 28, 1789. *Writings* (Ford), V, 112.

Chapter Four

THE EARTH BELONGS TO THE LIVING

THE REAL SUMMATION of Jefferson's and Madison's trans-atlantic debate on political theory occurs in an apparently new context. Just before leaving Paris, Jefferson wrote down his deepest philosophical critique of constitutions and the ultimate ends of good government in a letter he intended to send to Madison. It raised a question that Jefferson believed had never been raised before, but which, in his view, was one of the most fundamental in political philosophy: has one generation a right to bind another? This is the famous letter of September 6, 1789, usually identified by its powerful theme "The earth belongs always to the living generation." [1]

Jefferson held the letter until his arrival in America, intending to give it to Madison when they met. He therefore had several months to think over its contents. Second thought did not make him wish to revise or abandon his radical views, and Madison was to have received the letter at his first meeting with his friend. But after Madison's visit

[1] Jefferson to Madison, Paris, September 6, 1789. *Writings* (Ford), V, 115–24. Printed versions of this letter are not entirely correct. The Memorial Edition of Jefferson's *Writings* prints Jefferson's first version of this letter; but he corrected the important error of computing 34 years as the span of a "generation" to 19 years in the second version of the letter. There are other differences in this second version. The Ford Edition prints the corrected second version, but misreads several important sentences and phrases. For drafts, first version, and second version the Jefferson Papers at the Library of Congress must be consulted. For the original of the second version see Madison Papers, L.C.

was over, Jefferson recalled that while he had spoken of the letter, he had again forgotten to give it to him. He then sent it to him in New York on January 9, 1790, enclosed in a note which is a fresh endorsement of the theme. "After so long lying by me," Jefferson wrote, "and further turning the subject in my mind, I find no occasion to alter my mind. I hazard it therefor to your consideration." [2] When Madison finally received the long-overdue communication, he instantly wrote a searching reply.[3]

The two letters together (Jefferson scholars have failed to consider Madison's reply) constitute a brilliant finis for Jefferson's long and profitable tour of duty in Europe and Madison's supreme fight in America to establish a strong constitution and a stable new government. Nowhere in the friendship of fifty years can we find a better expression of intellectual reciprocity, enabling Madison to sparkle with borrowed warmth, and Jefferson to discipline the humane overambitiousness of his proposals. The perfect courtesy that pervaded this and other intellectual encounters made it possible for stringent criticism to be received without hurt, and philosophical prodding to be tolerated without injury to pride. The impression one gathers here—an impression reinforced in other exchanges—is that Jefferson is more speculative and more daring in putting forward dynamic generalizations, and that Madison is the more astute politician. Jefferson's liberated spirit made it possible for Madison to achieve the flair that required more than political intuition, while Madison supplied the means for Jefferson to remain a philosopher in politics—a philosopher, that is, charged with real power.

[2] Jefferson to Madison, Monticello, January 9, 1790. Madison Papers, L.C.

[3] Madison to Jefferson, New York, February 4, 1790. *Writings* (Hunt), V, 437–41, n.

2

Jefferson set up his argument in the letter on the "self evident" principle that the earth belongs to the living, and not to the dead. The dead have no powers and no rights, for they are nothing. Whatever powers or rights they had when alive cease naturally with their death. Therefore, since the dead have no rights, they have no right to bind the living.

The first application of this principle established that specific property rights are civil and not natural rights. The earth is made for the use of the living by natural law, but specific lands are owned by the living only by virtue of the laws of society. The portion of the earth occupied by any man ceases to be his with his death, and reverts to society. "Then no man can by *natural right* oblige the lands he occupied. . . . For if he could, he might during his own life, eat up the usufruct of the lands for several generations to come, and then the lands would belong to the dead, and not to the living, which would be the reverse of our principle. What is true of every member of the society individually, is true of them all collectively, since the rights of the whole can be no more than the sum of the rights of individuals." [4]

This distinction between natural and civil rights is basic in Jefferson's philosophy. Essential freedoms are personal and political. Inextricably connected with Jefferson's principle is his thesis that all men have a natural right to a share of the earth that, with proper cultivation, would take care of the primary needs. This principle enables Jefferson to criticize specific laws of landed property where these per-

[4] Jefferson to Madison, Paris, September 6, 1789. *Writings* (Ford), V, 116.

vert natural rights. Jefferson had developed the thesis two years before, in a letter to President James Madison of the College of William and Mary (the statesman's cousin). He wrote that in France he had seen the desperate need for society to devise laws to ensure a more equal distribution of the land. He now valued more than before his fight for the abolition of the feudal hangovers of primogeniture and entail in Virginia, although he clearly saw that the ease of finding a solution in America was a function of our great available land resources. But universally there was something *wrong* with man-made laws and governmental taxes that ended by disinheriting a considerable section of the population from the independence that came with working one's own property.

Jefferson formulated a principle to conform with these views that still carries a dynamic message: "Whenever there is in any country, uncultivated lands and unemployed poor, it is clear that the laws of property have been so far extended as to violate natural right." To justify this assertion, Jefferson next used a formula reminiscent of John Locke: "The earth is given as a common stock for man to labour & live on." [5] The chain of reasoning curiously reaches out to the future as well as to the past—for there is a distinctively modern ring to Jefferson's admonition: "If for the encouragement of industry we allow it [the earth] to be appropriated, we must take care that other employment be provided to those excluded from the appropriation. If we do not, the fundamental right to labour the earth re-

[5] Jefferson to Rev. James Madison, Paris, October 28, 1785. Ibid., VII, 35–6. Locke had written: "God, who hath given the world to men in common, hath also given them reason to make use of it. . . . The earth and all that is therein is given to men for the support and comfort of their being." John Locke: *Two Treatises of Civil Government*, Book II, Chapter v, paragraph 25, Everyman Edition, p. 129.

turns to the unemployed." While he did not wish to sound radical and admitted that it was "too soon" to say that those who cannot find employment should be at liberty to cultivate uncultivated land, "paying a moderate rent," he concluded his letter to the Reverend James Madison by observing: "But it is not too soon to provide by every possible means that as few as possible shall be without a little portion of land. The small land holders are the most precious part of a state."

The second application Jefferson made of the principle that the earth belongs to the living concerned the public debt. Since the dead have no right to bind the living, the living are under no obligation to pay the debts of the dead. The living have no right to burden posterity with their own debts and are morally bound to pay them within their own time. "I suppose that the received opinion, that the public debts of one generation devolve on the next, has been suggested by our seeing habitually in private life that he who succeeds to lands is required to pay the debts of his ancestor or testator, without considering that this requisition is municipal only, not moral, flowing from the will of the society . . . but that between society and society, or generation and generation there is no municipal obligation, no umpire but the law of nature." [6]

In presenting this argument for a natural limit on the public debt, Jefferson had in mind the perpetuation of debts by France and Great Britain. Because no limit was accepted, these countries witnessed the dissipations of their rulers and the corruptions of war. These in turn put the people under ever accumulating burdens of taxation, with resulting poverty and oppression. "By reducing . . . the faculty of borrowing within its natural limits, it would

[6] Jefferson to Madison, September 6, 1789. *Writings* (Ford), V, 120.

bridle the spirit of war, to which too free a course has been procured by the inattention of money lenders to this law of nature, that succeeding generations are not responsible for the preceding [7]. . . . and it will exclude . . . the contagious and ruinous errors of this quarter of the globe, which have armed despots with means not sanctioned by nature for binding in chains their fellow-men." [8]

To preserve the independence of the people and guard the rights of posterity, Jefferson proposed that governments should fix the ultimate term for the redemption of public debts within the limits of their rightful powers. The law of nature prescribes the limits of their powers within the period of the life of the majority. This rule would prevent the creation of a perpetual or unjust public debt. The point is so important for Jefferson that he urged the consideration of a fundamental provision in the new French constitution: ". . . would it not be wise and just for that nation to declare in the constitution they are forming that neither the legislature, nor the nation itself can validly contract more debt, than they may pay within their own age . . . ?" [9]

In writing to Madison, however, Jefferson had more immediate concerns than a declaration of rights in the French constitution. He proposed that Madison should consider the application of this principle to the United States. "It would furnish matter for a fine preamble to our first law for appropriating the public revenue. . . . We have already given, in example, one effectual check to the Dog of war, by transferring the power of letting him loose from the executive to the Legislative body, from those who are to spend to those who are to pay. I should be pleased to see this second

[7] Ibid., V, 121.
[8] Ibid., V, 123.
[9] Ibid., V, 120.

obstacle held out by us also in the first instance. No nation can make a declaration against the validity of long-contracted debts so disinterestedly as we, since we do not owe a shilling which may not be paid with ease principal and interest, within the time of our own lives." [10]

The third and most important application of the principle that the earth belongs to the living concerned the constitution and laws of any society. Since each generation is independent of the one preceding, it has a right to choose its own constitution and laws. No constitution, no law, is too sacred to be changed. This is the heart of Jefferson's philosophy of constitutions:

. . . no society can make a perpetual constitution, or even a perpetual law. The earth belongs always to the living generation. They may manage it then, and what proceeds from it, as they please, during their usufruct. They are masters too of their own persons, and consequently may govern them as they please. But persons and property make the sum of the objects of government. The constitution and the laws of their predecessors extinguished them, in their natural course, with those whose will gave them being. This could preserve that being till it ceased to be itself, and no longer . . . If it be enforced longer, it is an act of force and not of right. [11]

If the earth belongs to the living generation, it was important for Jefferson to determine the life of a generation. He correctly considered that this period is established by the laws of mortality. For this purpose, he turned to Buffon's mortality tables of 23,994 deaths and the ages at which they occurred. On this basis Jefferson set up two models for the succession of generations. In his first model he assumed a whole generation of men born on the same

[10] Ibid., V, 123.
[11] Ibid., V, 121.

day, reaching maturity at twenty-one years of age, and dying on the same day, thirty-four years later. Each successive generation was assumed to come on and go off the stage at a fixed and simultaneous time. On second thought, Jefferson corrected some of the features of this model in the final draft of his letter to Madison. In his second model Jefferson attempted to take account of the fact that people are born and die every year. He assumed a constant population defined by Buffon's mortality tables. He observed that of all the persons of all ages living at one moment, half would be dead within twenty-four years and eight months. By leaving out of account all minors, Jefferson estimated that one half of the adults (who have the power of self-government and constitute a majority of the voters) would be dead within eighteen years and eight months, or approximately within nineteen years. At the end of every nineteen-year period an entirely new majority will come into place, a new generation. Therefore, no debt, no constitution, and no law should validly extend beyond this period.

Naturally, all models have some degree of abstraction. But Jefferson sinned rather grossly on the side of abstraction, although his models were ingenious attempts to apply the best demographic data available in the late eighteenth century to the problem of defining a generation. In this attempt he manifested his normal experimental leanings in philosophy. Further, his effort was commendable for its intention to tie down elusive qualitative principles by quantitative demonstrations. But it should be noticed none the less that even the second model conjures up a forbiddingly unrealistic social situation—one which Madison spotted and which he called to Jefferson's attention. In both of his models Jefferson had computed the average life of a generation, and in applying the models to the political questions he raised he assumed a static society, with each generation born on the same day and maturing simultaneously at a fixed later time. But in fact births and deaths in any society form a continuum, and a new majority appears every year, and not simply every thirty-five or nineteen years. Jefferson confused a new majority with an *entirely* new majority.

In closing his letter, Jefferson had called on Madison to take up the thesis and promote it with "that cogent logic so peculiarly yours." Only Madison, Jefferson thought, could create the opportunity to "force" the subject into discussion—so high did Madison stand "in the councils of our country." Aware of the theoretical cast of his suggestions, Jefferson apologized for what would "at first blush. . . be laughed at, as the dream of a theorist"—an apology which he softened, in his second version of the letter, to "at first blush it may be rallied as a theoretical speculation." [12] These were very likely only conventional disclaimers, since Jefferson protested that examination would prove his theory "solid and salutary."

3

Despite Jefferson's friendly appeals, Madison was loath to employ his "cogent logic" in promoting a policy on the limits of constitutions, laws, and public debts that he considered unrealistic. The form taken by Madison in his reply was to agree in theory with his friend's fundamental principles, but to attack on the grounds of practicability virtually every specific proposal the letter contained. He detailed the reasons for his skepticism.

His first big gun was directed against Jefferson's recommendation that all constitutions require periodic revision

[12] Ibid., V, 123; and Jefferson Papers and Madison Papers, L.C.

every nineteen years in order to allow each generation to legislate for itself. Were such a limitation imposed on the fundamental laws of a society, what would be its effect? Madison objected that he could see three distinct disadvantages flowing from this mechanical limitation on constitutions. First, government would be subject to an interregnum, with all its attendant consequences. Secondly, a government "too mutable & novel" loses its tradition and the cumulative respect of a patriotic citizenry. Probably every government requires "that share of prejudice in its favor which is a salutary aid to the most rational government." Third, Madison suspected that periodic total revisions of a constitution might encourage "pernicious factions . . . and agitate the public mind more frequently and more violently than might be expedient." [13]

The second big gun was trained on laws carrying some stipulation rendering them irrevocable at the will of the legislature. "If the earth be the gift of *nature* to the living, their title can extend to the earth in its *natural* state only." In a civil state, Madison pointed out, the "improvements made by the dead form a debt against the living, who take the benefit of them." [14] Therefore, those who initiated the improvements can properly impose obligations upon the future generations who will gain by them. Especially is this true of debts incurred in wars of national defense. There are also debts incurred principally for the benefit of posterity, and not necessarily dischargeable within the term of nineteen years. In general, Madison concluded this series of objections by stating that upon investigation there seemed to be some "foundation in the nature of things" to support

[13] Madison to Jefferson, New York, February 4, 1790. *Writings* (Hunt), V, 438–9, n.
[14] Ibid., V, 439, n.

the "descent of obligations" from one generation to another.[15]

The third big gun of Madison's critique aimed at ordinary laws. Here Madison announced his objections were
"merely practical," but so strong that they constituted very
material objections indeed. Considering mainly positive
laws concerning property, Madison foresaw "the most violent struggles . . . between the parties interested in reviv-
ing & those interested in reforming the antecedent state of
property." [16] Anarchy, or at least a general confusion about
the state of things would then "discourage every useful effort of steady industry pursued under the sanction of existing laws." [17]

The burden of the final section of Madison's letter of
reply was philosophical. He properly interpreted Jefferson's
position to imply a doctrine of "overt or express" declaration of the public will on the part of each generation, for
constitutions and for laws affecting public debt and property. This assumption conditioned Jefferson's argument
throughout, and in Madison's opinion led to the "embarrassments" he had just reviewed in his threefold critique of
"the earth belongs to the living." The only escape from this
unworkable doctrine, Madison thought, was to endorse the
prevalent doctrine that there can be *tacit* assent to established governments and laws "and that this assent is to be
inferred from the omission of an express revocation." [18]
Without implied or tacit consent, civil society could not
exist. This principle, in fact, is at the heart of the republican belief that the voice of the majority binds the minority.

[15] Ibid.
[16] Ibid.
[17] Ibid., V, 440, n.
[18] Ibid.

If one asks *why* majority rule, the answer can hardly be that it is decreed by a law of nature! For, Madison pointed out, a law of nature would strictly imply unanimity rather than mere majority. The answer, Madison thought, must be derived from "compact founded on utility," not from natural law at all. Finally, if one were to suppose that tacit or implied assent could not be allowed, "no person born in Society, could on attaining ripe age, be bound by any acts of the majority, and either a unanimous renewal of every law would be necessary, as often as a new member should be added to the Society, or the express consent of every new member be obtained to the rule by which the majority decides for the whole." In this quite realistic fashion, anticipating the criticism of literal "natural rights" doctrine of a much later age, Madison depicted the *reductio ad absurdum* of the models that Jefferson used to establish that the earth belongs to the living. In this procedure he exposed the weakness of Jefferson's models by recalling that in any *actual* society a generation would not mature simultaneously and at fixed intervals; but daily and hourly, because of the stream of individuals passing from adolescence to adulthood.

The grander vision of Jefferson's startling proposal, however, did not escape Madison's consideration. He readily granted that Jefferson's principle was of general importance for philosophical legislators. In the main, he himself accepted Jefferson's objective: To make constitutions sensitive to the majority will of each successive generation—for without this, as Jefferson had pointed out, a constitution would be "an act of force and not of right." Madison further welcomed the principle, and said it would give him pleasure "to see it first announced to the world in a law of

the United States" to restrain living generations from plac-
ing "*unjust and unnecessary*" burdens on their successors.[19]
For the present generation is morally bound to respect the
natural rights—the basic needs—of coming generations,
however much positive laws in any given society may depart
from the moral ideal. In short, those who set the financial
policy of democratic countries would be doing well to bear
this principle in mind and apply it to the changing circumstances of their own day. But the limitation on debt policy,
or legal or constitutional policy, could not be mechanical or
automatic, restricted to nineteen or any other number of
years. Nor could debts be restricted in intention to the present generation if the object of the debts could *justly* be
claimed as a necessary burden on posterity, the debt having
been incurred principally for the benefit of posterity. The
debt incurred on account of the Revolutionary War, which
the United States was still struggling with at the time of
Madison's writing, was such a debt.

In general, the fundamental features of the theory that
proved acceptable to both Jefferson and Madison were forward-looking and generous in their regard for the liberty
and welfare of generations to come in America. Madison's
agreement with Jefferson in regarding constitutions as subject to principled alteration was one of many convincing
proofs that although he was a constitution-maker, he was
not a constitution-idolater. Both men were liberal and experimental in their effort to provide a society that would
meet the demands of each living being for conditions that
would encourage growth and self-respect. That was why
Jefferson really cared more for bills of rights than he did for
constitutions. Bills of rights, declarations of fundamental
political principles such as he had provided in the Declara-

[19] Ibid., V, 441, n.

tion of Independence and had promoted while in France, were salutary reminders of the ends of good government and the restraints upon power that every free society would honor.

While Madison underwrote what he considered to be the sound part of Jefferson's theoretical letter, he made it clear that he was in no position to assure his friend of the readiness of the new American government to accept the principles they both valued. It would. be a long time, he warned, before "truths . . . seen through the medium of Philosophy, become visible to the naked eye of the ordinary politician." [20]

4

One cannot properly appreciate Jefferson's perspective on the theme that the earth belongs to the living without reference to his recent experiences abroad. France, on the eve and in the dawn of revolution, was the climax of his exciting opportunity to gain "the knowledge of another world." In the midst of the American Minister's momentous last year in Paris, he was permitted to play a unique role as American adviser to a group of influential and enlightened French leaders. For the liberal reform group headed by Lafayette, the group Jefferson referred to as "the Patriot Party," he became a subtle brain-truster, counseling deftly, urbanely, and without a suspicion of egotism. He kept a steady head, placed an effective historical perspective on unprecedented and chaotic events, never wavered in his faith in free government.

With all his liberal enthusiasm, however, Jefferson was cautious in assessing the realistic limits of the reform that

[20] Ibid.

France could bear. Had he had his way, the French Revolution would have ended with a humane charter of rights, such as the one he prepared and sent to Lafayette and Monsieur de St. Etienne, for submission to the King.[21] The charter would have taken its place in a constitutional monarchy, Jefferson thought, designed to be no worse domestically than the British, and more restrained in its foreign ambitions. Possessed of a strong constitution of the sort Jefferson advocated, the French people, he decided, would have secured their basic liberties, and would be well placed for the gradual conquest of further popular rights and freedoms.

Quite spontaneously Jefferson was employing a political relativism that he had already encountered in theory in the writings of Montesquieu. But he really did not have to rely on Montesquieu for taking account of the obvious and vast differences between his own young country and an old and still feudal France. Consulting his own experience of two radically different worlds led Jefferson to wish that the cause of liberty would triumph in his "adopted" country, France, at the same time that he thought it vain to try to transpose literally the democratic experiment of America to French soil. The open lands of the North American continent, with their promise of a nation of independent, prosperous farmers, inclined Jefferson to believe that his country was singularly destined for earthly happiness. These same opportunities were lacking in France, where a much slower process would be required to liberate the oppressed peasantry, long ground under the heel of tax-hungry monarchs and a tithe-hungry church.

It was Europe, after all, that Jefferson had savagely

[21] Jefferson to M. de St. Etienne, Paris, June 3, 1789. *Writings* (Ford), V, 99–100.

characterized as a society where "every man must be hammer or anvil," and of which he wrote to Joseph Jones, James Monroe's distinguished uncle, that the comparison of our government with those of Europe was "like a comparison of heaven and hell." [22] Mindful of the compelling connection between economic sufficiency and public morality, Jefferson expected greater national virtue of America because she could avoid the "general prey of the rich upon the poor" —a harmony that he considered essential to republicanism.[23] The fact that the great mass of the population in the United States consisted of property-owning laborers, whose labor ensured them a minimum of their basic needs and moderate creature comforts as well, was his basis for hoping that America would never tolerate a government of men that devoured their own kind.[24] Since Jefferson thought it possible to have a society thus largely composed of one generally prosperous class, with no inner divisions of an inevitable sort between the rich and the pauper-poor, he could afford to be free of some of the fears of the "vengeful" majority that even his astute friend Madison had not been able to allay.

As the reform movement had gathered cumulative force in Paris, Jefferson's influence had even been felt in the French National Assembly. The opening of the fateful year 1789 found Jefferson busy with his intimate French friends, devising declarations of rights—the basic principles to guide a society that was ready to affirm the great truth that "the mass of mankind has not been born with saddles on their backs, nor a favored few booted and spurred, ready

[22] Jefferson to Joseph Jones, Paris, August 14, 1787. Ibid., IV, 438.
[23] Jefferson to Colonel Edward Carrington, Paris, January 16, 1787. Ibid., IV, 360.
[24] Jefferson to Dr. Thomas Cooper, Monticello, September 10, 1814. *Writings* (Memorial), XIV, 182.

to ride them legitimately, by the grace of God." [25] Having advised Lafayette on the chief principles to include in his declaration of rights, Jefferson was asked in turn to revise it. Penciled corrections of Lafayette's declaration on the copy Jefferson retained have been interpreted to be Jefferson's own. Jefferson must also have requested another good friend of his, Dr. Gem, to submit another version. Both declarations of rights Jefferson carefully copied in the original French and enclosed in a letter to Madison, so that America might study what the French intellectuals in the cause of liberty were turning their thoughts to. [26] In the summer of 1789 the French National Assembly in its pre-Revolutionary work became strikingly busy with similar declarations of rights. Jefferson's friends and disciples had not done their preparatory work in vain.

The penciled suggestions that are presumably Jefferson's have been taken to mean that he bracketed the word "property" in order to exclude it from the basic natural rights with which man was supposedly created. This is only a partially plausible interpretation. A vogue in historical interpretation in America has recently made much of the distinction between Locke's tradition emphasizing "property" and the American tradition, stemming from the Declaration of Independence, cleaving to the supposedly very different right, the "pursuit of happiness."

In the light of Jefferson's carefully elaborated thesis in "the earth belongs to the living" letter (a doctrine that he adhered to throughout his life) an elementary claim to some small portion of the earth is the inherent natural right of every individual. Thus Locke's famous trinity of rights—

[25] Jefferson to R. C. Weightman, Monticello, June 24, 1826. Ibid., XVII, 81–2.
[26] Jefferson to Madison, August ——, 1789. W. C. Rives Papers, L.C.

life, liberty, and property—is not far removed from Jefferson's philosophy of natural rights. For while Locke's "property" is thought to be a conservative and "bourgeois" interest, a close reading of Locke plainly shows that he used the term "property" in some contexts to mean far more than legal title to money, possessions, or credit. He sometimes meant it to include the product of a man's work—and every man, particularly in a "wilderness" like America (or in a "paradise" like it, for Locke uses both descriptions), had a natural right to work and to the fruit of his own labor. In this sense Locke speaks of a man having property *in his person*, in the faculties that he can employ to make the earth more productive. In this broad usage of the term "property" Jefferson, and the American tradition that stems from his writings, cannot be said to disagree.

While Jefferson recognized that the right to property could be alienated by society, or varied indefinitely by the specific civil laws of a society, he believed that the natural right to the means of subsistence should restrain the nature of those civil laws. Republicanism as a theory of society maintained the inviolability of property in this basic sense of embracing the satisfaction of the needs of the individual organism. In accordance with this important view, Jefferson wrote that "the true foundation of republican government . . . [is] the equal right of every citizen, in his person and property." [27] To improve one's material conditions as a result of one's own individual efforts was a further extension of the natural right to property.

The use of the phrase "the pursuit of happiness" in the Declaration is easily understandable, but only partly for theoretical reasons. There were practical reasons operating

[27] Jefferson to Samuel Kercheval, Monticello, July 12, 1816. *Writings* (Ford), X, 39.

too. Jefferson wanted moral, humane, and eloquent symbols in a manifesto that was expected to mobilize the thirteen colonies for war and win for them the sentiment of the civilized world. His rhetorical and stylistic sensibility alone might have made him prefer the phrase "the pursuit of happiness" over the uninspiring and legalistic term "property." Sense, however, strongly reinforced sound. Jefferson knew that the country would soon be asking loyal support from those without property as well as those with it, just as he knew that American Tories, who had refused to join the patriot ranks, might have their property confiscated. Still more sensible was his concern to avoid an appeal to property on the eve of repudiating Great Britain's complicated claims that the colonies, founded on the basis of royal grants in many cases, were and should remain *her* property! To all these substantial practical reasons, one should add the numerous precedents already in existence in American documents and political literature, as influential in making the term seem natural to the author of the Declaration of Independence: George Mason's Virginia Bill of Rights, notably, and James Wilson's pamphlet, *Considerations of the Nature and Extent of the Legislative Authority of the British Parliament*; plus a host of preceding English, Scottish, French, Swiss, Dutch, and classical sources where "happiness" is identified as the end-in-view of good government—all sources with which Jefferson was acquainted.

When Jefferson turned, some thirteen years after the Declaration of Independence, to his all-absorbing task of promoting declarations of rights for the French nation in its experiments for improved government, he probably enclosed the word "property" in Lafayette's Declaration for reasons similar to these earlier ones. Beyond these, the ambiguity in the term "property" was not a useful one. The natural right to property, as Jefferson distinguished it in his doctrine that the earth belongs to the living was not to be confused with the civil laws in society that fixed the particular property relationships that society saw fit to institute. In any event, the phrase Jefferson appears to have substituted for property in Lafayette's declaration, "*la recherche du bonheur*," did not appear in the Declaration of the Rights of Man and the Citizen that was presented to the Assembly and adopted by them on August 26, 1789. The disputed triplet had been replaced through the caprice or rationale of history by a quadruplet freighted with its own significant values, born of different fears than those that had possessed colonial America: "liberty, property, security, and resistance to oppression."

5

In so far as Jefferson's strictures on a short-term constitution were radical as well as experimental, it is valuable to see whether he was right in claiming originality for his philosophy. At the outset of Jefferson's letter, he stated that the question he was about to discuss "seems never to have been stated either on this or our side of the water." Since it was exceedingly rare for Jefferson to assert his originality, his pointed remark here should be heeded. The modest sanity with which he disclaimed any originality in the philosophy of the Declaration of Independence (indeed, he understated his contribution) is an outstanding illustration of his normal habit.[28] A close investigation of manuscript sources in an attempt to evaluate Jefferson's

[28] See Julian Boyd, ed.: *The Declaration of Independence* (Princeton University Press, 1945), pp. 11–13, for a convenient round-up of quotations on this question, and for an excellent comment thereon.

claim of originality revealed an absorbing interchange of ideas, which appears to confirm his claim.

The intellectual interchange began in February 1788, in Paris, in Jefferson's handsome house which he rented from the Count de Langéac. A visitor, one of the many whom the hospitable Virginian entertained, arrived to spend the late winter and spring in Paris. He was Thomas Paine, inspired revolutionary propagandist, the journalistic hero of the American Revolution. Apart from his pleasure at reunion with his good friends Jefferson and Lafayette, Paine had a project that had brought him to Paris: to get support from the French Academy of Sciences for his engineering venture to build the first iron bridge. He knew that Lafayette would be particularly helpful in this matter, and that Jefferson's enthusiasm almost matched his own. But after the business of the day was over, there was time for conversation. And conversation must often have centered on the unprecedented political developments taking place in two countries peculiarly interesting to the company, America and France.

During the course of Paine's visit, there is proof that Jefferson turned the discussion in his home one night to the subject of natural rights. The receipt of news regarding James Wilson's arguments, some months earlier, in the Pennsylvania Convention for the ratification of the Constitution appears to have occasioned the discussion. Wilson had urged that a bill of rights was not desirable in the Constitution. Paine, upon returning to his own lodgings after the evening's discussion, reflected further and composed a four-page memorandum on "natural and civil rights and the distinction between them." He sent this brief sketch of ideas to Jefferson "to see how nearly we agree." The main drift of Paine's memorandum was a sharp distinction between natural rights, which he called rights of "personal competency" (such as thinking, speaking, forming and giving opinions), and civil rights or rights derived from compact, which secured individuals personal protection for acquiring and possessing property.[29]

The discussion that interested these two doughty champions of republican theory did not die with that interesting evening. Jefferson's letter on the principle that the earth belongs to the living, and Paine's brilliant summation of republican political theory in his *Rights of Man*, took up the theme and developed it in accordance with the interests of the two authors. In developing the theme, Paine used language so strikingly similar to Jefferson's that one is forced to conclude that the similarity is more than coincidental. Paine wrote:

There never did, there never will, and there never can exist a parliament, or any description of men, or any generation of men, in any country, possessed of the right or the power of binding and controlling posterity to the "end of time" . . . therefore, all such clauses, acts or declarations, by which the makers of them attempt to do what they have neither the right nor the power to do . . . are in themselves null and void.

Every age and generation must be as free to act for itself, *in all cases*, as the ages and generation which preceded it. The vanity and presumption of governing beyond the grave, is the most ridiculous and insolent of all tyrannies.

Man has no property in man; neither has any generation a property in the generations which are to follow. . . .

It is the living, and not the dead, that are to be accommodated.[30]

[29] Jefferson Papers, L.C. Not dated on original. Formerly attributed to 1789. Probable date February or May 1788. (Most of March and April Jefferson was away from Paris, and the meeting referred to in the memo could not have taken place then.)

[30] *The Complete Writings of Thomas Paine* (New York: The Citadel Press; 1945), I, 251.

There is such a close parallelism between Jefferson's and Paine's formulation of the theme that the earth belongs to the living as to suggest that they continued their interchange on the elementary principles of good society and that one influenced the other. This suspicion is encouraged by the fact that when Paine returned to London in May 1788, he remained in close correspondence with Jefferson until the latter departed for America in the fall of 1789. His correspondence was concerned with political intelligence, unfailingly. Jefferson depended upon Paine for news of British politics, the more so since America had not replaced John Adams with a new American minister during this period. Jefferson himself feared that his mail would be pried into, and stated that he wrote to Paine less frequently than he wished because he waited each time for a trustworthy friend or acquaintance to carry his letter to Paine in England.[31] But this correspondence gives no clue for the present inquiry.

Further quest in the elusive matter whether Jefferson or Paine originated the striking idea that the earth belongs to the living led to the dim figure of Dr. Gem as a likely link in the transmission to Paine of Jefferson's elaboration of this idea. Dr. Gem seems to have been an Englishman residing in France, and is known to have been an intimate visitor at Jefferson's home. There is evidence that Jefferson was profoundly impressed with his sagacity in political theory, that Dr. Gem attended Jefferson and his daughters as a family physician, and that he was well acquainted with the personal affairs of the Jefferson household. It is further quite clear that Dr. Gem entertained ardent republican beliefs and was wholly in sympathy with the course of "reform" in the early phase of the French Revolution. Since

[31] Jefferson to Paine, Paris, December 23, 1788. Jefferson Papers, L.C.

Dr. Gem is little known and all of these statements are constructions from material that has not been worked with before, it is essential to submit corroborative evidence.

The first telling piece of evidence is a declaration of rights, in French, in Dr. Gem's hand (and endorsed by Jefferson as Gem's). This is one of the two sets of principles Jefferson sent to Madison to show what leading French thinkers were devising on the subject of fundamental rights. Although Gem's list is undated, it must have been written in the winter of 1788 or early in January 1789, because the date of Jefferson's copy of these same *"Principes généraux relatifs à un état politique"* was on or before January 12, 1789, when he sent it as an enclosure in his letter to Madison. Commenting to Madison on the two unusual enclosures, Jefferson identified Lafayette as the first author and Dr. Gem as the second:

The one is by our friend . . . [Lafayette]. You will see that it contains the essential principles of ours accommodated as much as could be to the actual state of things here. [No wonder, since Jefferson apparently helped Lafayette to compose it.] The other is from a very sensible man, a pure theorist, of the sect called the Oeconomists, of which Turgot was considered as the head. The former is adapted to the existing abuses; the latter goes to those possible as well as to those existing.[32]

The definitive connection between the physiocrat theoretician Dr. Gem and the theme "the earth belongs to the living" is established by a second remarkable document. This is a brief memorandum, in English, in Dr. Gem's hand (and again endorsed so by Jefferson). Although this document is still in the vast repository of Jefferson's papers at the Library of Congress, there is no entry to cover its receipt

[32] Jefferson to Madison, Paris, January 12, 1789. *Writings* (Ford), V, 64.

in Jefferson's scrupulous epistolary ledger. It is probable, therefore, that Dr. Gem gave it to Jefferson personally. The time must have been before September 6, 1789, when Jefferson worked out his letter to Madison. Gem had written:

That one generation of men in civil society have no right to make acts to bind another, is a truth that cannot be contested.

The earth & all things whatever can only be conceived to belong to the living, the dead & those who are unborn can have no rights of property.

Individuals have the power to alienate their property or to engage it for the payment of debts. Why may not a body [of] men, a nation, contract debts & engage their united property for the payment of them?

In this no rights of posterity seem to be violated; because the property of the present generation does not belong to them.

To repress the interested, ambitious & corrupt conduct of the administrators of nations, it may be expedient to declare by a law, that after a certain term of years the payment of a loan shall be void; creditors lending their money on these conditions suffer no wrong by the failure of payment.

As things are constituted in Europe, the indebted nations cannot without injustice refuse the payment of public debts." [33]

A close analysis of these critical notes indicates that Jefferson had already discussed these matters with Dr. Gem. The order in which the ideas are presented, and the language employed, partially substantiate this. The full substantiation is provided by the letter Jefferson sent to Dr. Gem on September 9, three days after Jefferson composed the final draft of the Madison letter. "The hurry in which I wrote my letter to Mr. Madison which is in your hands, occasioned an inattention to the difference between generations succeeding each other at fixed epochs, and generations

[33] Jefferson Papers, L.C. Undated, but probably August 1789.

renewed daily and hourly." [34] Since the final letter to Madison introduced the revised model of generations to which Jefferson referred, it is evident that Dr. Gem saw an earlier draft than the one dated September 6. Moreover, Jefferson's final draft of the letter to Madison apparently tried to answer Dr. Gem's principal criticism, to the effect that a nation may contract debts and engage its "united property" as payment. Although Jefferson recognized that individuals in private life have the power to engage their property to pay their debts, he asserted that this power is municipal only, not moral. "But a material difference must be noted between the succession of an individual and that of a whole generation. Individuals are parts only of a society, subject to the laws of a whole. . . . But when a whole generation, that is, the whole society dies . . . and another generation or society succeeds, this forms a whole, and there is no superior who can give their territory to a third society." [35] Therefore, there is no municipal obligation between society and society or generation and generation, "no umpire but the law of nature." [36]

One final item in this story of the interchange of ideas is a letter from Jefferson to Dr. Gem, some months after Jefferson had arrived in America and when he knew he would not be returning to Paris. The letter shows the affection and unusual regard Jefferson had for the doctor.

In bidding adieu, my dear Doctor, to the country which united our residence, I find the loss of your society and instructive conversation among the leading circumstances of regret. Be assured that I feel it most sensibly, and accept my warm ac-

[34] Jefferson to Dr. Gem, [Paris], September 9, 1789. Jefferson Papers, L.C.

[35] Jefferson to Madison, Paris, September 6, 1789. *Writings* (Ford), V, 117–18.

[36] Ibid., V, 120.

knowledgments for all your kindnesses and services to me and my family while at Paris. I hope that your philanthropy is by this time fully gratified by the final establishment of order, and equal government in a country which you love, and that you will still be pleased in seeing them extended to others—so as to found a rational hope that man is at length destined to be happy and free. . . .[37]

The case for Jefferson's influence on Paine through the intermediary of Dr. Gem can now be completed. All three were interested in natural rights and in the French cause of liberty. Jefferson had discussed these matters with each of them. It is probable that Dr. Gem met Paine when the latter visited Jefferson in Paris and that lively discussions ensued on the elementary principles of a good society. Dr. Gem, so far as we know, was the only one who had a copy of Jefferson's letter to Madison on "the earth belongs to the living." Soon after Jefferson drafted the letter and left France, Paine turned up in Paris, very much the favorite of the French liberal leaders. He would naturally have gravitated to another ardent British champion of the French Revolution, like Dr. Gem.

The hypothesis advanced here is that Paine saw a copy of Jefferson's letter to Madison. The vivid phrases would surely have appealed to Paine; and their reappearance in the *Rights of Man* would then be an altogether natural occurrence, an everyday borrowing from a cultural milieu to which Paine had contributed and in which he felt altogether at home.

6

The defense of the rights of the living, begun in Jefferson's letter, was brought into sharper focus in the contro-

[37] Jefferson to Dr. Gem, New York, April 4, 1790. Jefferson Papers, L.C.

versy that gave rise to the writing of the *Rights of Man* and that followed upon its publication in the United States. Paine's main purpose was to refute the reactionary political doctrine then being advocated in England by Edmund Burke. Paine had been taken up by Burke in the summer of 1788. But this odd alliance could not last long. Paine's vehement defense of everything American, which in itself had alienated some of his distinguished new British friends, became insufferable to Burke when it was coupled with an even more provoking defense of the accelerating French Revolution. Of the early stages of the Revolution, Paine had written to Jefferson that the year 1789 would be immortalized as an "Anno Mundi or an Anno Domini." [38] As for Burke, the former defender of the rights of the American colonies, the French Revolution was anathema primarily because it was a break with the past. His tolerant skepticism about philosophical abstractions in politics had given way under the pressure of the Revolution to an embittered metaphysical theory of society that outlawed all radical change. This theory was published, one year after Jefferson's forceful letter, in Burke's *Reflections on the Revolution in France.*

Burke's position was the perfect ideological opposite of the one defended by Jefferson and Paine. Contemptuous of the worship of "reason" and the large social and political innovations promoted by French Revolutionary republicans, he invoked the notion of a "Perpetual Charter" as a limit not only on revolutions, but on British reform movements as well. Rejecting all utilitarian approaches to society and politics, Burke made a mystical appeal to the spiritual partnership that was presumably the state's peculiar kind of contract. This contract was to be looked on with reverence

[38] Paine to Jefferson, London, February 16, 1789. Jefferson Papers, L.C.

since it extended beyond government to all science, all art, every virtue, and all perfection.

As the ends of such a partnership cannot be obtained in many generations, it becomes a partnership not only between those who are living, but between those who are living, those who are dead, and those who are about to be born. Each contract of each particular state is but a clause in the great primeval contract of eternal society, linking the lower with the higher natures; connecting the visible and invisible world, according to a fixed compact sanctioned by the inviolable oath which holds all physical and all moral nature, each in their appointed place.[39]

Nothing could be less palatable to Jefferson and Paine than Burke's trans-empirical political philosophy. According to the two defenders of the view that the earth belongs to the living, there was something better than a spiritualistic interpretation of civilization—the belief in the rights of men and their legitimate demand for favorable conditions to promote happiness in society. Freedom was hard enough to purchase, especially when its purchase price was blood. They were not inclined to defeat that freedom by obscurantist metapolitics that irrevocably bound the living to the dead and the future to the past. By some complex historical irony, in our own day the philosophy of natural rights is said to be "abstract" and "metaphysical." But as Jefferson and Paine held this philosophy, it was an operational approach to establish sound conditions for human security and growth. "Rights," in short, could listen to "Reason," and "Reason" had no quarrel with "Utility." But a "Perpetual Partnership" like Burke's looked down on "low" con-

[39] Edmund Burke: *Reflections on the Revolution in France* (1790). *Works* (Bohn Edition, London, 1861), II, 368.

cerns, was above mere reason, and was astrally removed from trading in "pepper and coffee, calico and tobacco." Burke's philosophy was what Jefferson elsewhere called the "Gothic" habit of mind, looking backward for its ideals, profoundly distrustful of keeping constitutions flexible to fit the changing needs of life. Truly, if Jefferson was not apprised of Burke's position when he wrote his forceful letter, he would have had to invent one like it for the sake of perfect opposition.

Jefferson soon had the opportunity, in an American setting, to endorse Paine's sharp attack on Burke in order to combat the developing opposition to true republicanism. After having read Paine's tract, Jefferson gave his blessings to the publication in a note that he intended to be private. As he wrote to Madison, he "was pleased to find that it was to be reprinted here, that something was at length to be publicly said against the political heresies which had of late sprung up among us, not doubting but that our citizens would rally again round the standard of Common Sense." [40] To Jefferson's great astonishment, however, the pamphlet appeared with his note employed for flamboyant advertisement. This indiscretion on the part of the printer was the origin of the open break between Jefferson and John Adams, since the "political heresies" referred to in Jefferson's note plainly characterized Adams's *Discourses on Davila.* In the ensuing criticisms Jefferson and Paine were coupled; to which Jefferson replied: "I certainly merit the same, for I profess the same principles." [41]

[40] Jefferson to Madison, Philadelphia, May 9, 1791. Writings (Ford), V, 331.

[41] Jefferson to James Monroe, Philadelphia, July 10, 1791. Ibid., V, 352.

7

The philosophy of the earth belongs to the living raises questions of such moment to the modern world that we must temporarily shift our focus. Jefferson was initially concerned with the purely economic aspects of the doctrine. This accounts for his basic analysis in physiocratic terms of the relation of man to nature and for his proposals on the public debt. It might be argued that this aspect of his doctrine has become outmoded by economic developments in which agriculture does not play the pre-eminent role it had in Jefferson's time. In particular, it might be argued that a literal interpretation of Jefferson's doctrine would have prevented the development of corporations, which became an integral part of capitalist economic development. Corporations were endowed with legal personality and with an extended life, normally beyond the life-span of a human being. Furthermore, the corporation was not treated as the sum of the individual stockholders and, by virtue of limited liability, the individual stockholders were not liable for the debts incurred. All this is clearly unnatural in Jefferson's terms; but it was an expedient legal or social mechanism that permitted the aggregation of large masses of capital and the resulting increases in productivity and the standard of living that characterized the nineteenth century.

Jefferson's basic doctrine, however, is not tied to its physiocratic trappings or to the artificial models for the succession of generations. The heart of his philosophy, as Madison sympathetically perceived, is the recognition that economic institutions may change and that no one is wise enough to fix perpetual laws of property that would serve the needs of posterity. This is the significance of his distinction between natural and moral rights, on the one hand, and municipal or civil laws, on the other. From this standpoint, the enormous concentration of capital by corporations poses a contemporary problem: the limits of the power of organized groups, whether of capital or of labor, to assure a balance between freedom and security. The Jeffersonian philosophy would defend, not the rights of private corporations as they are, but the right to modify our economic system so as to be better able to meet the needs of the living.

Jefferson's proposal on the public debt also has contemporary relevance. The public debt is a subject of popular controversy because it is already embarrassingly large and it is now generally recognized that government spending may be needed to assure full employment. Such spending is required in a private-enterprise economy in order to avoid the insecurity and cyclical turns of economic depression, and may be necessary in magnitudes and in timing that would prevent the resultant public debt from being repaid within a twenty-year period. As Madison recognized, certain kinds of public debt may be incurred for the benefit of posterity. Today these would include debts for fighting a defensive war, controlling depression, and protecting foreign democracies from outside conquest. These fiscal measures increase the chances of preserving democracy here and now and, to the extent that they succeed, will benefit posterity even though it may have to assume some share of the debts incurred. Here again, as Madison saw, Jefferson was criticizing unjust and unnecessary burdens; and for this purpose the use of his models for the succession of generations was too restrictive.

Some advanced economists today argue that the public debt is no burden so long as the government owes it to its own citizens—we owe it to ourselves. From this point of view, the only bad feature of a mounting public debt is our habit of worrying about it. All that we need to do is to get rid of this superstition and live with our debts cheerfully. If this were correct, both Jefferson and Madison were wrong in expressing a serious concern over the public debt. But further analysis establishes grounds for their concern. If the debt pays more than a nominal rate of interest, the concern is real and not simply superstitious. For if the government levies taxes to pay the interest, the additional taxes may become a factor limiting investment and production in the economy, especially at present high levels of taxation. Perhaps the convention of laying taxes to pay the interest is also a financial superstition. On this view, we should be just as ready to borrow to pay the interest as to pay for the original debt. The end result of this perpetual borrowing would be an economy with a growing distortion in the distribution of income, tending to increase idle savings by reason of the increased volume of payments going to the holders of the public debt. Thus the principal of a perpetual debt would have serious effects on our posterity, as Jefferson so strongly argued.

The contemporary discussion of these issues centers around the role of the state in the economy. The objective is to protect and promote the natural rights of the people, to assure that they are good and healthy, living lives of their own choosing, exercising and developing their capacities, protected against crippling ills. In short, the objective remains the protection of life, liberty, and the pursuit of happiness in changing social terms. Government has changed from a policeman to a positive economic agency.

The gist of Jefferson's letter is his philosophy that laws and constitutions must be revised in the light of our reason and experience for the peace and good of mankind. He returned to the thesis that the earth belongs to the living on numerous occasions throughout his life, the latest when he was in his eightieth year.[42] His last letter on this subject is notable for the clarity of its statement, the first significant omission of the time limits which he had used to define a generation, and the momentous revision of his original letter by the incorporation of Madison's principle of tacit assent.

That our Creator made the earth for the use of the living and not of the dead; that those who exist not can have no use nor right in it, no authority or power over it; that one generation of men cannot foreclose or burden its use to another, which comes to it in its own right and by the same divine beneficence; that a preceding generation cannot bind a succeeding one by its laws or contracts; these deriving their obligation from the will of the existing majority, and that majority being removed by death, another comes in its place with a will equally free to make its own laws and contracts; these are axioms so self-evident that no explanation can make them plainer; for he is not to be reasoned with who says that non-existence can control existence, or that nothing can move something. They are axioms also pregnant with salutary consequences. The laws of civil society indeed for the encouragement of industry, give the property of the parent to his family on his death, and in most civilized countries permit him even to give it, by testament, to whom he pleases. And it is also found more convenient to suffer the laws of our predecessors to stand on our implied assent, as if positively reenacted, until the existing majority positively repeals them. But this does not lessen the right of that majority to repeal when-

[42] There are a number of letters in which Jefferson presented the theme that the earth belongs to the living. The most important are: to John Eppes in 1813, to Samuel Kercheval in 1816, and to Thomas Earle in 1823.

ever a change of circumstances or of will calls for it. Habit alone confounds what is civil practice with natural right. . . .[43]

In this summing up, thirty-four years after the original letter to Madison, Jefferson reaffirmed his great theme and, by tacit assent, joined with Madison in a realistic appraisal of its operational meaning.

[43] Jefferson to Thomas Earle, Monticello, September 24, 1823. Writings (Memorial), XV, 470–1.

Chapter Five

LIBERTY AGAINST POWER

"What a perversion of the natural order of things! to make power *the primary and central object of the social system, and* Liberty *but its satellite."*
—MADISON, December 20, 1792

To BID ADIEU to France had been a hard decision for Jefferson to make. Personally, Jefferson had strong reasons to make him eager to return to France. There were his French friends, who depended on him for political guidance. There was the lovely Mrs. Maria Cosway, who engaged Jefferson's affections more than anyone had since his wife's death, with the exception of his ever-devoted daughters.[1] In addition, Jefferson's political predilections inclined him to France. He honestly thought that his best role at this critical juncture in European affairs would be to foster good diplomatic relations between America and an increasingly revolutionary France. In his past service he had negotiated good commercial treaties between America and France and had made himself the most cultivated and best-liked exponent of American republicanism on the Continent—second only to his fabulous predecessor, Dr. Franklin. Jefferson correctly judged that the good reputation he had won in France was important to use for his country. Philosophi-

[1] See Helen Bullock's *My Head and My Heart* for a charming and thorough study of Jefferson's "little history" with Maria Cosway (New York: G. P. Putnam's Sons; 1945).

cally, Jefferson had the highest motive for returning to France, to watch the course of the French Revolution, the most vital political experiment of the generation.

For all these reasons it is doubtful whether Jefferson would have been able to overcome the interests that drew him back to France without Madison's undeniably strong influence and counsel. At this period Madison enjoyed a singularly cordial relationship with President Washington, who relied on him for advice on legislation and appointments.[2] He had been consulted by the President about Jefferson's availability for an important post in the new government. To ascertain this, Madison had sent Jefferson a letter of inquiry while the latter was still in Paris, and had received the reply that continuance in his Paris post or retirement were the only alternatives he would consider. Therefore, when Jefferson left Paris it was in the full expectation of returning after his visit to Virginia was over and his daughters were safely deposited in their native state, where they could look forward to engagement and marriage with native Americans.

Although Jefferson had written unfavorably from Paris,[3] Madison was careful not to kill Washington's plan to get his best friend into the Cabinet as Secretary of State. He made sure to be the first emissary to consult with his friend at Monticello, where Jefferson was apparently still adamant against accepting a domestic post. This is clear from the tone of Jefferson's letter to Washington, in which he indicated that his preference was to continue in his European post, but in which he dutifully said that he would

[2] For an account of Madison's relationship with Washington, see W. C. Rives: *The Life and Times of James Madison* (3 vols. Boston: Little, Brown & Co.; 1868), III, 63–5.

[3] Jefferson to Madison, Paris, August 28, 1789. *Writings* (Ford), V, 114–15.

of course abide by "what you may be pleased to decide." [4] He had written the day before to William Short, who was still acting as his Secretary in Paris, that it was "impossible to give a flat refusal" to the President, but that he would indicate that his present office was more agreeable.

A glimpse of one aspect of the important discussion between Jefferson and Madison at Monticello late in December 1789 is afforded by Madison's report to President Washington:

A few days before I was allowed to set out for New York, I took a ride to Monticello. The answer of Mr. Jefferson to the notification of his appointment will no doubt have explained the state of his mind on that subject. I was sorry to find him so little biassed in favor of the domestic service allotted to him, but was glad that his difficulties seemed to result chiefly from what I take to be an erroneous view of the kind and quantity of business annexed to that which constitutes the foreign Department. He apprehends that it will far exceed the latter, which has, of itself no terrors to him. On the other, it was supposed and I believe truly, that the Domestic part will be very trifling. . . . After all, if the whole business can be executed by any one man, Mr. Jefferson must be equal to it; if not, he will be relieved by a necessary division of it. All whom I have heard speak on the subject are remarkably solicitous for his acceptance, and I flatter myself that they will not, in the final event, be disappointed.[5]

Once he had encouraged the President's interest in trying to obtain Jefferson for Secretary of State, Madison hastened to keep alive Jefferson's newly instigated and somewhat finicky appetite for the new job. Madison repeated in a letter to Jefferson what he had apparently al-

[4] Jefferson to the President of the United States, Chesterfield, December 15, 1789. Ibid., V, 141.

[5] Madison to George Washington, Georgetown, January 4, 1790. *Writings* (Congress), I, 501.

ready declared, that Jefferson's acceptance would "be more conductive to the general good, and perhaps to the very objects you have in view in Europe, than your return to your former station."[6] Madison's reasoning was, as usual, "cogent." Only Jefferson personally and his loyal circle of friends in Paris would suffer from Madison's reading of the score.

Unquestionably, Madison had played a key role in conditioning Jefferson's acceptance of the Secretaryship of State. Indeed, by sustaining the political move to bring Jefferson into Washington's Cabinet at this early date in the first administration of the new Republic, by arguing with Jefferson that the domestic position was matchless and that no other American statesman possessed the proper talents and qualifications to fill the post, Madison prepared Jefferson for the indispensable next stage in his development as a political leader. By this move, Madison also assured that a collaboration of momentous consequence between Jefferson and himself would develop. The two close friends were to work side by side to realize the ideal stated by Madison at the conclusion of his reply to Jefferson's philosophical letter on the principle that the earth belongs to the living: "that further light must be added to the Councils of our Country before many truths which are seen through the medium of Philosophy, become visible to the naked eye of the ordinary politician."[7]

2

Jefferson had seen the patent logic of Madison's arguments, that the great challenge for American statesmen in

[6] Madison to Jefferson, New York, January 24, 1790. Ibid., I, 502.

[7] Madison to Jefferson, New York, February 4, 1790. Writings (Hunt), V, 441, n.

the era when the federal government was first beginning to operate was to become influential in that government, right on the home scene. Madison had kept him very well informed of every turn and factional development in the American political world, and he had doubtless stressed the necessity of fighting incipient monarchism, aristocracy, and whatever newfangled name covered apostasy from genuine republicanism. Jefferson had reason to be apprehensive of the political sentiments of some of his countrymen.

In the opening days of the first session of Congress, Madison had claimed the floor to protest measures inimical to the spirit of republicanism. It was apparently necessary as early as this to recall the errant to the ideals they were already beginning to forget. Behind him Madison had the wealth of experience he had gained by his leadership in the Constitutional Convention. He was now master enough in parliamentary debate to embroider the theme of republicanism with ease, evident scope, and effective assurance. One notable protest against incipient aristocracy Madison voiced in his speech against titles. While Jefferson was still in Paris, Madison had written him the news that John Adams, the Vice-President, and R. H. Lee had sponsored titles in the Senate, recommending that Washington be given the splendid designation "His Highness the President of the United States and protector of their liberties." Had the project succeeded, Madison commented, "It would have subjected the President to a severe dilemma, and given a deep wound to our infant Government." [8] The irony of the situation was not lost upon Jefferson, who quickly wrote, excoriating John Adams, his former friend, as he never had before: "The President's title . . . was the most superlatively ridiculous thing I ever heard of. It is a proof the more of the justice of

[8] Madison to Jefferson, New York, May 23, 1789. Ibid., V, 370, n.

the character given by Doctor Franklin of my friend. Always an honest man, often a great one but sometimes absolutely mad." [9]

Madison's tactical advance in the debate on titles was adroit. He began by reminding Congress that "the nature of our Government" and "the genius of the people" are not suited to shows of power and prestige. He asked whether titles are "dangerous," as many had asserted. Hardly. The fact that one of the "most impotent sovereigns in Europe has assumed a title as high as human invention can devise" had in no way conferred too much power on him. No, Madison objected to titles "in principle." Instead of increasing, they "diminish the true dignity and importance of a Republic, and would in particular, on this occasion, diminish the true dignity of the first magistrate himself." What American, asked Madison, appealing to his countrymen's horror of cutting an effeminate figure, would want some "splendid tinsel or gorgeous robe" to disgrace "the manly shoulders of our chief." He concluded with: ". . . the more simple, the more Republican we are in our manners, the more rational dignity we shall acquire." [10]

Despite these early intimations that Jefferson would not find simon-pure republicans staffing the government, he could not suppress a shock of displeasure when he arrived in New York in the spring of 1790 to take up his new duties as Secretary of State. The change in atmosphere between the liberal, enlightened circles he had frequented in France, in the first year of its Revolution, and the reactionary neo-Anglican moneyed groups in New York was oppressive. Jef-

---

[9] Jefferson to Madison, Paris, July 29, 1789. Slight inaccuracy in Ford's text; therefore see Jefferson Papers, L.C.

[10] Madison's Speech on Titles in First Congress, first session, May 11, 1789. *Writings* (Hunt), V, 356–7.

ferson's own description of his experience cannot be bettered:

I had left France in the first year of its revolution, in the fervor of natural rights, and zeal for reformation. My conscientious devotion to these rights could not be heightened, but it had been aroused and excited by daily exercise. . . . The courtesies of dinner parties given me as a stranger newly arrived among them, placed me at once in their familiar society. But I cannot describe the wonder and mortification with which the table conversations filled me. Politics were the chief topic, and a preference of kingly, over republican, government, was evidently the favorite sentiment. An apostate I could not be; nor yet a hypocrite: and I found myself, for the most part, the only advocate on the republican side of the question, unless, among the guests, there chanced to be some member of that party from the legislative Houses.[11]

Had Jefferson's shock not been cushioned by the friendship and guidance of Madison, who knew every current of opinion, he might have quit New York to retire to his civilized mountaintop on the outskirts of Charlottesville.

3

One of the foremost issues on which Madison briefed Jefferson as his friend took his important place in the Cabinet was the question of the public debt. Madison had risen in Congress to attack Hamilton's proposal for the support of the public credit and, in doing so, helped to define the principles of republicanism that were later to become the standard of the original Republican Party. A review of this clash is offered here only to the extent that it is the back-

[11] Jefferson: *Anas. Writings* (Ford), I, 159–60.

ground for the maturing of republican ideology in the United States.

The gist of the recommendations made by the Secretary of the Treasury had been that the government debt, both national and state, should be funded at par, to maintain the sanctity of contract and to ensure that the United States would be respected for having observed its debt of honor. Madison allowed several weeks of clamorous debate on Hamilton's plan to pass before he entered the lists. He had not forgotten that his own position in the Continental Congress in 1783 had been opposed to discrimination among the holders of the debt; but as he conscientiously noted in his papers, "At that time the debts were due to the original holders." [12] He accordingly paid tribute to the importance and difficulty of the subject of public debt before declaring his own views.

No one cognizant of political duty, Madison declared, would deny the validity of all debts contracted by the United States, regardless of the fact that the nation was now represented by a new form of government. "No logic, no magic," he flatly stated, "can diminish the force of the obligation." The only question at issue, then, is to whom the payment is really due. The great mass of the debt he described as divided between different classes of creditors, ranging from the original creditors to present holders of alienated securities. The only principles that could govern the provision for these different groups of creditors, Madison stated, were public justice, public faith, public credit, and public opinion. On that basis, it was evident that original holders, who had been forced to part with their securities at desperately low prices because of the impaired credit

[12] Nathan Schachner: *Alexander Hamilton* (New York: D. Appleton-Century Co.; 1946), p. 255.

under the Articles of Confederation, should receive some compensation for their losses. Madison recommended "discrimination" to this effect: to pay the present holders the highest price that had prevailed in the market prior to the proposed funding of the debt, and to pay to the "original sufferers" the residue between the highest price and the face value of securities.

This compromise Madison anticipated would be called "impracticable." Were it really proved unworkable he would abandon it. But, point by point, Madison rebutted every serious argument that might be advanced against his proposal. Since the present case was extraordinary, he thought ordinary maxims were hardly applicable. The proposed "discrimination" required "nothing more than a knowledge of the present holders, which will be shown by the certificates; and of the original holders, which the office documents will show." [13] Others might demur that if the government in this case went beyond "the literal into the equitable claims against the United States," it ought to go back to every case of injustice. To this, Madison sensibly replied that the magnitude, practicability, and insistence of the present case set it apart from others.

The following week Madison presented his case more dramatically than he had earlier, calling attention to the pitiable situation of the original holders, who would stand to lose by a universal funding at par. "A debt was fairly contracted: according to justice and good faith, it ought to have been paid in gold or silver; a piece of paper only was substituted. Was this paper equal in value to gold or silver? It was worth, in the market . . . no more than one-eighth or one-seventh of that value. Was this depreciated paper freely

[13] Madison's Speech on Public Credit, February 11, 1790. First Congress, second session. *Writings* (Hunt), V, 441–5.

accepted? No. The Government offered that or nothing. The relation of the individual to the Government, and the circumstances of the offer, rendered the acceptance a forced, not a free one. The same degree of constraint would vitiate a transaction between man and man before any Court of Equity on the face of the earth." [14] Madison begged the Congressmen to consider the substance as well as the form, the equity as well as the letter of the claims—not "the bark," but "the pith of the business." This great and extraor- dinary case ought to be decided on the great and funda- mental principles of justice. He confessed he had been reproved for appealing to the heart as well as the head. He would be bold to repeat "that in great and unusual ques- tions of morality, the heart is the best judge." [15] By this ex- plicit statement Madison fixed as one quality of republican ideology a permanent concern for the welfare of honest but underprivileged citizens.

Despite the liberal idealism of Madison's protest, Ham- ilton's plan for securing public credit was finally enacted by Congress; but the accompanying proposal that the state debts be assumed was at first rejected, largely through Mad- ison's efforts. It might have foundered permanently, since Virginia and other states that had liquidated nearly all of their Revolutionary debts were unwilling to be taxed to pay the debts of poor or laggard states, had not Jefferson been influenced by Hamilton to effect a historic compromise.[16] Jefferson proposed that Hamilton dine with him for a "friendly discussion of the subject" and thought that "the first step towards some concilation of views would be to bring Mr. Madison & Colo. Hamilton together." The com-

[14] Madison's Speech on Public Credit, February 18, 1790. First Con- gress, second session. Ibid., V, 448.

[15] Ibid., V, 449.

[16] Jefferson: *Anas. Writings* (Ford), I, 162–4.

promise involved an agreement to remove the capital to the Potomac, another measure long and diligently nourished by Jefferson and Madison, to sweeten the "peculiarly bitter" pill that the Southern states would be asked to swallow with the assumption of state debts.[17] Madison acquiesced, but stipulated that he would not vote for the modified assumption plan, although he would no longer strenuously oppose it.

Jefferson could not recall whether Madison or Hamilton proposed this *quid pro quo*—but it is not hard to guess that both Virginians had more than a passive role in this "sweetening." Subsequently, two Representatives (whose districts lay on the Potomac!) were induced to change their votes, and the modified assumption bill was passed. The removal to the Potomac, however, did not find favor with the Pennsylvania delegation, and, according to Jefferson's account, Hamilton "took on himself" to arrange for an intermediate ten-year residence of the capital at Philadelphia, the move to Washington being reserved for the opening of the new century. Jefferson never ceased to lament "the unfairness" of the assumption of state debts. Without the good grace to accept the consequences of a compromise to which he had been a party, he complained that because of it Hamilton was able later to carry his bank project, which in turn eventuated in "that speculating phalanx" both in Congress and out, which designed to change "the political complexion of the Government of the U. S." [18]

Locating the capital on the Potomac was important to Jefferson and Madison for several reasons. If it were to be located in a city run by powerful financial circles, the dele-

[17] Jefferson: *Writings* (Ford), VI, 172–4. This account is more accurate than the details given in the *Anas*.

[18] Ibid., VI, 174.

gates were likely to be unduly influenced by immediate "public opinion." The very worst cities from this point of view were New York and Philadelphia. The second factor was the undeveloped transportation of the 1790's. It made a difference to Southern delegates how many days the trip to and from Congress would consume on the road. Madison argued that the Potomac was desirable for this reason because it was geographically the center. He computed that there were roughly 12,700 miles to the south of the proposed location, and about 12,400 to the north, so that "if any arguments could be brought against it, it is its being too far to the Northward." [19] Jefferson, of course, agreed with Madison and urged similar views in letters to friends at about this time.

4

The climax of the joint Jefferson-Madison struggle against Hamilton's financial measures came when the Secretary of the Treasury issued his report recommending the creation of a national bank (December 13, 1790). The purpose of the proposed bank was primarily to expand the amount of money in circulation in the United States and to establish paper notes of uniform value to facilitate this object. As Hamilton conceived it, however, the Bank of the United States was to be a joint-stock concern, privately owned—on Hamilton's theory that government ownership and management could never be as effective as private—the government to derive a share in the bank's profits, based upon its original investment in it. Hamilton defended the proposal on "implied powers" in the Constitution and cited the Bank of England for precedent.

[19] Madison's Speech "Location of the Capital," First Congress, second session, *Writings* (Hunt), VI, 17.

Both Madison and Jefferson saw the dynamic charge carried in this important bank bill. With perfect accord they used their different positions in the government to expose its "unconstitutionality"—Madison in a speech to Congress early in February 1791, and Jefferson in an "Opinion on the Constitutionality of a National Bank" prepared for President Washington and submitted on February 15.

Madison reminded his colleagues of the "peculiar manner in which the Federal Government is limited"—by a grant of particular powers only, leaving the general mass of powers in the hands of the states and the citizens. A review of the Constitution nowhere validates Congress's power to incorporate a bank, Madison declared. Indeed, a power to grant charters of incorporation had been proposed "in the General Convention and rejected." [20] The legislation that would sanction the incorporation of a national bank would therefore undermine the original intention of the framers of the Constitution and beget a monopoly that would jeopardize the equal rights of every citizen.

To incorporate a national bank, Madison contended, was a substantive prerogative, not among those enumerated in the Constitution, nor to be deduced by implication as a mere accessory "evidently and necessarily involved in an express power." [21] The terms "necessary and proper" in the Constitution could never be interpreted to accord with the language of the bill on the bank, which in its preamble stated that any means could be used that might be conducive to the successful conducting of the finances, or that would tend to facilitate obtaining loans. Nor could the phrase "common defense and general welfare" be relied

[20] Madison's Speech, "Bank of the United States," February 2, 1791. First Congress, third session, ibid., VI, 26.
[21] Ibid., VI, 32.

upon to justify the bank bill, since the power here referred to in the Constitution was limited to taxation for those ends.[22]

Madison, in a compendious conclusion, summed up his objections: the power exercised by the proposed bill was "condemned by the silence of the Constitution . . . by the rule of interpretation arising out of the Constitution . . . by its tendency to destroy the main characteristic of the Constitution; by the expositions of the friends of the Constitution . . . by the apparent intention of the parties which ratified the Constitution; by the explanatory amendments proposed by Congress themselves to the Constitution." Therefore he hoped that the extraordinary power invoked by the proposed bill would receive its "final condemnation by the vote of this House."

When, less than a week later, Madison took up his objections to the bank bill, he elaborated on the enormous influence of corporations ("incorporated societies") in the history of Europe. "They are powerful machines," he warned, "which have always been found competent to effect objects or principles in a great measure independent of the people." [23] He then moved that the bill undergo a revision and amendment, but the vote went against him.

In the heated clash of opinion between Hamilton and Madison, President Washington found no easy guide to his own decisions. Washington requested opinions from Jefferson and Edmund Randolph in his Cabinet as well as from the author of the bill, the Secretary of the Treasury. He turned to Madison, requesting him to prepare a veto message in case he should decide to use his veto. Madison's message, although very brief, was an important restatement,

[22] Ibid., VI, 28.
[23] February 8, 1791. Ibid., VI, 37.

in terms compatible with the executive authority, of the central objections he had already advanced on the floor of Congress.[24]

Jefferson, in advising that the bill was unconstitutional, agreed with Madison that if the "general welfare" clause were used to sanction a corporation like the bank, one might as well reduce the whole constitutional instrument to the single statement that a Congress be instituted with power to do whatever would be for the good of the United States. In that event, he warned, "as they would be the sole judges of the good or evil, it would be also a power to do whatever evil they please."[25] He further argued that the proposed congressional legislation would conflict with "the most ancient and fundamental laws of the several States," such as those of mortmain, alienage, descents, forfeiture and escheat, distribution. Again in agreement with Madison, he declared the national bank would form the subscribers into a corporation, give them the sole and exclusive right of banking under the national authority, and be so far against the laws of monopoly.[26]

Foreseeing the battle of constitutional construction ahead, Jefferson put his cards on the table and indicated what he thought to be the proper rule of "construction." He thought it an established rule "where a phrase will bear either of two meanings, to give it that which will allow some meaning to the other parts of the instrument, and not that which would render all the others useless." On this logical method, he found that establishing a bank was not only incompatible with the first general phrase, "to lay taxes to

[24] Copy of a paper sent to the President at his request by Madison, February 21, 1791. Ibid., VI, 42, n.1.

[25] Jefferson's "Opinion on the Constitutionality of a National Bank," February 15, 1791. *Writings* (Ford), V, 286.

[26] Ibid., V, 284–5.

provide for the general welfare of the United States," but with the second, "to make all laws necessary and proper for carrying into execution the enumerated powers." The intention of the Constitutional Convention with respect to Congress, he understood to have been to "lace them up straitly within the enumerated powers" and to confine congressional legislation to the *indispensable* means to carry the enumerated powers into effect. No doubt echoing Madison's information, Jefferson then recalled that the proposal in the Convention to authorize Congress to open canals and empower them to incorporate had been rejected, for one reason, because it was feared that Congress might then also have the power to erect a bank! [27]

Hamilton was far from mild in his resentment of the opinions rendered by Jefferson and by Edmund Randolph, the Attorney General. With obvious irritation, he first called attention to his own principled disinterestedness in the issue of the bank. He then reduced Jefferson's objections to a "general denial of the authority of the United States to erect corporations." To controvert this, Hamilton proclaimed it an "axiom" that from the very *definition* of government it followed that "every power vested in a government is in its nature sovereign, and includes . . . a right to employ all the *means* requisite and fairly applicable to the attainment of the ends of such power, and which are not precluded by restrictions and exceptions specified in the Constitution, or not immoral, or not contrary to the *essential ends* of political society." [28]

Thus, to the "strait lacing" interpretation of powers advocated by Jefferson and Madison, Hamilton opposed a

[27] Ibid., V, 286–7.

[28] Hamilton to President Washington: "Opinion as to the Constitutionality of the Bank of the United States," February 23, 1791. Works (Lodge), III, 446–7.

broad construction of the powers of the national government. The opposed views had, of course, two utterly different objectives. Jefferson and Madison were trying to safeguard the people's liberty and expected the states to help protect the rights of citizens. Hamilton hoped to protect the national government from the "depredations" of the states and the untrustworthy people they represented.

A year later Hamilton seriously doubted that the general government would be "able to maintain itself" against the influence of the states. He saw their influence already "penetrating into the national councils and preventing their direction." Hamilton was again dubious about the success of republicanism: "It is yet to be determined by experience whether it be consistent with that stability and order in government which are essential to public strength and private security and happiness." [29]

In contrast to these Hamiltonian doubts, the ideology of Jefferson and Madison was solidly republican. Constitution-wise, this meant "limited" or "equipoised" government. The tendency of the doctrine of implied powers, as Hamilton used it, was exactly antithetical to limited government. It would end, Madison warned, by forging a chain of implications that would "reach every object of legislation, every object within the whole compass of political economy." Madison therefore took pains to demonstrate the indefinite applicability of Hamilton's means-ends reasoning in the bank bill: "To borrow money is made the end, and the accumulation of capitals implied as the means. The accumulation of capitals is then the end, and a Bank implied as the means. The Bank is then the end, and a charter of incorporation, a monopoly, capital punishments, etc., implied as the

[29] Hamilton to Colonel Edward Carrington, Philadelphia, May 26, 1792. Ibid., IX, 533–4.

means." Thus the broad use of implied powers begets a slippery logic that ends in an all-sovereign government, controlled by no check, whether regional, state, or from the people.[30]

5

Under the stress of this political tempest, Jefferson and Madison developed a more intimate friendship than ever before, meeting daily, dining, planning the next day's strategy. Within a year of having taken office, Jefferson sent a charming note to Madison urging him to desert his own lodgings, particularly since he had been informed that Colonel Beckwith, the unaccredited British agent who cultivated Hamilton's friendship, was going to be "an inmate" in the house where Madison was staying. This fact encouraged Jefferson to "make a proposition" to Madison "which I did not venture as long as you had your agreeable Congressional society about you, that is, to come and take a bed and plate with me. I have four rooms of which any one is at your service. Let me intreat you, my dear Sir, to do it, if it be not disagreeable to you. To me it will be a relief from a solitude of which I have too much." Nor, he courteously fibbed, would an extra guest increase his expenses "an atom." Jefferson's library would be a convenience, and "the approaching season will render this situation more agreeable than fifth Street, and even in the winter you will find it not disagreeable. Let me have I beseech you a favorable answer. . . ."[31] For reasons that Madison did not put in writing, this warm invitation was not accepted.

[30] Madison's Speech, "Bank of the United States," February 2, 1791. First Congress, third session. Writings (Hunt), VI, 31.
[31] Jefferson to Madison, March 13, 1791. Jefferson Papers, L.C.

Shortly thereafter, Jefferson conceived another project, to which Madison readily assented—a vacation and tour through the Northern states, which gave them ample opportunity to discuss their political ideas fully while sharing enthusiastic discoveries about the unfamiliar countryside. The plan for the trip was to proceed together from New York to Albany and Lake George, crossing over to Bennington, Vermont, through Vermont to the Connecticut River, down to Hartford and New Haven, and back to New York and Philadelphia.[32] The itinerary must have sounded most attractive to Madison, for Congress was over more than two months before Jefferson was able to get away from his crowded desk at the Department of State, and Madison waited for his friend. They were gone a day under four weeks,[33] and while they probably mended fences and utilized every available opportunity for political visits with Republican leaders like Burr and Livingston in New York and Governor Clinton in Albany, the New England jaunt seems to have been, as Madison said, primarily for "health, recreation & curiosity."[34] After the trip Jefferson announced that the severe headaches that had plagued him for several months had vanished.

Letters from the New England trip are full of sparkling accounts of lakes and mountains, sugar maple, the silver fir, aspen with a velvet leaf, wild gooseberries, strawberries in blossom, fishing for speckled trout, salmon, sailing on Lake Champlain.[35] Political maneuvers could hardly have been

[32] The trip began on May 20 and ended June 16, 1791.

[33] Jefferson to Mary Jefferson, Philadelphia, May 8, 1791. In Sarah N. Randolph: *The Domestic Life of Thomas Jefferson*, (Cambridge, Mass.: Harvard University Press; 1939), p. 165.

[34].Madison to Jefferson, New York, May 12, 1791. *Writings* (Hunt), VI, 51, n.

[35] Jefferson to Martha Jefferson Randolph, Lake Champlain, May 31, 1791. Randolph, op. cit., 166–7.

the chief goals of a trip that led two curious travellers to visit "the principal scenes of General Burgoyne's misfortune . . . the encampments at Saratoga in ground where the British piled their arms, and the field of the battle of Bennington . . . We have also visited Forts William Henry and George, Ticonderoga, Crown Point, etc. which have been scenes of blood from a very early part of our history." [36] This pleasant excursion in good company reminded Jefferson of his European travels—in Italy, France, and Germany—and upon returning home he hastened to lend his detailed travel journals to Madison.[37]

6

Another joint adventure soon engaged the two friends. Both Jefferson and Madison had an extremely modern (and that is to say keen) respect for public opinion. Madison was perhaps a trifle more scientific in approaching public opinion; but Jefferson was personally more gifted in devising dramatic opportunities for "informing" the people. Together they managed to keep in touch with politically influential friends in Virginia like Edmund Randolph, George Mason, Edmund Pendleton, and Henry Lee; and by the time the fight with Hamilton and his anti-republican followers was under way, they worked energetically to arrange for a "voice" that would present the republican case to circles closer to the capital.

Directly after the close of Congress in the late spring

[36] Jefferson to Thomas Mann Randolph, Bennington, June 5, 1791. *Writings* (Ford), V, 340–1.

[37] Madison to Jefferson, July 31, 1791. Madison Papers, L.C. Madison comments that, to enjoy the travel memorandums fully, "I must repeat them with a map of France before me, which I cannot at present command."

of 1791, Madison had gone to New York and talked with his old college classmate Philip Freneau about a small post as translator in the State Department (at the annual salary of $250) that Jefferson had "allotted for him," and about their hopes that the Republican paper he had planned to locate in New Jersey he would print in Philadelphia instead. Freneau appeared reluctant to move to Philadelphia, but listened to Madison's arguments about its advantages. To Jefferson, Madison wrote: "The more I learn of his character, talents and principles, the more I should regret his burying himself in the obscurity he had chosen in N. Jersey. It is certain that there is not to be found in the whole catalogue of American Printers, a single name that can approach towards a rivalship." [38] Jefferson's desire to secure this unrivaled "Printer" increased with Madison's praise, but he reported a week later that Freneau had not communicated with him: "I suppose therefore he has changed his mind back again, for which I am really sorry." [39]

How sorry he was became clearer to him with each passing day, for the tempest started by Jefferson's endorsement of Thomas Paine's new pamphlet, *The Rights of Man*, reached its height shortly after. However much criticism Jefferson's praise of Paine's work brought him, he regretted only the accidental manner in which it had been made to seem a campaign against John Adams, with whom Jefferson certainly differed but, as he explained to President Washington, "we differ as friends should do." [40] Jefferson

[38] Madison to Jefferson, New York, May 1, 1791. *Writings* (Hunt), VI, 47, n.
[39] Jefferson to Madison, Philadelphia, May 9, 1791. *Writings* (Ford), V, 330.
[40] Jefferson to the President of the United States, Philadelphia, May 8, 1791. Ibid., V, 329. See entire letter for an explanation of the involved circumstances of Jefferson's endorsement of *The Rights of Man*.

did, however, agree with Paine's charge that John Adams's *Defence of the Constitutions of the United States* had preached the heresy of "Kings, lords, & commons." Adams's *Discourses on Davila* continued the controversy. Finally, John Quincy Adams, John Adams's talented son, rushed into the fray with his "Publicola" papers, which were so cogent that many Republicans, including Jefferson, believed them to have come from the pen of the father—and indeed that John Adams's pen had improved its style!

Truly, the republican cause in the United States sadly required a vigorous newspaper. Jefferson wanted Madison to point out that John Fenno, editor of the *Gazette of the United States*, was already condemned for his Toryism and identified with the anti-republican Hamilton faction. Freneau would find the ground of republicanism "as good as unoccupied." [41] A few weeks later Madison sent a heartening report, and observed that if Freneau came to Philadelphia, he would have the financial assistance of Childs, who had been one of his employers in New York, but that the "conduct and title of the paper . . . will be altogether his own." [42]

At last Freneau saw his way. In the late summer he took up residence and occupation in Philadelphia, where by the end of October he printed the first number of his *National Gazette*. By late summer of 1791 Jefferson and Madison knew they were no longer limited to undercover attempts to stop the Hamiltonian "phalanx." They now had an official organ, dedicated to republican principles, and edited by a talented and experienced journalist. Vehement attacks against Jefferson and Madison were to increase.

[41] Jefferson to Madison, Philadelphia, July 21, 1791. Madison Papers, L.C.

[42] Madison to Jefferson, New York, July 24, 1791. Madison Papers, L.C.

Hamilton himself concocted virulent articles for Fenno's *Gazette* charging the two friends from Virginia with a plot against "the government" in backing Freneau's paper. But these articles were highly questionable in being issued to the American public pseudonymously (under the signature of "American" and "Catullus"); and the author himself was open to charges of dominating Fenno's paper, which had blasted the opponents of Hamilton's measures for two years without an opposition press in Philadelphia able to reply. Little more was accomplished by Hamilton's protest, therefore, than to heat the political temperature, already sizzling, one degree higher.

Shortly after, friend Edmund Randolph wrote to Madison asking for the facts in the affair with Freneau. Madison replied, defending Freneau as a man of talent, whose "merit and sufferings in the cause of the Revolution" were widely known, and whose appointment to the present clerkship was by no means an adequate recognition of his merits. He admitted having advised Freneau to establish a press at Philadelphia instead of in New Jersey, partly because Madison thought Freneau's own interests would be advanced by the change. Secondarily, he said (the primary and secondary reasons may perhaps be profitably switched), he had certainly hoped that "a free paper" meant for general circulation, and edited by a "friend to the Constitution," would provide an antidote to the doctrines circulating in favor of monarchy and aristocracy.[43] He emphatically denied that he had negotiated an "illicit or improper connection between the functions of a translating Clerk in a public office and those of an Editor of a Gazette." This, in sum, was the public position of Jefferson and Madison. To determine the

---

[43] Madison to Edmund Randolph, Orange, September 13, 1792. *Writings* (Hunt), VI, 117n.–118n.

degree to which it was justified remains the task of historians who will piece together the complicated details of the Freneau episode.[44]

7

Madison lost little time in using Freneau's *National Gazette* to protest the growing speculation in stocks encouraged by the policies of the Secretary of the Treasury. During the summer of 1791 the abuses of the new funding system had Jefferson and Madison smarting under the "daring depravity of the times." "The stock-jobbers will become the pretorian band of the Government, at once its tool & its tyrant; bribed by its largesses, & overawing it by clamours & combinations," Madison predicted.[45] Not quite two years after the launching of the new federal government, under a Constitution Madison had personally helped to fashion in the image of limited government, it was apparent to him that the fiscal policy and its attendant practices could, given time and favorable circumstances, undermine the democratic victory of the American people.

Accordingly, Madison wrote a series of brief political essays for the *Gazette*, to recall the fundamental nature of republican government. One essay on "Consolidation" described the natural tendency of government to follow a self-directed course when "the public mind" had no voice or was apathetic. This general tendency of consolidation could be countered only by an alert and united body of citizens

[44] See Gaillard Hunt's note to this letter, loc. cit., n.1. Recent studies of Freneau have not settled this question. For a good Freneau bibliography see Robert E. Spiller and others, eds.: *Literary History of the United States*, (3 vols. New York: The Macmillan Company; 1948), III, 517–20.

[45] Madison to Jefferson, New York, August 8, 1791. *Writings* (Hunt), VI, 58–9, n.

whose devotion to local or state governments permitted them to express effectively the "sense of the people." "Let it be the patriotic study of all," Madison entreated, "to maintain the various authorities established by our complicated system, each in its respective constitutional sphere; and to erect over the whole, one paramount Empire of reason, benevolence, and brotherly affection." [46]

The empire of reason and affection as an element of Republican theory was further discussed in an essay on "Public Opinion" printed in the same paper two weeks later.[47] Here Madison declared that public opinion, which sets bounds on every government, is the real sovereign in every free government. The function of declarations of principles and rights, he now asserted, is to influence public opinion, and thus, in turn, to influence every free government. Certain dangers to liberty arise from an extensive country, where size makes it difficult to ascertain public opinion and dwarfs each man's estimate of his own significance. To counteract this, every means to "a general intercourse of sentiments" becomes a vital aid to liberty—"good roads, domestic commerce, a free press, and particularly a circulation of newspapers through the entire body of the people, and Representatives going from, and returning among every part of them," Madison pointedly enumerated.

In the following year Madison contributed an unusually stimulating short article on liberty and power. In Europe, he wrote, charters of liberty had been granted by power. America had established a new and revolutionary practice, which had been followed recently by France, of issuing "charters of power granted by liberty." "Liberty

[46] "Consolidation," in *National Gazette*, December 5, 1791. Ibid., VI, 67–9.
[47] December 19, 1791. Ibid., VI, 70.

against power, and power against licentiousness" were forever to be the moral heritage of republicans. The enlightened public opinion of the United States could not help resenting recent trespasses upon constitutional provisions for liberty and order. "Every citizen," Madison urged, with a rhetorical flourish not usual to him, must be "an Argus to espy . . . an Aegeon to avenge" such inroads on liberty.[48]

Toward the close of January 1792 Madison was trying his hand on an article defining the differences between the Republican and the "anti-Republican" parties. Madison granted that parties were unavoidable. They grow from real or supposed differences of interest; and they have always existed in society and probably always will. The best strategy for combating the evil effects of parties is to establish political equality, reduce inequality of property, legislate justly among competing interests, and where interests cannot be compromised, make one party a check on the other. "If this is not the language of reason," Madison added, "it is that of republicanism." The opposite view, of increasing inequalities, of artificially stimulating the growth of parties and the intensity of their conflicts, "is as little the voice of reason, as it is of republicanism." [49]

Still another provocative piece, deliberately entitled "Spirit of Governments," continues the exposition of the republican ideology by criticizing the work of Montesquieu. Montesquieu had devised three pat principles of government (fear, honor, virtue) that supposedly characterized the three fundamental types of government: monarchy, aristocracy, republics. Disapproving these categories, Madison substituted three supposedly more fundamental govern-

[48] "Charters," in *National Gazette*, January 19, 1792. Ibid., VI, 83–5.
[49] "Parties," in *National Gazette*, January 23, 1792. Ibid., VI, 86.

mental forms: military despotisms ("under which human nature has groaned through every age"); money despotisms, which mask themselves under an apparent liberty, but rely upon an army of interested partisans to defend the domination of the few over the freedom of the many; and republican governments, "which it is the glory of America to have invented, and her unrivalled happiness to possess." In this interesting political hierarchy, the best governments are those which derive their energy "from the will of the society." They govern by reasonable measures, conformed to the different interests in society.[50]

As for the occupational affinities of republicanism, Madison suggested agriculture. Health, virtue, intelligence, and competency in the greater number of citizens were the obvious ideals for a free and safe society. On each count he found "the life of the husbandman . . . pre-eminently suited." In discussing intelligence (the only quality that might not improve with withdrawal from cities) Madison conceded that the mind might be less susceptible of polish in rural retirement than in an urban crowd, but he thought it "more capable of profound and comprehensive efforts. . . . It is more ignorant of some things? It has a compensation in its ignorance of others." Essential manufacturing and professional services will exist, and adjust their numbers to the circumstances and demands of society. But public policy will vaunt the life of the great prosperous farming class and recall the imperfections of other modes of living "as long as occupations more friendly to human happiness, lie vacant." [51]

Having in this way raised the question of property,

[50] "Spirit of Governments," in *National Gazette*, February 20, 1792. Ibid., VI, 93–5.

[51] "Republican Distribution of Citizens," in *National Gazette*, March 5, 1792. Ibid., VI, 96–9.

Madison composed a brilliant short piece showing that there are two basic senses of property. First, he identified the "particular" sense of property, by which we commonly understand money, possessions, the right to exclude others from the external objects we own. But second, there was a "larger and juster" concept: it included everything to which we attach values and in which we have rights— limited only by the general recognition of "the like advantage" to everyone else. This second, broader meaning implies that men have "property" in their religious opinions, in the liberty and safety of their persons, in the free use of physical and mental faculties. Governments that maintain excessive concentrated power leave no man safe in his opinions, his person, his faculties, his possessions. On the other hand, too much liberty might incur a similar insecurity. When it is said that government is instituted to protect property, Madison insisted it is the broad signification of property that is intended. Just governments, then, will not violate the freedom to enjoy and communicate opinions, to differ in religious views and "conscience," and to be secure from arbitrary seizures, and will not permit citizens to suffer under arbitrary restrictions, exemptions, monopolies, or unequal taxes. When governments pride themselves on guarding the inviolability of property, let them see to it that they respect the property in rights as well as the rights of property, narrowly conceived! [52] With this subtle warning, Madison concluded his reflections on a theme central to the welfare of democratic society.

In the fall of 1792, after Jefferson had raised the issue of his retirement from office, and the anti-republican forces led by Hamilton and Adams had gathered more strength, Madison wrote another article. This one, "A Candid State

[52] "Property," in *National Gazette*, March 29, 1792. Ibid., VI, 101–3.

of Parties," attempted the valuable task of reviewing the short history of political parties in the United States. Madison found three important line-ups. First, the cleavage in the era of revolution, between the patriots of the Revolution and the "disaffected class" of Tories who adhered to the British Empire. This first division was meaningless after the Revolution was won. The second cleavage was occasioned by the federal Constitution and was by no means clear in "party" membership. The effectual establishment of the federal government in 1788 disposed realistically of the second line-up. The third party division and the most permanent (because "natural" to the majority of political societies) was between those who would narrow government into fewer hands and approximate it to a hereditary form and those who believe that mankind is able to govern itself. The "anti-republican" party Madison characterized further as encouraging the influence of money and emoluments, and the terror of military force, as principal aids to governmental energy. Anti-republicans wish to "point the measures of government less to the interest of the many than of a few, and less to the reason of the many than to their weaknesses." The republicans respect the rights of man and are offended at public measures that do not appeal to the understanding and to the general interest of the community.[53]

The "summing up" Madison reserved for a final imaginary dialogue between a "Republican" and an "Anti-republican." The latter had argued that the government must be strong above all, and the people submissive. To which the faithful Republican retorts: "What a perversion of the natural order of things! . . . to make *power* the primary

[53] "A Candid State of Parties," in *National Gazette*, September 26, 1792. Ibid., VI, 106–19.

and central object of the social system, and *Liberty* but its satellite." [54]

In these later articles, one cannot help being impressed with Madison's determination to show that republican ideology is first and last on the side of "the people." The formulation is clearly in terms congenial to Jefferson's democratic version of republicanism. Doubtless Hamilton and his "pretorian band" were the inciting cause of this alteration in Madison's previously more conservative brand of republicanism. By 1792 Madison was so deeply engaged in fending them off that he was prepared to assert that "each generation should be made to bear the burden of its own wars, instead of carrying them on, at the expense of other generations. And . . . each generation should not only bear its own burdens, but . . . the taxes composing them, should include a due proportion of such as by their direct operation keep the people awake, along with those, which being wrapped up in other payments, may leave them asleep to misapplications of their money." These reflections, obviously echoing Jefferson's theme, "the earth belongs to the living," appeared in Madison's essay promoting the republican ideal of peace. A primary responsibility of republican government is there declared to be to help curb ambitious wars, and to inaugurate the type of government reform that subdues the will of the government in order to heed better the will of the people. The people are better off with government policies that confine the living generation to the payment of its own debts. These policies ultimately fortify the hope of more continuous peace; and this is a sounder objective, Madison

[54] This dialogue, entitled "Who Are the Best Keepers of the People's Liberties" was the last of Madison's contributions to the *National Gazette*, appearing December 20, 1792. Ibid., VI, 120–3.

suggests, than the visionary illusion of "Universal and Perpetual Peace." [55] On this democratic ideal of peaceful society Madison was temporarily content to rest his defense.

8

Jefferson and Madison reached the high point of their opposition toward the policies of the Secretary of the Treasury when Hamilton's classic *Report on Manufactures* was presented to Congress on December 5, 1791. In the opposition the *Report* engendered we see reflected every basic issue of Republican ideology in its first historic phase.

The *Report* proposed the encouragement of infant manufactures in the United States by using the taxing powers of Congress. Among specific devices recommended were subsidies, tariffs, and the prohibition of competitive imports. Hamilton argued that funds can be so used because the "National Legislature has express authority 'to lay and collect taxes, duties, imposts, and excises, to pay the debts, and provide for the common defence and general welfare.' " He asserted that there was "no room for a doubt, that whatever concerns the general interests of learning, of agriculture, of manufactures, and of commerce, are within the sphere of the national councils, as far as regards an application of money." The only qualification Hamilton conceded on the generality of these spending powers was "That the object, to which an appropriation of money is to be made, be general, and not local; its operation extending, in fact, or by possibility, throughout the Union, and not being confined to a particular spot." [56]

[55] "Universal Peace," in *National Gazette*, February 2, 1792. Ibid., VI, 88–91.
[56] Hamilton: *Report on Manufactures*. Works (Lodge), IV, 151–2.

Jefferson and Madison heatedly took issue with this doctrine—a doctrine that is still considered extreme by American liberals today. To the two Republican statesmen, at any rate, it represented the final position of unlimited power, subverting all the effective restraints on totalitarian power so carefully provided for in the Constitution.

Madison sounded off, a few weeks after the *Report* had been presented, in a letter to the influential Virginia Republican, Henry Lee, then Governor of Virginia. He asked: "What think you of the commentary . . . on the terms 'general welfare'?—The federal government has been hitherto limited to the specified powers, by the Greatest Champions for Latitude in expounding those powers—If not only the *means*, but the objects are unlimited, the parchment had better be thrown into the fire at once." [57] Cueing Edmund Pendleton, whose prestige with Virginia Republicans was great, Madison suggested that the *Report on Manufactures* needed to be exposed to the public. Its doctrine, he again said, was contrary "to the true and fair, as well as the received construction, and as bidding defiance to the sense in which the Constitution is known to have been proposed, advocated and adopted. If Congress can do whatever in their *discretion* can be *done* by *money*, and will promote the *general welfare*, the government is no longer one possessing enumerated powers, but an indefinite one subject to particular exceptions." [58] As for the "general welfare" clause itself, Madison pointed out that it had been copied from the Articles of Confederation, "where it was always understood as nothing more than a general caption to the specified powers, and it is a fact that it was preferred

[57] Madison to Henry Lee, Philadelphia, January 1, 1792. *Writings* (Hunt), VI, 81, n.

[58] Madison to Edmund Pendleton, January 21, 1792, Philadelphia. *Writings* (Congress), I, 546.

in the new instrument for that very reason as less liable than any other to misconstruction." [59]

Madison did more than write to influential politicians in Virginia. His debate in Congress was luminous and effective. He objected: "If Congress can apply money indefinitely to the general welfare, and are the sole and supreme judges of the general welfare, they may take the care of religion into their own hands; they may establish teachers in every State, county, and parish, and pay them out of the public Treasury; they make take into their own hands the education of children, establishing in like manner schools throughout the Union, they may undertake the regulation of all roads, other than post roads. In short, everything, from the highest object of State legislation, down to the most minute object of police, would be thrown under the power of Congress; for every object I have mentioned would admit the application of money, and might be called, if Congress pleased, provisions for the general welfare." [60] As a result, the *Report* was pigeonholed, the first major defeat for one of Hamilton's most cherished policies.

In the midst of these ideological battles, Jefferson found his position vis-à-vis Hamilton difficult to bear. In a conversation with Washington on February 29, 1792, Jefferson alluded to his wish to retire from the Secretaryship of State. Profoundly concerned, Washington pressed Jefferson to explain the "symptoms of dissatisfaction" that had been noticed in the government. Jefferson stressed two charges in his reply: that the Secretary of the Treasury had contrived a financial system that encouraged gambling on the part of the citizens, and had "introduced it's poison into

[59] Ibid.
[60] *Annals of the Congress of the United States* (Gales and Seaton, eds.; 1834), III, 363ff.

the government itself. . . . Particular members of the legislature, while those laws were on the carpet, had feathered their nests with paper, had then voted for the laws, and constantly since lent all the energy of their talents, & instrumentality of their offices to the establishment and enlargement of this system." In short, Jefferson's first argument was that particular Congressmen stood to profit financially from Hamilton's measures, and that therefore the Secretary of the Treasury was extending his influence unconstitutionally, reaching out from the executive agency he headed, into the national legislature. Secondly, Jefferson protested that Congress would be endowed with vast powers to appropriate money for anything "*they* should deem for the *public welfare*" if the *Report* prevailed. And he thought this far graver than the question of the Bank of the United States, "which was thought an incident to an enumerated power." [61]

Six months later Jefferson wrote a long, explanatory letter to Washington, summing up the causes of his unhappiness in remaining in the government. He denied ever having intrigued against the Secretary of the Treasury to defeat his plans. That he had disapproved utterly the system Hamilton was promoting, he fully admitted. Deploring a system that flared from principles adverse to liberty, Jefferson bitterly described its object to be: "to draw all the powers of government into the hands of the general legislature, to establish means for corrupting a sufficient corps in that legislature to divide the honest votes & preponderate, by their own, the scale . . . & to have that corps under the command of the Secretary of the Treasury for the purpose of subverting step by step the principles of the con-

[61] Jefferson's note in the *Anas*, dated March 1, 1792. *Writings* (Ford), I, 177.

stitution, which he has so often declared to be a thing of nothing which must be changed." [62]

The *Report on Manufactures* purported to be a plan that would increase "the total mass of industry and opulence," being "ultimately beneficial to every part" of the nation.[63] Hamilton offhandedly declared that arguments which implied a "contrariety of interests between the Northern and Southern regions of the Union are . . . unfounded and mischievous . . . the aggregate prosperity of manufactures and the aggregate prosperity of agriculture are intimately connected." In fact, however, there was no immediate or short-run conciliation of the Southern agrarian interests with the Northern manufacturing interests; and the *Report* unquestionably favored the North at the expense of the South. When Jefferson and Madison protested that a few merchants and financiers only would benefit by Hamilton's plan, they had a legitimate concern for nine tenths of America's population, who were then engaged in agriculture. In the long run Hamilton's position that the whole nation might be benefited by extensive manufacturing was right—but "in the long run," Jefferson and Madison could argue, in the words of John Maynard Keynes, "we are all dead." Meanwhile speculation was rife, panic and failure a familiar phenomenon in New York and Philadelphia.

Joined to this realistic reluctance to allow agriculture to suffer for the profit of a few who would make the machine the new staff of life was the fear on the part of Republican leaders like Jefferson and Madison that farmers, and even the mobs of workers in cities, would be lost to the

[62] Jefferson to the President of the United States, Monticello, September 9, 1792. Ibid., VI, 102–3.
[63] Hamilton: *Report on Manufactures.* Works (Lodge), IV, 140.

cause of free government. Unless workers and farmers were independent, informed, and vigilant, the government might call itself flattering names like "democracy" or "a Republic," but would in fact be a government *over*, instead of *by*, the people. For a complex of economic, political, and moral reasons, then, Jefferson and Madison regarded rapid and intense industrialization with profound distrust. Two radically different kinds of society could manage to defeat the republican experiment: a feudal agrarian society, where the mass of people were serfs in name or in fact, burdened with debts and committed to hopeless poverty; or an unthinking, greedy, industrialized world, where the mass of workers were dependent upon the will of a privileged few for their sustenance. In both cases the greatest number of people would be too oppressed, too early cast into the pit of labor, too ignorant, and too fearful of their economic needs to make dependable citizens of a strong democracy.

This is the meaning of Jefferson's celebrated or despised "agrarianism"—most boldly expressed in his early book, the *Notes on Virginia*, written in 1781. Here he had vaunted the American "immensity of land" not yet cultivated nor "locked up against the cultivator." And he had eulogized the "cultivators of the earth" as "the chosen people of God . . . whose breasts he has made his peculiar deposit for substantial and genuine virtue." This was also the passage where he had inveighed against the corruption of morality in those who labored, dependent on "the venalities and caprice of customers." The oppressed wage-slaves of the great cities Jefferson had there repudiated as the mobs who "add just so much to the support of pure government, as sores do to the strength of the human body." [64]

[64] *Notes on Virginia. Writings* (Ford), III, 268–9.

Jefferson's belief in the moral values of a life close to the soil had deep roots in his early education and natural preferences, as did Madison's similar sentiment. They had read the Roman poets and had early in their education become enamored of antiquity's idealization of the Arcadian way of life, an ideal that a boyhood on Virginia plantations would encourage rather than dispel. To this personal love of the land the Republican leaders joined their bookish convictions that free society and the fate of a large, prosperous small-farmer class, "freeholders," were indissolubly linked. As Madison had phrased it in the Constitutional Convention: "Viewing the subject in its merits alone, the freeholders of the Country would be the safest depositories of Republican liberty." [65] It would never have been thinkable for Jefferson and Madison to write, as Hamilton did, that among the benefits of widespread manufacture were the employment offered to women and children and to cite favorably, as he did, the example of the British cotton mills, where "four-sevenths, nearly, are women and children, of whom the great proportion are children, and many of them of a tender age." [66]

But Jefferson and Madison were no rigid agrarians of the doctrinaire sort. As national statesmen they rarely acted for purely sectional interests, clearly recognized the role of manufacturing and commerce, and even promoted it. Jefferson in France, as an official representative of his country, and later as Secretary of State, vigorously protected the interests of Northern fishermen, shippers, and manufacturers. Both favored bounties to cod fisheries in New England in 1792, Jefferson by recommending it in his report

[65] *The Journal of the Constitutional Convention*, Madison: *Writings* (Hunt), IV, 120.

[66] Hamilton: *Report on Manufactures*. *Works* (Lodge), IV, 87.

on the fisheries, Madison by voting for it in Congress.[67] They were even to move noticeably further in the direction of encouraging manufacture, navigation, and the appropriation of money by Congress for public works. But they were to do this only after two conditions of great importance had come about: (1) when national self-preservation had made it imperative to stimulate home manufacture, during the Embargo and the War of 1812; (2) when they no longer feared an unprincipled faction in control of Congress, or of one of the major government departments, which would rapidly "manage" the American Republic out of the liberties it had but recently wrested from the British Empire.

Nor were Jefferson and Madison acting as doctrinaire agrarians in fighting Hamilton's *Report on Manufactures*: their opposition was more fundamental and flowed from their republican ideals. They saw Hamilton's proposal as the culmination of a financial and political program that would give unconstitutional power to the general government to be used mainly for the protection of speculators, promoters, and moneyed merchants at the expense of more than nine tenths of the people. The logic of their protest was suited to a government of, by, and for the people and is a significant early phase of Republican ideology in this country.

[67] For a valuable appraisal of the difference between Jefferson and Madison as national political leaders and the sectional politics of the ordinary Virginia leaders, see Harry Ammon: "The Republican Party in Virginia: 1789 to 1824." A Ph.D. Dissertation in typescript, University of Virginia, June 1948 (especially pp. 126–8).

Chapter Six

KEEPING OURSELVES IN THE RIGHT

". . . we shall keep the people on our side by keeping ourselves in the right."
—JEFFERSON to MADISON, August 11, 1793

JEFFERSON AND MADISON might criticize the corruption inherent in too much power; but they were not absolutists about "the right." In the heated controversies of Washington's first administration they had played a role in behalf of what was then roughly formulated as "the republican interest." The remaining eight years of the century would witness the hardening of lines of interest into bona fide political parties. Jefferson and Madison were to divide the responsibilities of general management of the vigorous new national Republican Party. More important still, they were determined to work out a set of principles that would elevate their party above merely political considerations. The practical problems of general management are not of primary interest to us here. The growth of a political ideology, however, is decidedly so.

Party lines were already evident in the election year, 1792, when the Vice-Presidency became a contest between John Adams, the incumbent, and the Republican candidate, Governor George Clinton of New York. In this year Jefferson complained that Hamilton had dared to call the Republican Party a *faction* in Fenno's *Gazette of the*

United States.[1] Despite his longings to escape from political office, Jefferson continued to carry the staggering load of his duties as Secretary of State. His continuance in office was partly owing to pressure put upon him to remain by President Washington,[2] and partly to his irrepressible desire to work out a genuine republican ideology with his resourceful and invaluable friend Madison. The turn taken by foreign affairs in the years of Washington's second administration gave international vision to the policies of the party that wished to speak for the American populace. Hamilton's party, the Federalists, developed their own distinctive ideology during these same years. The characteristics of the two opposition parties are best understood by sampling the political developments of the time.

Since the American Revolution, there had been an almost national affection for France. In the days of the debate over the federal Constitution, it became clear that Hamilton and other strong-government men and conservatives favored the British monarchical form of government over a republic. But the republican form won. Its victory, however, did not still the murmurs or gloomy predictions of those who now added to their former admiration for the English model the increasingly radical and bloody course of the French Revolution. Alarmed at the emerging sans-culotte attack on the bourgeoisie, the Federalists, like Burke and conservatives everywhere, could use the terms "democrat" with loathing, and "Jacobin" with horror. The Republicans they considered "Francomen," democrats, Jacobins, atheists—partisans of upheaval, an-

[1] Jefferson to Madison, Philadelphia, June 29, 1792. *Writings* (Ford), VI, 95.
[2] For a study of Jefferson as Secretary of State see Samuel Flagg Bemis: *The American Secretaries of State and Their Diplomacy* (New York: Alfred A. Knopf; 1927–9), Vol. I.

archy, and Satan. Leading the heretical, Jacobinical ranks were the mild Jefferson and the even milder Madison: "Mad Tom" and his apprentice!

In ideological contexts, however, Jefferson and Madison were quite at home. Lampooning the "Anglomany" of their "monocratic" friends, the Republicans created an uneasy atmosphere for reactionaries and the would-be managerial élite who had to survive in what was still a *republican* world. "Would you believe it possible," Jefferson wrote to Paine, "that in this country there should be high and important characters who need your lessons in republicanism . . . we have a sect preaching up and pouting after an English constitution of king, lords, and commons, and whose heads are itching for crowns, coronets, and mitres." [8]

Probing for causes of the hardened enmity between the pro-British Federalists and the pro-French Republicans, one encounters two different philosophies of human nature, similar to the divided beliefs of political leaders in the separate states before the Union. By and large, the Republicans tended to be pro-French because they believed that people could govern themselves. Reason, discussion, and compromise were real and almost sacred activities—not reserved for the few, but attainable by the many; whereas the people who were rallying to the Federalist Party were privately and sometimes publicly convinced that the mass of men were fools. The people were in general too hasty, venal, and stupid ever to play a responsible role in governing themselves. The last decade of the eighteenth century, however, was close enough to the American Revolution, with its equalitarian ideals of "natural rights," to prevent any view contemptuous of average human beings from finding favor with the majority of the people. Nor did Jefferson

[8] Jefferson to Thomas Paine, June 19, 1792. *Writings* (Ford), 87.

fear that the people would ever buy this cynical philosophy of leadership. He declared repeatedly that the bulk of the people were sound, true to republican principles as before. What he feared was that disillusioned leaders, devoid of faith in the common man, would capture the reins of government first, and then subvert the Constitution, until they had made their own rule a hereditary aristocracy or worse.

Was this exaggerated and far-fetched? It did not seem so to Jefferson and Madison and their friends, who listened to the private comments of important Federalists like Hamilton, John Adams, Rufus King, Fisher Ames, and their satellites. Hamilton could hardly make a secret of his views, since he had stated in the Constitutional Convention that he had no scruple in declaring the British government "the best in the world" and had confessed his doubt "whether anything short of it will do in America." [4] The basis of this disagreeable avowal was Hamilton's fear of the "amazing violence & turbulence of the democratic spirit," [5] and his diagnosis that the American people would soon be cured of "their fondness for democracies." [6]

Vice-President John Adams, a far more principled and subtle mind than Hamilton, grounded his version of aristocratic political theory in what he thought to be the history of republics since the experiments of ancient Greece and Rome. More benevolent toward the people than Hamilton, Adams still regarded them mistrustfully and was pleased, in his Puritan political way, to take stewardship over them. In a highly significant note that should be part of Jefferson's memoir, *The Anas*, but thus far has been omitted from printed versions, Jefferson entered the record

[4] Madison's *Journal of the Constitutional Convention. Writings* (Hunt), III, 189–90.

[5] Ibid., III, 191.

[6] Ibid., III, 194.

of Adams's bias against democracy. Adams had delivered himself of the following tirade:

that men could never be governed but *by force*, that neither virtue, prudence, wisdom nor anything else sufficed to restrain their passions, that the first National conventn. of France had establd. a constn., had excluded themselves from it's admn. for a certain time, a new set of successors had come, had demolished their constitution put to death all the leading characters concerned in making it, were now proceeding to make a new constn. & to exclude themselves for 6. years from it's admn. that their successors would in their turn demolish, hang them, and make a new constn. and so on eternally till a force could be brought into place to restrain them.[7]

Views like these, expressed by the most responsible leaders of the Federalist Party, had warned the Republicans to keep close watch on seemingly innocent technical administrative measures. A society that could only be governed by force would naturally spell the end of the liberties the American Revolution had won for Americans. When Jefferson and Madison fought tooth and nail against Hamilton's financial policies, and against his encroachments upon the jurisdiction of the State Department and elsewhere in the administration,[8] they were acutely conscious of the large stakes they were protecting. For if the administration and Congress were captured by a clique believing in force,

[7] Jefferson, January 16, 1793. Jefferson Papers, L.C. Jefferson adds to his account of this conversation that "E. R. [Randolph] took notice of this declaration."

[8] The most recent biography of Hamilton and the most recent favorable study of the administration of the Federalist Party admit Hamilton's grave interference in the affairs of Jefferson's Department of State. See Schachner, op. cit., pp. 296–8; Leonard D. White: *The Federalists* (New York: The Macmillan Company; 1948), pp. 224–36. According to White, who minutely details Jefferson's sins against Hamilton, it was "Hamilton's active intervention in the field of foreign affairs, a field peculiarly Jefferson's," that set off the administrative feud between them (p. 224).

it might refuse to be turned out with the next election. What we now call "totalitarianism" was in truth possible then, in the days when democratic government had so little precedent to make it firm. This was the private anxiety of the Republican leadership, as Jefferson revealed when he wrote in cipher to his friend Short: "It is prognosticated that our republic is to end with the President's life." [9]

Republicans who advocated that men could be governed by reason welcomed with genuine enthusiasm every effort in other countries to overthrow tyranny and proceed with government "friendly to the rights of man." It was in this spirit that Jefferson sympathized with France's cruel trial as it struggled to hack its way free of monarchical shackles. So robust a spirit was not present in his former secretary and friend, William Short, who watched the mounting wave of terror that closed over many of his and Jefferson's friends in Paris. Short turned against the Jacobins, sending home strong and bitter condemnations of the French Republic in official communiqués. For this, in the beginning of 1793, Jefferson rebuked his young friend, disapproving the "extreme warmth" with which his letters had "censured the proceeding of the Jacobins of France." Jefferson emphatically stated that he considered the Jacobins "as the same with the Republican patriots" whom he had known in the early part of the Revolution; and he traced the events that he thought had shown the Jacobins that harsh measures were needed in order to prevent "the reestablishment of despotism." Deploring that the innocent had fallen with the guilty in the ensuing struggle, Jefferson recalled Short to his "pure republicanism." Innocent victims were like men who had fallen in battle; history would

[9] Jefferson to William Short, Philadelphia, July 29, 1791. *Writings* (Ford), V, 362n.

"embalm their memories." But "the liberty of the whole earth was depending on the issue of the contest. Rather than it should have failed," Jefferson concluded, "I should have seen half the earth desolated. Were there but an Adam & an Eve left in every country, & left free, it would be better than as it now is." It was also significant that Jefferson thought this ardent faith in political liberty belonged to "99 in an hundred of our citizens," and therefore felt it binding upon Short as a representative of the United States.[10]

2

Unhappily for the Republicans, the first diplomatic representative of the new French Republic to arrive in this country was the young and vainglorious "Citizen Edmond Genêt." Regarded with open hostility by the Federalists even before he arrived in Washington, the only Cabinet member to welcome him was Jefferson. Part of the trouble ahead was in no way connected with the envoy's unsuitable personality. Genêt had arrived at a strange juncture in American affairs. The outbreak of war between monarchical England and Revolutionary France occurred early in 1793. Eager to keep out of the crushing embrace of the European combatants, Washington, after prior consultation with his Cabinet, had issued a so-called "Neutrality Proclamation," in which, thanks to Jefferson's influence, the word "neutrality" nowhere appeared. Jefferson had fought to prevent putting England and France on the same footing in this official declaration. Overtly, in Cabinet meetings, he had argued that both England and France would be tempted to

[10] Jefferson to William Short, Philadelphia, January 3, 1793. Ibid., VI, 153–4.

make better concessions to America if they remained un-
certain about her intentions. Hamilton had argued boldly
that the treaty of amity with France did not oblige America
in any way now that the French government had been
taken over by a radical Revolutionary clique. The proclamation that terminated these differences in the Cabinet was
substantially Hamilton's victory.

Thus Genêt would have encountered difficulties if he
had been the most circumspect and supple of diplomats.
In truth, of course, he was anything but that. He was
determined to commit America to open support of France,
and proceeded in a well-known series of high-handed tactics
to embarrass the very men who were trying to help him.
One device, which has since become a stock device for
"psychological warfare" when nations are at war, was to
appeal to "the people" over the head of the chief executive
of the nation. Genêt's diplomatic impudence in the realm
of propaganda came on top of his unprecedented violations
of this country's sovereignty, including fitting out ships of
war in American ports and capturing British vessels in
American waters. The American people were in no mood
to sympathize with the rash French envoy.

Devoted as they were to the French cause, Jefferson
and Madison drew back in alarm. In the hot month of
August the situation had got under Jefferson's skin, and
although he had written a previous letter to Madison on
the same day, he wrote a second confidential one. The
message Jefferson was anxious to get to Madison was that
the time had come for the Republicans to change their
policy on Genêt. Genêt, he charged, was working not only
against himself but against the republican interest. Because
of his outrageous conduct, a popular swing to the support
of the President's neutrality policy, and to the President

personally, was in progress. "The towns are beginning generally to make known their disapprobation of any such opposition to their government by a foreigner," Jefferson wrote. The time to cavil about small points was past. It would be "true wisdom in the Republican party to approve unequivocally of a state of neutrality" and to "abandon Genêt entirely, with expressions of strong friendship & adherence to his nation and confidence that he has acted against their sense." To this major directive Jefferson added an arresting comment: "In this way we shall keep the people on our side by keeping ourselves in the right." [11]

Jefferson justified the new policy by reviewing the causes of his "cruel dilemma." He had adhered to Genêt as long as he could reasonably hope to bring him around to the right behavior "because I knew what weight we should derive to our scale by keeping in it the love of the people for the French cause & nation, and how important it was to ward off from that cause and nation any just grounds of alienation." But Genêt was "absolutely incorrigible," and the Republicans had better "quit a wreck which would sink all who clung to it." The last point of Jefferson's message was that Genêt would be recalled, and Jefferson himself would prepare the official statement of his conduct for President Washington.

This letter clarifies the nature of Jefferson's pro-French sentiment. It shows that republicanism and the cause of free government at home took precedence over all foreign attachments. Operationally, he was willing to do everything in his power to benefit the "cause of the French nation" and Revolution, even submitting to the galling charges of bloody Jacobinism, atheism, and un-American-

[11] Jefferson to Madison, Philadelphia, August 11, 1793. (This is Jefferson's second letter to Madison of that date.) Madison Papers, L.C.

ism that the Federalists heaped upon him. He had in fact prevented American foreign policy from moving closer toward Great Britain. But he was no "idealist" in the soft-headed sense of the term. Keenly watchful over public opinion, Jefferson saw Republican interests in this country would suffer more from having the people alienated from the Republican Party than by a temporary estrangement from France.

Madison's foresight prevented this policy change regarding Genêt from driving the people into an anti-French and pro-British mood. As Jefferson labored over his desk in the rapidly emptying city of Philadelphia in the fall of 1793, Madison concocted a plan to "call out the real sense of the people" before they should be misled. He had written to John Taylor suggesting "a proper train of ideas" and he counted on the co-operation of Edmund Pendleton, Archibald Stuart, and a few other important Virginia Republicans in other counties.[12] His object was to get public endorsements at a local and state level for the new policy; and he thought he could do this best by stressing the distinction between a nation and its agent, between principles and events. Americans should be wary lest they be led by the enemies of France in this crisis "into the arms, and ultimately into the Government, of Great Britain." [13] While Madison saw the necessity for abandoning Genêt, he thought it expedient to recall the errors on America's part that had contributed to the debacle. These were: "the refusal, in the outset of the government, to favor the commerce of France more than that of Great Britain; the unfortunate appointment of Gouverneur Morris to the former;

---

[12] Madison to Jefferson, August 27, 1793. *Writings* (Congress), I, 595–6.

[13] Madison to Jefferson, September 2, 1793. Ibid., I, 596–7.

the language of the proclamation; the attempts of Pacificus [Hamilton] to explain away and dissolve the Treaty [with France] . . . and the appearance of its being an informal manifestation of the views of the Executive, &c." [14] The eminent aids rendered by the French to the United States in the Revolution ought "ever to be remembered and acknowledged with gratitude, and . . . the spectacle exhibited by the severe and glorious contest in which it [France] is now engaged for its own liberty . . . must be peculiarly interesting to the wishes, the friendship, and the sympathy of the people of America." [15]

In the "Pacificus" essays Hamilton had insinuated that Jefferson and other friends of France were either subverting the Neutrality Proclamation by seeking war with Great Britain, or seeking "a pretext for censuring the conduct of the Chief Magistrate, for some purpose very different from the public good." This caused Jefferson too much anguish to bear in silence. He dispatched a dramatic note to Madison, imploring his harassed friend to "take up your pen, select the most striking heresies, and cut him to pieces in the face of the public." [16] This, an unusually vengeful statement for the urbane Jefferson, could hardly be ignored. Much as Madison was loath to undertake the "grating" task of entering the lists with Hamilton,[17] he did so, composing a series of papers signed "Helvidius." Thus the two former collaborators in the *Federalist* papers were now openly pitted against each other in print. Jefferson declared himself satisfied, and Madison felt he had done something to

[14] Ibid., I, 598.

[15] The entire sketch is printed in Madison's *Writings* (Congress), I, 599–601.

[16] Jefferson to Madison, Philadelphia, July 7, 1793. *Writings* (Ford), VI, 338.

[17] Madison to Jefferson, [Orange], July 18, 1793 and July 30, 1793. *Writings* (Hunt), VI, 135, 138, n.

defend United States treaty obligations with Revolutionary France. Years later he excused this venture in printed fireworks by saying the articles were written "under an excitement stimulated by friends, against a publication not only breathing the intemperateness of party, but giving a perverted view of President Washington's Proclamation of Neutrality and calculated to put a dangerous gloss on the Constitution of the United States." [18]

The "Helvidius" papers sought to expose the heresies from republicanism in Hamilton's defense of the Neutrality Proclamation. The power to declare war and make treaties is, according to the Constitution, not solely an executive power, Madison reminded his readers. Hamilton himself had acknowledged this in No. 75 of *The Federalist*. "Pacificus" had most likely borrowed his notion, Madison hinted, from the British example of regarding war and treaties as within the *royal prerogative*. In the third paper of the series the author reminded "Pacificus" that "every nation has a right to abolish an old government and establish a new one." The fourth paper admonished that "in no part of the constitution is more wisdom to be found than in the clause which confides the question of war or peace to the legislature," because war is the "true nurse of executive aggrandizement." [19] But it was the fifth paper that "charmed" Jefferson,[20] with its effective critique of Hamilton's repeated use of the phrase "the government" whenever he discussed the issues of the Neutrality Proclamation. Madison pointedly asked whether it was proper in a republican government to call the chief executive *the government*?

[18] Note among Madison's "detached memoranda" [1817]. W. C. Rives, L.C.

[19] Madison's *Writings* (Hunt), VI, 174.

[20] Jefferson to Madison, Philadelphia, September 8, 1793. *Writings* (Ford), VI, 417.

Obviously not; but this singular style, he recalled, was the usual "phraseology of a foreign government"— namely, the British monarchy.

3

The culmination of the Republican-Federalist split over the French-British issue was fought on an apparently quiet battleground: tariff and tonnage rates on imports into the United States. At the end of 1793, just prior to leaving the State Department, Jefferson prepared a report for Congress on "The Privileges and Restrictions on the Commerce of the United States in Foreign Countries." For this purpose Madison had contributed voluminous notes that described the actual movement of United States trade in the summer of 1792, with Spain, Portugal, France, Great Britain, the United Netherlands, Denmark, and Sweden. The report quickly proceeded from the trade résumé to the major theoretical question: how best to remove, modify, or counteract the restrictions on the U. S. commerce and navigation previously described? Before answering the question, Jefferson stated his ideal for international trade: freedom from all shackles everywhere, "every country . . . producing that which nature has best fitted it to produce, and . . . free to exchange with others mutual surplusses for mutual wants." [21] Such friendly relations among all nations would result in "the greatest mass possible . . . of those things which contribute to human life and human happiness." More important still, "the numbers of mankind would be increased, and their condition bettered."

[21] "Report on the Privileges and Restrictions on the Commerce of the United States in Foreign Countries," transmitted to Congress December 16, 1793. Jefferson: *Writings* (Ford), VI, pp. 470–84. Quotation above from p. 479.

Unfortunately, these optimum conditions, Jefferson saw, were not suited to a world that perpetually preyed on American shipping. He therefore conceded that for nations not yet "ripe for free commerce in all its extent" fewer restrictions and liberalized regulations were the best that could be negotiated. Since the United States was a customer that offered principally the "necessaries of life, or materials for manufacture" in exchange for manufactured products and luxuries, Jefferson thought it could expect "welcome and friendly treatment at every market." [22] In the worst case, of a nation determined to continue its system of prohibitions and duties, Jefferson recommended economic warfare. For "it behooves us to protect our citizens, their commerce and navigation, by counter prohibitions, duties and regulations, also. Free commerce and navigation are not to be given in exchange for restrictions and vexations." Navigation as a branch of industry was valuable, but as an instrument of defense, essential. Arguing at some length for the need for an independent shipbuilding industry in the United States, and a "respectable body of citizen-seamen," the supposedly "agrarian" Jefferson ranged himself with all those who since have preached the independence and defensive strength of this country.

In arguing for counter-prohibitions and discrimination, Jefferson was mindful not only of recent shipping losses, but of British exclusion tactics, such as prohibitive duties, refusal to consider a vessel as American that had not been built within our territories, refusal to allow American vessels to carry American products "to certain countries under their domination." Concretely, he proposed one set of moderate duties for nations that favored American products and shipping. For nations that hindered our shipping and com-

[22] Ibid., VI, p. 480.

merce, he advocated a fixed advance over the moderate duties on certain articles and an absolute prohibition on others.

While Jefferson wanted "all the liberality and spirit of accommodation which the nature of the case will admit," [23] he would not tolerate appeasement of systematic aggression by militant nations. Here, as in his policy on France, Jefferson was a sound American—protective of national interest, grateful to friendly countries, solicitous for the general improvement of conditions in America and in all nations that had proved themselves co-operative. The example of France, who of her own accord "proposed negotiations for improving, by a new treaty on fair and equal principles, the commercial relations of the two countries," Jefferson eagerly cited in concluding his report. The once friendly disposition of the French government to the United States he hoped would be resumed now that "internal disturbances" in France were expected to disappear.

Jefferson sent in his formal resignation as Secretary of State to President Washington on December 31, 1793. Before he could properly leave Philadelphia, to "estrange" himself from politics, he awaited the outcome of Madison's sponsorship of the commercial resolutions in Congress. These propositions, similar to an earlier set prepared by Madison and like the recommendations in Jefferson's report, were introduced by Madison in January 1794, after considerable delay contrived by the Federalists. The resolutions obtained a favorable vote from the House of Representatives and were fortified by the passage of a non-importation bill against British products, but events were moving faster than resolutions. New British outrages on American shipping destined for the West Indies put the

[23] Ibid., VI, p. 484.

entire administration on its mettle to try to stop British marine aggression.

Again Hamilton precipitately charged (in articles signed "Americanus") that Madison's commercial resolutions were "a covert design to embark the United States in the war" on the side of France.[24] He, however, like all the Federalist leaders, was tense and worried about British depredations. Out of their worry came a plan from a small caucus of Federalist Senators to send Hamilton, the arch-friend of England, to negotiate a new treaty with Great Britain. When it was realized that Hamilton, in the opinion of the country, would not be a suitable envoy, the Federalist caucus agreed on John Jay, who could be relied on to work for substantially Hamiltonian policies.

5

While Jay was occupied with his commission in England, the Republicans, already distrustful of every new measure in Washington's troubled second administration, judged themselves to be overwhelmed in federal politics. The outward sign of the diminution of Republican power in policy formation was Hamilton's established domination of Washington and his Cabinet.

A dramatic incident proved beyond a shadow of doubt that the administration was performing as Hamilton wished. The incident was the so-called "Whisky Rebellion" in western Pennsylvania in the late summer and fall of 1794. Trouble had been brewing since the first news of the excise taxes on whisky had hit these Western farmers, whose only portable product to Eastern outlets was the liquid, not the grain from which it had been distilled. Lib-

[24] February 1 and 8, 1794. Hamilton: *Works* (Lodge), V, 74–96.

erty poles, mass meetings, and riots in the four western counties of Pennsylvania, in western Virginia, and south as far as South Carolina, were the sum and substance of the rebellion. On an earlier occasion when trouble had broken out in Pennsylvania over the same cause, Hamilton had urged military intervention. The Secretary of the Treasury took a particularly hostile view of the popular uprising because he was the author of the financial system, part of which was being attacked. Hamilton was quick to find that the rioters were "Jacobins," riotous democrats, in his thinking, typical of Jefferson's followers. He urged Washington to issue a call for twelve thousand militia. For a pseudonymous article in the newspapers Hamilton formulated the issue as: "Shall there be government or no government?" [25] Temporarily assuming the office of Secretary of War, Hamilton rode at the head of the large militia force assembled to squelch the riots.

Fortune favored the Republicans in one detail. The riots had virtually subsided by the time Hamilton set out to subdue the insurrection. Despite the distressing absence of an enemy—Hamilton's troops everywhere encountering commissioners who proclaimed the restored peace—Hamilton pressed on farther, panting for "rigor everywhere." The army, under Hamilton's direction, made hundreds of arrests, and Hamilton himself made Washington believe that the rebellion had been systematic and political in origin, started by the democratic societies of Jacobin clubs to overthrow the government. As a national figure, Hamilton suffered in prestige from his role as an inquisitional knight. He had been a formidable political opponent in his economic and administrative measures. Now, as a leader on horseback warring on a vanishing handful of outraged farm-

[25] Schachner, op. cit., p. 335.

ers, he was the joke of sharp-witted newspapers and com-
mon-sensical Americans.

Madison and Jefferson reaped the profit of the contre-
temps of Hamilton's maneuvers. Madison, at first worried
about the rebellion, was happy and relieved to be able to
report that "It happened most auspiciously . . . that with
a spirit truly Republican, the people everywhere and of
every description condemned the resistance of the will of
the Majority, and obeyed with alacrity the call to vindicate
the authority of the laws." [26] If the insurrection had not
been crushed quickly by popular action, rather than from
above, it would have encouraged a "formidable attempt
. . . to establish the principle that a standing army was
necessary for *enforcing the laws*." Madison testified that
exactly this had been the "fashionable language" in Philadelphia in the middle of October.

Following Hamilton's attack on the democratic societies as "self-created Societies," President Washington had
been influenced to denounce them in a speech. Madison
pronounced this the "greatest error of his political life." [27]
For Washington's sake, he said, he hoped it would be
passed over in silence by the House of Representatives,
for even the President's popularity could not survive such
an anti-democratic outburst. The principle that Madison
judged to be inviolable with a free people, and that the
President's words had threatened, was the right of citizens
to enter into voluntary organizations or societies and the
further right of such societies to censure the government
or particular measures of the government as they saw fit.

[26] Madison to Monroe, Philadelphia, December 4, 1794. *Writings*
(Hunt), VI, 220–1.
[27] Ibid.

Arbitrary denunciations from the chief executive cannot deprive the people of what the law permits "& what the Legislature has not right by law to prohibit," Madison declared. Once the government set itself up as judge and censor of lawfully permitted sources of criticism, it could easily move on from the denunciation of particular organizations to attacks upon private individuals and the press.

Jefferson was more wrathful than Madison at the high-handed charge that the democratic societies had fomented the rebellion. To one of the Virginia Republican leaders in Congress he fumed that it was a move "to restrain the liberty of our citizens meeting together, interchanging sentiments on what subjects they please, & stating their sentiments in the public papers." This repression had been foisted upon the American Republic "a full century earlier than I expected." Jefferson intimated that by this play the Federalists had overreached themselves. The "tide against our constitution is unquestionably strong, but it will turn. . . . Hold on then like a good & faithful seaman till our brother-sailors can rouse from their intoxication & right the vessel." And, as a realistic afterthought, he advised: "Make friends with the trans-Alleganians. They are gone if you do not. Do not let false pride make a tea-act of your excise-law." [28]

To Madison, Jefferson commented bitterly on President Washington's willingness to carry out Hamilton's bold political attack on the Republicans in denouncing the democratic societies. He called it "wonderful indeed, that the President should have permitted himself to be the organ of such an attack on the freedom of discussion, the freedom

[28] Jefferson to William Branch Giles, Monticello, December 17, 1794. *Writings* (Ford), VI, 515–16.

of writing, printing & publishing." He was curious to see "what line their ingenuity would draw between democratical societies, whose avowed object is the nourishment of the republican principles of our constitution, and the society of the Cincinnati, a *self-created* one, carving out for itself hereditary distinctions, lowering over our Constitution eternally, meeting together in all parts of the Union, periodically, with closed doors, accumulating a capital in their separate treasury, corresponding secretly & regularly, & of which society the very persons denouncing the democrats are themselves the fathers, founders, & high officers. Their sight must be perfectly dazzled by the glittering of crowns & coronets, not to see the extravagance of the proposition to suppress the friends of general freedom, while those who wish to confine that freedom to the few, are permitted to go on in their principles & practices." [29]

Jefferson was quite sincere in drawing this contrast between the democratic societies and the military society, the Cincinnati. From the very first he had looked on the Cincinnati as an institution inimical to republican habits, copied from societies where military aristocracies were appropriate, but entirely unbecoming to a nation of free men who had together shared the burdens and dangers of winning the independence of their country. While he had been preparing to leave for Paris, Washington had written to Jefferson asking him what he thought of the proposed society and of his own membership in it. Jefferson had written immediately advising strongly against countenancing it.[30] And when he learned, a few years later, that the

[29] Jefferson to Madison, Monticello, December 28, 1794. Ibid., VI, 516–17.

[30] Jefferson to General Washington, Annapolis, April 16, 1784. Ibid., III, 466–7.

most enlightened Europeans he knew were, if anything, more opposed to such societies, his judgment was reinforced.[31]

Soon Madison was able to send Jefferson good news. The attack on the democratic societies had miscarried. Apparently even the more conservative Republican newspapers had co-operated with the active democratic societies in appealing to public sentiment; and quite apart from how citizens felt personally about the democratic societies, the majority seemed to agree about the value of the freedom to organize. By a strange juxtaposition of information, Madison's letter also contained the news that "Hamilton is to resign, according to his own notification the last of Feby." [32] Thus in rapid succession after the unheroic militia advance into western Pennsylvania, the Secretary of the Treasury and his devotee the Secretary of War withdrew from the Cabinet. Jefferson's guess had not been bad. The tide seemed to be turning against high-handed Federalism.

5

Not until the late spring of 1795 did the Republicans encounter the delayed bombshell of Hamilton's machinations, in the form of the Jay treaty, submitted to the Senate in special session in June, but negotiated in England some seven months earlier. This most disputed of all American treaties immediately became the subject for satiric poems, countless newspaper articles (including bold defenses of it by Federalist chiefs Hamilton and Rufus King), several full-

[31] Jefferson to George Washington, Paris, November 14, 1786. Ibid., IV, 327–29.

[32] Madison to Jefferson, Philadelphia, December 21, 1794. *Writings* (Hunt), VI, 229.

length books, and even a play. But whatever literary excitement the treaty could arouse, it could not really boast a single gain on the principal issue of securing Great Britain's abandonment of the spoliation of American shipping. Federalist defenders tended to excuse it in terms of its usefulness in preserving peace and maintaining the credit stability of the United States—admirable objectives, to be sure, but hardly the immediate answer to America's grievance against British interference with her rights as a sovereign and independent nation.

So far as Republican ideology was concerned, the Jay treaty was the last straw. No longer could the Federalists pretend that they were free from the corrosion of Anglomany. Madison now opened all stops. He proclaimed that the "true key" to the unparalleled proceeding of the Federalists and of their spokesman, Jay, was that these men were a British party "systematically aiming at an exclusive connection with the British government & ready to sacrifice to that object as well the dearest interests of our commerce as the most sacred dictates of National honour." [33]

Jefferson was naturally as belligerent about the betrayal of the Jay treaty as Madison. He used the occasion to express his now famous view on "rogues" in history. In general, he said, men are not rogues; but rogues are usually uppermost, nestling themselves into places of power and profit. "These rogues set out with stealing the people's good opinion, and then steal from them the right of withdrawing it, by contriving laws and associations against the power of the people themselves." The Jay treaty had been foisted upon a busy nation—Jefferson used the metaphor

[33] Madison to Robert R. Livingston, [Orange], August 10, 1795. Ibid., VI, 236.

of a busy crew, tending its proper tasks, the captain at his log book, while "a rogue of a pilot has run them into an enemy's port." [34]

Full-blown protest did not come until a strange circumstance forced President Washington's hand, making him put his signature to the treaty he had distrusted and disliked. A scandal, involving Secretary of State Edmund Randolph,[35] apparently unjustly, revealed that in an intercepted communiqué of Fauchet, the French Minister to the United States, the President was described as an enemy of Great Britain's and a particular friend of France. To show that this accusation was without foundation, Washington waived his own severe reservations about the Jay treaty and signed.

The substantial arguments shared by Jefferson and Madison on the Jay treaty were first set forth by Madison in an impressive letter of more than five thousand words, which he sent to several politically useful correspondents.[36] Essentially, the criticism ran that by the proposed treaty the commerce of the United States would be more open to seizure on the high seas and confiscation at British-controlled ports than ever before; that the effect of its unequal privileges to Great Britain would be to discourage any other nation, and particularly France, from giving the United States favored-nation advantages; that its observance of the modern law of nations was limited to those cases precisely that benefited Great Britain; and that the entire spirit of the treaty was incompatible with the national

[34] Jefferson to Mann Page, Monticello, August 30, 1795. *Writings* (Ford), VIII, 25.

[35] For an account of Randolph's innocence, see W. C. Rives: *Life and Times of James Madison* (3 vols. 1859–68), III, 519–23.

[36] To ——, Orange, August 23, 1795. *Writings* (Hunt), VI, 238–57.

rights of an independent people. Finally, Madison spurned the notion that although the treaty was injurious to the United States, it ought to be ratified in order to avoid Great Britain's future aggressions. He warranted that there was no evidence "either in History or Human nature, that nations, are to be bribed out of a spirit of encroachment & aggressions by humiliations which nourish their pride, or by concessions which extend their resources & power." A forceful statement, and one that suited exactly the Republican leader who had genuine concern for American national character and for what he called the "genius of their Government & people." [37]

Earlier Hamilton had tried to speak in defense of the Jay treaty, but had been met by the boos of the angry New York crowd he was addressing, and finally by a volley of stones, one of which struck his forehead. He had retired, "prudently," but in haste. A series of articles signed "Camillus," however, succeeded in impressing public opinion as his earlier speeches had not. They took the forceful position that the treaty, imperfect as it was, was essential to keep the United States out of war. At least another decade was necessary for the United States to acquire the maturity that would authorize it to take a "higher and more imposing" tone in national discussions, Hamilton estimated. A master at special pleading, Hamilton ignored the objectionable features of the treaty and plugged its few advantages: England's agreement to evacuate the Northwest frontier forts, and the sound principle that British creditors be compensated.

In counterattack, Madison this time preferred to eschew the press, although Jefferson had begged him "For

[37] This paragraph is based on the letter cited above. The quotations, ibid.

God's sake, take up your pen and give a fundamental reply to Curtius [Noah Webster] & Camillus [Hamilton]." [38] The congressional campaign Madison fostered in the House of Representatives in the spring of 1796 was his answer—and it converted a session that Washington had feared would be "hot" into one that literally sizzled. The particular events of the Madison campaign that nearly upset the Federalist applecart in the spring of 1796 were principally the issue of a call from the House of Representatives to the President to submit all papers regarding the Jay treaty to the lower house. President Washington refused to comply with this unprecedented request, referring in his message to the constitutional intention that the treaty-making power be confined to the President and the Senate. Madison responded that treaties were a special kind of law and properly require the sanction and co-operation of the House of Representatives. Otherwise the country could be committed to war, or to financial, commercial, or military preparedness measures, solely on the decisions of the executive and the Senate.

In a tightly compressed outline for one of his many speeches at this time, Madison noted: "It is easy to say President & Senate have power to Treaty & treaties supreme laws." But it is "equally easy to say Congress have power to legislate." The question is, how to solve the collision between the above two "easy" statements about power. When treaties are to be enforced, they operate within the sphere of Congress, and inevitably affect primary objects of domestic legislation like commerce. If treaties are to be the supreme law of the land, can they invalidate earlier legislation enacted by Congress? Madison concluded that it was

[38] Jefferson to Madison, September 21, 1795. *Writings* (Ford), VII, 32.

"Not conceivable that the people so jealous of the sword & the purse shd. have intended to put both into the hands of President and Senate and make Congress—the mere heralds to proclaim war—the agents—to recruit armies and the Cashiers, to pay out money for them." [39]

Madison's dual strategy to block the Jay treaty and formulate a democratic theory of limited executive authority was instructive for the future—but its immediate outcome was defeat. Madison hoped that "rash councils" would not prevail with France as a result of unfriendly American actions. He could see no escape from the truth that while the war lasted, England would continue to command most attention, "because she can do this country most harm." In peace, however, France would move up in the public interest, "because she can do it most good." [40]

Meanwhile, one piece of news, packed with political implications, temporarily took priority over the Jay treaty. "It is now generally understood that the President will retire," Madison wrote. "Jefferson is the object on one side Adams apparently on the other." The presidential election came forward to absorb the thought and future planning of Jefferson and Madison.

6

By innumerable signs, plainly evident in Jefferson's correspondence in his three years of retirement as a "private citizen," the former statesman was trying to be a busy and contented farmer. In the summer of 1793 he had consulted Madison on a detailed plan he had worked out for

[39] "Notes for a speech on the Jay Treaty." *Writings* (Hunt), VI, 295, n.–300, n.

[40] Madison to James Monroe, Philadelphia, May 14, 1796. Ibid., VI, 301, n.–2, n.

the succession of crops "for a farm of red highland of about 500 acres of open land fit for culture." [41] He had appealed to his friend, then home from Congress on vacation, as to a superior farmer. To a friend whom he had last seen in France, Jefferson later wrote that he could be seen at Monticello "in my farmer's coat, immersed soul and body in the culture of my fields, and alive to nothing abroad except the successes of the French revolution, and the welfare of my friends." [42] In fact, he never tired of assuring friends that he was "wholly absorbed by the concerns of a farmer." [43]

Actions in part bore out the sincerity of Jefferson's protestations. Happy in the bosom of his family, Jefferson managed his farm in the best scientific spirit of the eighteenth century—inventing, experimenting, planning. In 1795 he installed a nailery at Monticello, partly for experimental purposes, to bear out his favorite belief that every large farm or plantation could manufacture its principal necessities at home, and partly for profit. These were the years also when Jefferson perfected his famous mold-board plow, for which he received international awards.[44] What he had observed abroad was used to enrich his farming in America, even to the extent of adding European grains and vegetables and choice livestock like Merino sheep. When he wrote to Madison that he would not exchange his life of retirement for "the empire of the universe," he thought

[41] This section is omitted from Ford's printing of Jefferson's letter to Madison, June 29, 1793. The entire letter is in Madison Papers, L.C.

[42] Jefferson to Colonel Blockden, December 11, 1794. Jefferson Papers, L.C.

[43] Jefferson to Rittenhouse, Monticello, February 24, 1795. Jefferson Papers, L.C.

[44] For an account of Jefferson's achievements as an experimental agriculturist see August C. Miller, Jr.: "Jefferson as an Agriculturist," *Agricultural History* (1942), XVI, 65–78; M. L. Wilson: "Thomas Jefferson—Farmer," American Philosophical Society, *Proceedings* (1943), LXXVII, 216–22.

he meant what he said; yet Jefferson could not abandon the powerful interests of political leadership. A few days after he had described himself as "immersed soul and body" in farming, he wrote importunately to Madison, pleading that he stay at his post in the capital: "Hold on then, my dear friend, that we may not shipwreck." Nor did he refrain from the ultimate appeal one man can make to a friend, the request that his friend's wife encourage the project. "Present me respectfully to Mrs. Madison," Jefferson added, "and pray her to keep you where you are for her own satisfaction and the public good." [45]

The appeal to Mrs. Madison was psychologically correct on Jefferson's part. His best friend, long a shy bachelor whose self-esteem had been injured by the refusal of his first suit more than a decade earlier,[46] at the age of forty-three made an unusually happy marriage. Madison's second and successful attempt at courtship involved a personable, vivacious, and warmhearted young widow, Dolly Payne Todd. Jefferson knew of his friend's intentions and approved. Madison, deeply in love, and exultant at having at last broken free from the "single state," which both he and Jefferson considered unhappy for a man, announced his marriage with evident embarrassment. In the third paragraph of a matter-of-fact letter to his dearest friend, Madison confessed in dry, almost legalistic language that he was writing from "the seat of Mr. G. Washington of Beckeley . . . where I have remained since the 15th ult: the epoch at which I had the happiness to accomplish the alliance

---

[45] Jefferson to Madison, December 28, 1794. Jefferson Papers, L.C. A large part of this important letter is printed in Ford, VI, 516–19, but the the sentence quoted and interesting "small news" on a closing page is omitted.

[46] The fullest and best account of this early "romance" of Madison's is in Irving Brant's *James Madison: The Nationalist*, pp. 283–7.

which I intimated to you I have been sometime soliciting." [47] Madison went on to state that he and his bride would set out for Philadelphia in nine or ten days, that he would as always receive Jefferson's commands with pleasure, and write often. In short, he was reassuring Jefferson that his marriage would not interfere with their friendship and the political trust that sustained it.

7

Private life was soon pushed to one side by the early discussion of the Republican slate for the Presidential campaign, some two years off. The two undisputed leaders of the Republican cause in America were our two friends, who for once had very different initial plans about the best candidate for president. It is usually overlooked that Jefferson wrote first to Madison, urging him to prepare himself for that role. A highly amusing, if utterly serious, Alphonse-Gaston interchange between Jefferson and Madison developed, wherein each argued the other's case. At the close of 1794 Jefferson wrote a forward-looking letter to his friend, warning him against retirement, and suggesting that the only valid excuse for retiring from Congress would be "retirement . . . to a more splendid & a more efficacious post" where Jefferson assured his friend he would rejoice to see him. Under no circumstances would he forsake his own retirement.[48]

On the question of the Presidency Madison wrote that his mind was shut "against the admission of any idea such as you seem to glance at. I forbear to say more . . . with respect to myself; and because the great deal that may and

[47] Madison to Jefferson, Harewood, October 5, 1794. Madison Papers, L.C.
[48] Jefferson to Madison, December 28, 1794. Jefferson Papers, L.C.

ought to be said beyond that restriction will be best reserved
for some other occasion, perhaps for the latitude of a free
conversation. You ought to be preparing yourself however
to hear truths which no inflexibility will be able to with-
stand." [49]

Jefferson would not give up so easily. Although he
must have realized that his own prestige was unmatched in
the estimation of Republicans throughout the country, he
appreciated Madison's role as leader of the Republicans in
Congress, his genius for shrewd publicity, his ability in po-
lemical writing, and his general management in organizing
Republican leaders and local groups. Jefferson assured Madison that there was not "another person in the US. who
being placed at the helm of our affairs" would so well ensure the fortune of "our political bark." [50] He protested that
the wish to see Madison as candidate was pure and unmixed
on his part.

The greater conviction, however, was Madison's. The
reasons he must have marshaled in his "free conversations"
with Jefferson were probably the obvious ones. Jefferson had
been more brilliant in his outward career: he had a famed
felicity of expression and he had authored the Declaration
of Independence; he had held more exalted posts, including
the Ministry to France, and France was clearly to become
the great symbol in the coming campaign. Personally, Jefferson was Madison's senior. He was more commanding,
more popular, and more attractive. Thanks to Madison's
able services, he had been able to refrain from overt polemi-
cal writing or political propagandizing, and his retirement
had given him an aura of impartiality.

[49] Madison to Jefferson, Philadelphia, March 23, 1795. *Writings*
(Congress), II, 38.
[50] Jefferson to Madison, Monticello, April 28, 1795. *Writings* (Ford),
VII, 8–10.

Jefferson's reluctance was also affected by the objective difficulties he saw ahead for the new executive. The rising tension caused not only by British assaults on American shipping, but now by the increasing hostility of the French, whose hopes for a Franco-American entente had been shattered by the Jay treaty, was already being felt in the period preceding the presidential election. Jefferson conceded the point that Madison had hastened to drive home, that to offset French resentment against America, "wise councils and healing measures" were imperative on the part of the new administration—and that the presence of a Republican president or vice-president would be the sole guarantee of such measures. Short of this, America and France could develop into perpetually alienated countries, and the long-time consequences of this would be disastrous to the interests of America.[51] Ultimately Jefferson relented enough to become interested in the lighter role of vice-president.

Of the greater desirability of the Vice-Presidency Jefferson had little doubt. At the end of November he wrote to his son-in-law that few would believe the true dispositions of his mind on that subject. "It is not the less true however that I do sincerely wish to be the second on that vote rather than the first. The considerations which induce this preference are solid, whether viewed with relation to interest, happiness, or reputation. Ambition is long since dead in my mind. Yet even a well-weighed ambition would take the same side."[52] All through the month of December, Madison anxiously posted notes to Jefferson giving him whatever scraps of information he could glean about the way the voting would fall, whether to John Adams, the Federalist

[51] Madison to Jefferson, Philadelphia, December 5, 1796. *Writings* (Congress), II, 106–7.

[52] Jefferson to Thomas Mann Randolph, Monticello, November 28, 1796. Jefferson Papers, L.C.

candidate, or to Jefferson. Apprehensive that Jefferson might yet balk at the lesser role, he wrote that the final result was still in doubt, but that "You *must* reconcile yourself to the secondary as well as the primary station, if that should be your lot." [53] Two weeks later Madison outlined his friend's obvious duty: "The new President whoever he will be will have much in his power; and it is important to make as many circumstances as possible conspire to lead him to a right use of it." [54]

To strengthen his position, Madison warned Jefferson that the British party had been emboldened by America's recent difficulties with France to propagandize for a British-American alliance in the event of an actual rupture with France. Madison knew well that any danger to the independence of the American Republic was a powerful argument. In fact, Jefferson had rashly written to Philip Mazzei a bold picture of the growth of apostasy from republicanism in America, binding the country in "Lilliputian cords," which he hoped the great mass of Republicans would soon awake to snap apart. In the course of this letter Jefferson allowed his hatred of the "Anglican monarchical, & aristocratical party" to break loose and injudiciously penned these lines: "It would give you a fever were I to name to you the apostates who have gone over to these heresies, men who were Samsons in the field & Solomons in the council, but who have had their heads shorn by the harlot England. In short, we are likely to preserve the liberty we have obtained only by unremitting labors & perils." [55] This letter, with its

[53] Madison to Jefferson, [Philadelphia], December 10, 1796. *Writings* (Congress), II, 107.

[54] Madison to Jefferson, Philadelphia, December 19, 1796. Ibid., II, 108.

[55] Jefferson to Philip Mazzei, Monticello, April 24, 1796. *Writings* (Ford), VII, 76–7. This is the letter that leaked into the Italian and

rash criticism of Washington, provided a source of great embarrassment to Jefferson as it found its way into print. At any rate, Jefferson proved in it that he was prepared to assume the task Madison had so energetically presented to him as his "historical" duty.

The strongest demonstration of Jefferson's feeling about the Presidency was his readiness to influence the vote in Adams's favor in case the awkward method of designating president and vice-president that was then in effect should prevent a clear victory for either. The fact that he specifically instructed Madison to inform other influential politicians of his wishes on this matter cannot readily be interpreted as only a graceful gesture or a political move, since its object, if attained, would have been self-defeating. In case of an equal division of votes, Jefferson "prayed" and "authorized" Madison fully to "solicit on my behalf that Mr. Adams may be preferred." [56] An enthusiastic appreciation of Adams, as Jefferson's senior in political experience as well as in life, followed.

The impulse to welcome Adams won over any lingering resentment when Jefferson heard the news of Adams's victory. Once more Jefferson assured Madison not only that he preferred the office of vice-president to that of president, but that the main purpose, "to put our vessel on her republican tack before she should be thrown too much to leeward of her true principles," [57] might be realized if there could be good working relations with the new president.

French press and occasioned a storm of two-sided recrimination and protest. Jefferson maintained that his letter had been distorted in its bad and free translations, and that he had not referred to Washington. The Federalists blasted him for it in their papers.

[56] Jefferson to Madison, Monticello, December 17, 1796. Ibid., VII, 91–2.

[57] Jefferson to Madison, Monticello, January 1, 1797. Ibid., 98–9.

In this spirit Jefferson had written to his once good friend John Adams, but, not content with his own judgment, he sent the letter to Madison, asking him to decide whether or not it should be posted to Adams. In this instance Madison employed the authority Jefferson had given him to withold the letter, revealing in his reasons for doing so a shrewder sense of politics than Jefferson had. One must admit that in certain highly charged political situations Jefferson had a worthy but impractical tendency to resort to the "higher" ground of the speculative thinker or the friend who is large enough to be above political animosities. He fostered the quixotic desire for a life of political leadership and adventure without the soiling enmities and cruelties that invariably accompany it. Yet he was not entirely firm in resisting "the call" to political power, and it was galling to his enemies that, once Jefferson had accepted political power, he would on occasions act as a man does who is free of all but philosophical or humanistic interests. In very carefully worded language, therefore, Madison had to point out to Jefferson that his letter to Adams would be a political mistake. He thought that Adams was already well aware of Jefferson's friendly feelings for him (he had been given definite recent information to that effect). He feared that protesting this friendship now might irritate Adams's well-known "ticklish" temper. In addition, Madison reminded Jefferson that while Adams appreciated "the candid manner in which your friends had in general conducted the opposition to him," he could hardly be expected to have enjoyed the activities of "the zealous & active promoters of your election." Nor, Madison warned, could Jefferson afford to disown the latter (however much he might be inclined to do so), since they were already "sore" at having exposed themselves to the enmity of the President-elect.

Above all, there was a probability, Madison reminded Jefferson, that the course of Adams's administration might arouse the opposition of the Republicans, and that a written testimonial of "the degree of compliment and confidence which your personal delicacy and friendship have suggested" might prove distinctly embarrassing.[58]

One reason for Jefferson's friendly sentiments toward Adams had a clearly political origin. Although John Adams was known to be stubbornly independent in his views, he was anathema to Hamilton, who suspected that the proud "John Yankee" (as Adams liked to refer to himself) would not make a good puppet. Hamilton's first attempt to wrest the Presidency from Adams, by arranging to have votes switched to Pinckney, had just failed. Jefferson saw the chance for a dividing wedge in the Federalist administration and valued Adams as "the only sure barrier against Hamilton's getting in." [59]

The political world quickly welcomed Jefferson as the new Vice-President. From his good friend Benjamin Rush, Jefferson received a letter early in January gracefully congratulating him "upon your election to the Vice President's Chair of the United States, and upon your *escape* of the Office of President. In the present situation of our country it would have been impossible for you to have preserved the credit of republican principles, or your own character for integrity, had you succeeded to the *New York* Administration of our government." [60] These were exactly Jefferson's own sentiments, and there was more comfort still in Rush's

---

[58] Madison to Jefferson, Philadelphia, January 15, 1797. *Writings* (Hunt), VI, 303–4.

[59] Jefferson to Madison, [Monticello], January 1, 1797. *Writings* (Ford), VII, 99.

[60] Benjamin Rush to Thomas Jefferson, Philadelphia, January 4, 1797. Jefferson Papers, L.C.

perceptive remark that John Adams had spoken with pleasure of the "prospect of administering the government in connection with you.—He does you justice upon all occasions.—And it is currently said, views the attempt which originated in New York to prefer Mr. Pinckney to him, in its proper light."

An alarming turn in foreign affairs soon confirmed the wisdom of Jefferson's foreboding that it would be best to avoid the nation's highest office. France and Spain, Jefferson thought because of America's "own follies," were behaving so badly that it was feared that they might try to ruin our commerce or start a war. "The President is fortunate," Jefferson complained, in an outburst at the retiring President Washington, "to get off just as the bubble is bursting, leaving others to hold the bag. Yet, as his departure will mark the moment when the difficulties begin to work, you will see, that they will be ascribed to the new administration, and that he will have his usual good fortune of reaping credit from the good acts of others, and leaving to them that of his errors." [61] These were hardly generous thoughts, and yet they were partly correct. The second President of the United States, John Adams, took possession of an administration that was torn by internal dissension and external problems of a chronically incurable kind. In many ways the party strife that had begun to ferment in Washington's two administrations was to mount to new highs of nightmarish grandeur.

Madison, divining Jefferson's fears, lost no time after the election in urging Jefferson to come to Philadelphia before the adjournment of Congress in order to be qualified. He recommended that despite the expense involved

[61] Jefferson to Madison, [Monticello], January 4, 1797. Jefferson Papers, L.C.

for Jefferson, it would be wise to make the trip to avoid an "interregnum" without a Republican in high office on the scene.[62]

Jefferson took Madison's advice, but meant to arrange his entry into office in a fashion that the world has learned to identify as typically Jeffersonian. "I mean to get into Philadelphia under shadow of the stage," he wrote, "and unperceived to avoid any formal reception . . . I do not let it be known that I go in the stage, and have announced a later arrival there than I mean actually to effect. . . ." This was the style congenial to an aristocratic democrat who hated ceremony and found it possible to be dignified without any formal trappings of rank. In further confirmation of his republican spirit was the remark that despite the fact that John Adams had revived "all the feelings of antient friendship towards me, and a wish to conduct the government in concurrence with me," it would not be possible for Jefferson to enter the executive Cabinet. "The constitution makes me the member of a legislative house, and forbids the confusion of legislative & executive functions except in the person of the President. . . ."[63]

Just one month after the election of the new President, Madison notified Jefferson that he would reserve for oral communication what he judged to be the trend of the new administration. He ventured no further in writing than dryly to comment that the prospects were not flattering.[64] Less than a week later Madison speculated on Adams's intention of taking the advice of the Senate on whether the

[62] Madison to Jefferson, Philadelphia, January 8, 1797. *Writings* (Congress), II, 110–11.

[63] Jefferson to Thomas Mann Randolph, Monticello, January 22, 1797. Jefferson Papers, L.C.

[64] Madison to Jefferson, Philadelphia, February 5, 1797. *Writings* (Congress), II, 115–16.

offices held during pleasure were or were not vacated by the political demise of his predecessor. Did this show, Madison asked, that "the maxims of the British Government are still uppermost" in Adams's mind [65] or that the Senate would be involved in the executive agency more than heretofore. None of the implications Madison could draw seemed to be "flattering."

Madison himself was worn out by the terrific burdens that had been placed on him by his participation in Congress, and seemed to feel, now that Jefferson was so near to the center of government, that a period of retirement was in order for him. He therefore emphatically instructed his father that he did not wish to have his name up for the county election. In almost weary repetition he warned against the friendly prerogative that Jefferson might exercise: "If Mr. Jefferson should call & say anything to counteract my determination I hope it will be regarded as merely expressive of his own wishes on the subject, & that it will not be allowed to have the least effect. In declining to go into the Assembly . . . I am sincere & inflexible." [66] When Madison spoke in tones like these, he could not be swayed.

Madison's brief retirement lasted longer on the open record than it did as an operational reality. On paper, it looked like a retirement beginning March 4, 1798, and lasting until he attended the House of Delegates at Richmond in December of 1799. At least for this brief period he was able to live at home in Orange with his newly-wed wife. But once the Adams administration, just one year after Madison's withdrawal from politics, hit the shoals of civil

[65] Madison to Jefferson, Philadelphia, February 11, 1797. Ibid., II, 117.
[66] James Madison, Jr., to James Madison, Sr., Philadelphia, March 12, 1797. *Writings* (Hunt), VI, 307–8.

liberties, Jefferson's call for help could not be pigeon-holed as "merely expressive of his own wishes."

Meanwhile, for Jefferson the *entente cordiale* with Adams had evaporated into thin air only a few months after the opening of the administration. There were no open hostilities as yet; but Jefferson now feared that the President would turn the dispositions of Congress toward war with France, and he saw many followers for this aggressive course in those who wished "the Executive to be the sole power in the government." [67] The struggle to keep free of war would be "arduous and doubtful." So Jefferson developed his normal symptoms of distate for politics. Impatient to meet his family at Monticello, he longed "to exchange the turbulence & hatred of faction for the delights of domestic affection & tranquility." [68]

[67] Jefferson to Thomas Mann Randolph, Philadelphia, May 10, 1797. Jefferson Papers, L.C.
[68] Ibid.

Chapter Seven

THE VIRGINIA AND KENTUCKY RESOLUTIONS: IN DEFENSE OF CIVIL LIBERTIES [1]

THE CRISIS in America's foreign affairs that made Jefferson loath to enter again upon the national stage at the beginning of the Adams administration was to deepen. What started as sharp disagreement over foreign policy developed into a series of notorious acts, described by Jefferson as "worthy of the 8th and 9th century." [2] These Alien and Sedition Acts were immediately viewed by the Republican leaders as an attempt to stifle Republican criticism of the administration and thereby to destroy the two-party system. They were the occasion for the Virginia and Kentucky Resolutions. New materials have made it possible to give a fresh account and a reappraisal of the significance of these Resolutions and the exact nature of Jefferson's and Madison's participation in the strategy of devising them.

The rift between Republicans and Federalists had been widened by the Federalist-inspired recall of James Monroe as Minister to France, on grounds of excessive attachment to France. Once he was at home in Virginia, Monroe busied himself during the late summer and fall of 1797 with the writing of a long "pamphlet" on his trouble-

[1] Much of the material in this chapter appeared as a joint article by Adrienne Koch and Harry Ammon entitled "The Virginia and Kentucky Resolutions: An Episode in Jefferson's and Madison's Defense of Civil Liberties," William and Mary Quarterly, April 1948, pp. 145–76.

[2] Jefferson to T[homas] M[ann] R[andolph], Philadelphia, May 9, 1798. Jefferson Papers, L.C.

174

laden mission to the French Republic.[3] Madison and Jefferson read the manuscript and eagerly awaited its publication. After it appeared, Jefferson reported "unqualified eulogies both on the matter and manner by all who were not hostile to it from principle." [4] But even the hostility to Monroe's *View* delighted Madison. He thought the attack on it was "aided by an official source and is a proof that . . . [the pamphlet] bites." [5] It had clearly caused consternation in the little band of Secretaries (in Adams's Cabinet) who were out-and-out Hamilton men. The unjust treatment of Monroe and further antagonistic acts against France by President Adams made it really impossible for Jefferson to maintain "the pleasure of cordiality" that he had first tendered him. Adams's messages to Congress and his public speeches in the critical years 1797 and 1798, when America teetered on the brink of a war she could not well have survived, were intolerable in the judgment of Jefferson and Madison. In a public speech Adams attacked the cordial audience of leave granted Monroe by the French Directory; he stormed that it was an "insult" to America, and that Monroe had been "recalled in displeasure for misconduct" and was therefore a "disgraced minister." [6]

Monroe's successor, Federalist Charles C. Pinckney, had the unique fate not only to be refused welcome but to be expelled from French territory by order of the French Directory. To clear up this situation a peace commission,

[3] *A View of the Conduct of the Executive in the Foreign Affairs of the United States, connected with the Mission to the French Republic during the years 1794, 5 & 6* (Philadelphia, 1797).

[4] Jefferson to Monroe, Philadelphia, December 27, 1797. *Writings* (Ford), VII, 183.

[5] Madison to Jefferson, Orange, January 21, 1798. *Writings* (Congress), II, 121.

[6] Quoted in W. P. Cresson: *James Monroe* (Chapel Hill: University of North Carolina Press; 1946), p. 173.

composed of John Marshall and Elbridge Gerry as well as Pinckney, was sent to Paris. But again, after months of waiting, bad news arrived. The American commissioners had not been granted an official hearing by the headstrong and temporarily powerful Directory; and the most callous proposals for a bribe had been made to them through go-betweens of Talleyrand, known in the dispatches to America as "X, Y, and Z."

The more strained Franco-American relations appeared to be, the more Adams inclined to show the cutting edge of his "John Yankee" temper. Madison, quite out of patience, characterized Adams as headstrong, quick to insult public opinion, ready to gamble on his private beliefs at the cost of plunging the country into war, hostile to "the smallest disturbance of the ancient discipline, order and tranquillity of despotism"—in short, "a perfect Quixote of a statesman." [7] Jefferson, in turn, termed a message that President Adams had delivered to both houses of Congress on March 19 "almost insane." [8] In this message, the President announced the failure of the peace mission to France, reviewed the series of American mistakes and mishaps in dealing with France as a "liberal and pacific policy," and concluded that since it had failed, he would exhort Congress to "adopt, with promptitude, decision and unanimity, such measures as the ample resources of the country afford, for the protection of our seafaring and commercial citizens, for the defence of any exposed portion of our territory, for replenishing our arsenals, establishing founderies and military manufactories, and to provide . . . revenue

[7] Madison to Jefferson [Orange], February 1798. *Writings* (Congress), II, 12.

[8] Jefferson to Monroe, Philadelphia, March 21, 1798. *Writings* (Ford), VII, 221.

. . . to defray extraordinary expenses." [9] This was so close to being a declaration of war on France, that Jefferson felt "the question of war and peace depends now on a toss of cross and pile." [10]

Taking advantage of the public anger and astonishment at the insolent treatment of America by the French, Federalist merchants began to circulate war-petitions; and wavering members in the House of Representatives went over to the war party.[11] In quick succession came Adams's vigorous refusal ever to send another minister to France "without assurance that he will be received, respected, and honored as the representative of a great, free, powerful, and independent nation." [12] Legislation in conformity with this policy was rapidly passed. A navy was created, the construction of new ships authorized, a large "provisional" army approved. On July 2 Adams had no hesitation in nominating Washington as Commander of the Army, although he deliberated for a long and stubbornly silent period over Hamilton's ardent wish to be the next in command. With Washington's backing, Hamilton finally won the coveted place; but not without Adam's full realization of Hamilton's profound enmity for him.

It was in the midst of these ominous preparations, in the first weeks in July, that the most dictatorial measures of the nation's history were put on the statute books: the "Alien and Sedition Acts." The first Alien Act authorized

[9] *The Works of John Adams*, edited by Charles Francis Adams (10 vols. Boston: Little, Brown & Company; 1850–6), IX, 156–7.

[10] Jefferson to James Madison, Philadelphia, March 29, 1798. *Writings* (Ford), VII, 225.

[11] Jefferson to James Monroe, April 19, 1798. *Writings* (Ford), VII, 240.

[12] Message to both houses of Congress, June 21, 1798. *The Works of John Adams*, IX, 159.

the President to order "dangerous" aliens to be deported from United States territory. Who was "dangerous" and whether there were reasonable grounds to suspect complicity in treasonable or secret machinations against the government of the United States would be determined by the President. The second, the Alien Enemies Act, empowered the President, in the event of a declaration of war, to have the subjects of the hostile government "apprehended, restrained, secured, and removed, as alien enemies." The Sedition Act declared it an offense and stipulated the punishment for combining and conspiring "with intent to oppose the government, to incite riots or insurrections against the laws of Congress; or to publish false, scandalous, and malicious writings against the government, either House of Congress, or the President, with intent to bring them into contempt, to stir up sedition, or to aid or abet a foreign nation in hostile designs against the United States."

At the first news of the intended laws against civil liberties, Jefferson wrote to Madison indicating the objects against which he thought they were directed.[13] The aliens aimed at were principally Republicans and pro-French: men like Volney, the French social philosopher and writer; Dr. Joseph Priestley, the English Unitarian scientist and clergyman, who had sought asylum in the United States; his fellow expatriate Dr. Thomas Cooper, who had founded a Republican newspaper in Pennsylvania; Victor du Pont, founder of the American explosives firm, and son of Jefferson's French friend, the educator, du Pont de Nemours; and even Albert Gallatin, top economist of the Republican Party, who was Swiss by birth.

Jefferson regarded the Sedition Act as a device for the

[13] Jefferson to James Madison, Philadelphia, April 26, 1798. *Writings* (Ford), VII, 245.

suppression of the "whig presses" and their contributors, supporters, and friends.[14] He developed his views in another letter to Madison: "They [the Federalists] have brought into the lower house a sedition bill, which among other enormities, undertakes to make printing certain matters criminal, tho' one of the amendments to the Constitution has so expressly taken religion, printing presses &c. out of their coercion. Indeed this bill & the alien bill both are so palpably in the teeth of the Constitution as to show they mean to pay no respect to it." [15]

In these bills the Republicans sensed a double threat to their existence. Clearly, the Federalists were closing the avenues of ordinary political propaganda to their enemies in the crucial years before the presidential election of 1800. If the Republicans were to be silenced, they could not win. Secondly, there was acute fear that these laws revealed a move on foot to alter the structure of the Republic in order to establish a monarchy in its place. Henry Tazewell, Republican Senator from Virginia, refused to be deluded by small alterations to the original Sedition Act and charged pointedly that laws such as these could only serve to "indulge that appetite for tyranny that alone could have occasioned the introduction of the principle." [16]

So rapidly had "the reign of witches" encamped itself that John Taylor, ever alert to criticism and protest, recommended that it was "not unwise now to estimate the separate mass of Virginia and North Carolina, with a view to their separate existence." [17] Jefferson hastened to calm Tay-

[14] Ibid.
[15] Jefferson to Madison, Philadelphia, June 7, 1798. Ibid., VII, 266–7.
[16] Tazewell to Madison, Philadelphia, July 12, 1798. Rives Papers, L.C.
[17] The Taylor letter has become the subject of controversy. For a guide to the controversy see Ford's note in Jefferson's *Writings*, VII, interleaving pp. 262 and 263.

lor on this dangerous point. He agreed that "we are completely under the saddle of Massachusetts and Connecticut, and that they ride us very hard." [18] Nevertheless, Jefferson argued, in every "free and deliberating society, there must, from the nature of man, be opposite parties, and violent dissensions and discords." This party divison may, in fact, be salutary, since it implies that no party can proceed unwatched and unnoticed. "But if on a temporary superiority of the one party, the other is to resort to a scission of the Union, no Federal government can ever exist."

Jefferson reinforced this positive statement by a persuasive set of questions that showed the weakness of Taylor's argument for separation. Would the evil stop with one break? Would not the passions of men be the same in a smaller segment as they were in the Union, and would not these generate party spirit in the "residuary confederacy"? What would a country be like where one party could eternally threaten the opposition to join the residuary confederacy or create still new ones? "Seeing, therefore, that an association of men who will not quarrel with one another is a thing which never yet existed . . . I had rather keep our New England associates for that purpose. . . ." [19] At this time Jefferson had confidence that even if there were to be war (in which event both parties would give unquestioned loyalty to its prosecution), in the long run the domestic situation would improve and the government be restored to its true principles, for, he wisely reflected, "this is a game where principles are the stake."

Apart from purely political considerations, it should not be forgotten that Jefferson saw in the Sedition Act a denial of one of the philosophic principles he held most

[18] Jefferson to John Taylor, Philadelphia, June 1, 1798. Ibid., VII, 263.
[19] Ibid., VII, 264–5.

sacred. Knowledge and freedom of inquiry—the submission of man-made truths to man-made confirmations or disproofs—were valued by him not only as a means but also as a noble human end. The independent dignity of mankind and of the individual were derived from the searching human mind. This belief was naturally not unique. It was a time that would later be typed as "the Age of Enlightenment"—an age distinguished by its faith in scientific methods of establishing hypotheses and in supporting them by firm clusters of "facts." Politically a republic was considered by liberal thinkers superior to a monarchy, an oligrachy, or an aristocracy exactly because of its commitment to the freedom of the human mind and its respect for "natural rights." Jefferson had, in this vein, regarded religion as his foe in earlier years, because it presumed to have a patent on truth and its methods were evil, sanctioning the suppression of free inquiry and criticism.

Jefferson's philosophic view was eloquently stated when he wrote, in June 1799, to William Green Munford, a student at William and Mary:

I join you . . . in branding as cowardly the idea that the human mind is incapable of further advances. This is precisely the doctrine which the present despots of the earth are inculcating, and their friends here re-echoing; and applying especially to religion and politics: "that it is not probable that anything better will be discovered than what was known to our fathers." We are to look backwards then and not forwards for the improvement of science, and to find it amidst feudal barbarisms and the fires of Spital-fields. But thank heaven the American mind is already too much opened, to listen to these impostures, and while the art of printing is left to us, science can never be retrograde; what is once acquired of real knowledge can never be lost. To preserve the freedom of the human mind then and freedom of the press, every spirit should be ready to devote itself to martyrdom; for as long as we may think as we will, and speak as we think the condition of man will proceed in improvement. The generation which is going off the stage has deserved well of mankind for the struggles it has made, and for having arrested that course of despotism which had overwhelmed the world for thousands and thousands of years. If there seems to be danger that the ground they have gained will be lost again, that danger comes from the generation your contemporary. But that the enthusiasm which characterizes youth should lift its parricide hands against freedom and science would be such a monstrous phaenomenon as I can not place among possible things in this age and this country.[20]

But the price of freedom, as Jefferson so rightly put it, was eternal vigilance. Some time before the Alien and Sedition Acts, Jefferson had detected a maneuver to make use of the federal courts in Virginia to curb the activities of Republican publicists. This little-known incident took place in the spring of 1797. In that year the grand jury of the federal circuit court of Richmond "presented" Samuel Jordan Cabell, the Republican Representative from the district of Albermarle, because he had sent to his constituents circular letters violently attacking the Adams administration. The grand jury declared: "We . . . present as a real evil the circular letters of several members of Congress, and particularly . . . of Samuel J. Cabell, endeavoring at a time of real public danger to disseminate unfounded calumnies against the happy government of the United States . . . and to increase or produce a foreign influence ruinous to the peace, happiness and independence of these United

[20] Jefferson to William Green Munford, Monticello, June 18, 1799. MS. letter, Teachers College Library, Columbia University. This interesting letter was called to my attention through the courtesy of the editors of *The Papers of Thomas Jefferson.*

States." [21] Jefferson at once labeled this presentment as the "perversion" of a legal institution into a political one.[22]

When Jefferson returned to Monticello, he drafted a petition denouncing the presentment. In August he sent his petition to Madison for revision, proposing that it should be submitted, when completed, to the people of the congressional district of Albermarle by his nephew, Peter Carr.[23] Approving Jefferson's petition, Madison made only a few verbal changes.[24] Monroe was also consulted; but he made no contribution beyond pointing out that perhaps the state had no power to act on a question involving a federal agency.[25] Jefferson's petition was then submitted to the state legislature, its real authors remaining unknown.

The petition did more than condemn the presentment; it charged that the proper relations between a representative and his constituents had been obstructed and it reaffirmed the Republican principle that there be no extension of the judicial power into the legislative branch of government.[26] The petitioners requested the legislature to "redress" their grievances. No suggestions were made about how this should be done, and the House of Delegates contented it-

[21] Presentment of the Grand Jury of Richmond, May 22, 1797, Norfolk, Va., *Herald*, May 29, 1797. This presentment was never acted upon, for Cabell was never tried.

[22] Jefferson to Peregrine Fitzhugh, Philadelphia, June 4, 1797. Photostat in the University of Virginia Library, from the original in the Duke University Library.

[23] Jefferson to Madison, Monticello, August 3, 1797. *Writings* (Ford), VII, 164–5.

[24] Madison to Jefferson, August 5, 1797. Draft, Madison Papers, L.C.

[25] Monroe to Jefferson, Albemarle, September 5, 1797. James Monroe: *Writings*, edited by Stanislaus Murray Hamilton (New York, 1898), III, 85.

[26] The petition of the subscribers, inhabitants of the counties of Amherst, Albemarle, Fluvanna, and Goochland. *Writings* (Ford), VII, 158–64.

self with passing a resolution that "said presentment is a violation of the fundamental principles of representation . . . an usurpation of power . . . and a subjection of a natural right of speaking and writing freely." [27]

In the harsh light of the Alien and Sedition Acts, Jefferson had reason to consider his earlier strategy in the matter of the jury petition wise. Returning to this subject in October 1798, with Madison's aid he drafted a new petition, this time proposing a practical remedy. The petition urged the legislature to provide for the election of jurors by the people and to abolish the practice of allowing the agents of the court to pick the jurors. [28] On the surface this petition was non-political. Actually it aimed at ensuring a proper percentage of Republican jurors, proportioned to their popular strength in Virginia. With a heavy representation of Republican jurors Jefferson foresaw that the activities of Federalist-dominated courts would be effectively hamstrung. In truth, the jury petitions were the modest trial balloons of the Republican leaders as they jockeyed to circumvent the obnoxious federal influence that had clamped down the Alien and Sedition Laws upon a "free" people.

2

The Virginia and Kentucky Resolutions were Jefferson's and Madison's sweeping protest to the Federalists' Alien and Sedition Acts of July 1798. These two sets of Resolutions closed the century in prophetic tones, displaying an oracular logic about constitutional law—a logic that the next century was partly to misread and liberally to misuse in

[27] *Journals of the House of Delegates of Virginia for 1797*, pp. 55–8, December 28, 1797. These resolutions were not transmitted to the Senate.
[28] Petition on the Election of Jurors. *Writings* (Ford), VII, 284–7.

contexts foreign to the original intent. From their first conception in the late summer of 1798 to their acceptance by the Virginia and Kentucky legislatures, elaborate trappings of secrecy surrounded the proceedings connected with the Resolutions. John Breckinridge sponsored the resolves for Kentucky and John Taylor for Virginia. But for almost a quarter of a century the authors, Jefferson and Madison, never acknowledged the part they had played to any but the few who were directly involved in the public presentation of the Resolutions.[29]

As the disturbing Resolutions of '98 made their way through the country, traveling from Kentucky and Virginia to every state legislature in the Union, they appeared on the surface to be nothing more than two impersonal messages from two apparently eloquent Southern assemblies, asking for corroboration from their several sister states. With no exceptions, the immediate comment was hostile. As political propaganda, however, the Resolutions were tremendously effective, frightening the Federalist ranks and uniting, as Hamilton feared they might, the Republicans into a determined party with "body and solidity."[30]

The ethics of secrecy may be questioned, but in this case the necessity for the real authors to conceal their identity was plain. It should be recalled that all Republicans had

[29] For a detailed account of the mystery of the Virginia and Kentucky Resolutions and its solution, see Koch and Ammon, loc. cit., pp. 145–76.

[30] Hamilton to Oliver Wolcott, June 29, 1798. Alexander Hamilton: Works (Lodge), X, 295. Hamilton's position is interesting. At first jubilant over the Federalist mood in Congress that permitted the Alien and Sedition Acts to be introduced, Hamilton grew worried that they might be a "false step." Objecting to "tyranny" largely because of its powers of uniting the opposition, he pointed out that "Energy is a very different thing from violence." But by February 2, 1799, he admitted in a letter to Theodore Sedgwick that he would be ready to use the militia against Virginia if necessary; for the time, he thought it unadvisable. Ibid., X, 340–2.

taken to caution and secrecy since the bitterly anti-French Congress first began to consider the repressive legislation. As John Taylor put it, "government is getting into the habit of peeping into private letters, and is manufacturing a law, which may even make it criminal to pray to God for better times." [31] The war fever which resulted in the Alien and Sedition Acts would have mounted to a threatening new high had the principal author of the Kentucky Resolutions been publicly identified as Thomas Jefferson, then Vice-President in the John Adams administration. And if Madison's name had been officially connected with the slightly more temperate Virginia Resolutions, which he wrote shortly after Jefferson had completed the ones for Kentucky, the known personal and political alliance of the two Republican leaders would have served to link Jefferson's name with the Resolutions for *both* Kentucky and Virginia. Indeed, the possibility might well have occurred to these two legally astute statesmen that the second highest officer in the United States government might be charged with sedition if he overtly associated himself with a movement to declare two measures of the current Congress "unconstitutional." [32]

Jefferson drafted the Kentucky Resolutions in the early fall of 1798 with the close co-operation of Madison. The collaboration is indicated by analysis of Jefferson's epistolary ledger. Usually, when Jefferson and Madison were in Virginia at the same time, they would write each other numerous notes and letters, at least several times a month. In the

[31] [John Taylor] to Jefferson [June 25, 1798]. Jefferson Papers, L.C.
[32] This idea does not appear in the correspondence between Jefferson and Madison. Madison, however, seems to have feared that the Federalists would stop at nothing. When it was proposed that Monroe should publicly defend his conduct in France, Madison cautioned Jefferson that care should be exercised lest "the spirit of party revenge may be wreaked thro' the forms of the Constitution." Madison to Jefferson, June 10, 1798. *Writings* (Hunt), VI, 324.

critical months directly after Congress passed the suppresive legislation that dismayed the Republicans, there was not a single entry to or from Madison in Jefferson's ledger, between July 21 and October 26. Yet when correspondence was resumed, it is clear that Madison was fully aware of all that Jefferson had done.[33] In a step as precipitous as issuing a defiant new declaration of rights, a step involving the future existence or survival of the Republican Party, it would be absurd to assume that Jefferson would have acted alone. The hypothesis here advanced is that although there is only one *known* meeting [34] recorded in the period when Jefferson was busying himself with drafting the Kentucky Resolutions, there were probably frequent meetings and secret messages exchanged, which may have been instantly destroyed and were never recorded in Jefferson's epistolary ledger, in order to guard the secrecy they so much required.

When the draft of the Kentucky Resolutions was ready, Jefferson gave them to Wilson Cary Nicholas with the advice that he entrust them to some reliable Republican member of the legislature of North Carolina. Nicholas departed from Jefferson's plan by giving them instead to John Breckinridge of Kentucky. Nicholas confessed to Jefferson in writing that he had revealed to Breckinridge the name of the real author, receiving complete assurances of secrecy. Probably Breckinridge had been visiting Nicholas (they were interested in joint land-speculating ventures); and after Breckinridge had received his historic mission to introduce the Resolutions in the Kentucky legislature, both men apparently agreed that it would be unwise for Breckinridge to call on Jefferson—what with the efficient spying

[33] Jefferson to Madison, October 26, 1798. *Writings* (Ford), VII, 287.

[34] This was the meeting that occurred a few days before October 26. Ibid.

of Charlottesville Federalists and their henchmen—and Breckinridge returned directly to Kentucky bearing Jefferson's draft with him. Jefferson approved Nicholas's choice of Breckinridge in a letter written in early October, which ended with the request that Nicholas visit Madison, and the very significant comment: "You know of course that I have no secrets from him. I wish him therefore to be consulted as to these resolutions." [35] In Kentucky, Breckinridge lost little time in putting Jefferson's Resolutions to work. With only a few slight changes, the resolutions were passed by the Kentucky House of Representatives on November 10, 1798, with only three dissenting votes. Three days later the Senate concurred unanimously with the lower house.

These Kentucky Resolutions of '98 were not the first legislative protest against laws that were charged with being "unconstitutional." They were, however, the first statement of this grievance that recommended a method of redress other than their repeal by Congress (such an appeal would have been worse than futile at the time). It is this new mode of redress that gives Jefferson's Kentucky Resolutions their original significance in the history of America. As is well known, the Kentucky Resolutions formulated the explicit doctrine that the Union is a compact among the states. In the "compact" only limited powers were assigned to the created federal government, the residue being reserved to the states or to the people. Since the Constitution was founded on a "compact" among the states, each state retained the right "to judge for itself, as well of infractions [of the compact] as of the mode and measure of redress." Having started with so sweeping a definition of the power of the states, the Resolutions nevertheless concluded quietly

[35] Jefferson to Nicholas, Monticello, October 5, 1798. *Writings* (Ford), VII, 281-2.

by requesting the other states to assist Kentucky in securing the repeal of the Alien and Sedition Acts.[36]

This conclusion was different from the one Jefferson had put into his draft; for Jefferson had invited the states to "concur in declaring these acts void and of no force." And the states were expected, in Jefferson's draft, to take measures for providing that neither these acts "nor any others, not plainly and intentionally authorized by the Constitution, shall be exercised within their respective territories." [37] Jefferson, in short, had gone much further in his version than the Kentucky legislature wished to go; his original eighth Resolution (which appeared in the set adopted by Kentucky as the ninth) was therefore altered by the omission of the two passages just cited. In dropping these phrases, Kentucky deliberately occupied a more moderate ground than that proposed by Jefferson.

3

In the middle of November 1798 the subject of the Virginia and Kentucky Resolutions was first mentioned explicitly in writing by Jefferson or Madison. At that time Jefferson wrote to his collaborator saying he was enclosing a copy of the draft of the "Kentucky resolves." He proceeded to recommend a technique of studied ambiguity. "I think we should distinctly affirm all the important principles they contain," he advised Madison, who was about to draw up the Virginia Resolutions, "so as to hold to that ground in future, and leave the matter in such a train as that we may not be committed absolutely to push the matter to extremities, & yet be free to push as far as events will render pru-

[36] The Kentucky Resolutions of 1798, and Jefferson's drafts for them, are printed in Jefferson's *Writings* (Ford), VII, 288–309.
[37] Ibid.

dent." [38] As Jefferson said, placed within the original letter was his final draft of the Kentucky Resolutions plus a manuscript copy of the Resolutions as they passed the Kentucky House of Representatives. In the latter the variations from Jefferson's original are set aside carefully from the main body of the text. From Jefferson's comments in the letter just quoted it is clear that he sent these copies so that Madison could refer to them for guidance while drafting his resolutions for the Virginia legislature.

There is good reason to believe that Jefferson saw Madison's draft of resolutions for Virginia before they were sponsored in the House of Delegates by John Taylor, who had earlier expressed his abhorrence of resolutions. More than that, Jefferson took the liberty of making an important change while the resolutions were on their way to Taylor. This time again the go-between proved to be Colonel Nicholas. At the end of November 1798 Jefferson wrote to him briefly but urgently, saying: "The more I have reflected on the phrase in the paper you showed me, the more strongly I think it should be altered. Suppose you were instead of the invitation to cooperate in the annulment of the acts, to make it an invitation 'to concur with this commonwealth in declaring, as it does hereby declare, that the said acts are, and were ab initio, null, void, and of no force, or effect.' " [39] As he had distinctly stated to John Taylor in a letter three days earlier, it was his policy "for the present" to resolve the Alien and Sedition Laws to be "against the constitution & merely void, and for addressing the other States to obtain similar declarations; and I would not do anything at this moment which should commit us further, but reserve our-

[38] Jefferson to Madison, Monticello, November 17, 1798. W. C. Rives Papers, L.C.

[39] Jefferson to Wilson Cary Nicholas [Monticello], November 29, 1798. *Writings* (Ford), VII, 312–13.

selves to shape our future measures or no measures, by the events which may happen." [40] Jefferson was hoping that public opinion would rise against "arbitrary" government, which, he commented, even the English had blushed and wept to see develop so rapidly in America.

The wording Jefferson suggested in his urgent note to Nicholas appeared in the Virginia Resolutions as introduced into the House of Delegates on December 10, 1798 by John Taylor. On Taylor's own motion, however, just before the final vote was taken (December 21), the phrase was stricken out. Taylor's change restored Madison's original wording, inviting the states to "concur with this commonwealth in declaring as it does hereby declare, that the aforesaid acts are unconstitutional." Since Taylor himself would have preferred an even stronger declaration than the one Jefferson had suggested, it is not likely that he was responsible for the motion to restore Madison's, which purposely omitted the critical word "null," which Madison deeply distrusted. Most likely Madison alone, or Madison with Jefferson grudgingly won over to his view, suggested that Taylor make the motion to amend the Resolutions as noted. Years later, when Madison was rescuing the Virginia Resolutions from the construction put upon them in the nullification controversy, he pointed to the deletion of the phrase "null, void, and of no effect" as proof that the Virginia legislature was expressing only its opinion and not attempting to invalidate a federal law. [41]

Madison's Virginia Resolutions summarized in the brief compass of a few hundred words the illicit manipulations of the Constitution with which he charged the Fed-

[40] Jefferson to John Taylor, Monticello, November 26, 1798. Ibid., VII, 311.

[41] Madison to James Robertson, March 27, 1831; Madison to Nicholas P. Trist, December 1831. *Writings* (Congress), IV, 166–7, 204–5.

eralists leaders. Significantly, the Resolutions began with a declaration of loyalty to the Union. They announced that the federal compact derived its existence from the states that were parties to it, and that "in case of a deliberate, palpable, and dangerous exercise of powers not granted by the said compact, the States . . . have the right . . . to interpose for arresting the progress of the evil and for maintaining . . . the authorities, rights, and liberties appertaining to them." [42] An enumeration of the abused powers followed. First, Madison censured the effort to extend the powers of the general government by forced constructions of the Constitution and wholesale interpretations of certain general grants which destroyed the meaning of the specific enumeration. The tendency of these unconstitutional procedures would be to "transform the present Republican system of the United States into an absolute, or at best, a mixed monarchy." In further demonstration of this unconstitutional centering of power, the Resolutions maintained that the executive and judicial power had been united in passing the Alien Act; while the Sedition Act had been passed in direct contradiction to the amendment that guaranteed freedom of the press to the people of the United States.

Thus Madison's Virginia Resolutions differed from Jefferson's draft of the Kentucky Resolutions in being more cautious and less forceful. Their inconclusiveness expressed Madison's doubt about the legality of the stronger doctrine. He was certain that it was a good Republican tactic to pillory the Federalists for barbaric laws infringing civil liberties; but what about the propriety of appealing to the constitutional position of the states? He scrupulously stated his

[42] The Virginia Report of 1799–1800 . . . together with the Virginia Resolutions of December 21, 1798 . . . (Richmond, 1850), p. 148.

grounds for disagreeing with Jefferson after the first set of Kentucky and Virginia Resolutions had passed. "Have you ever considered thoroughly," he asked Jefferson, "the distinction between the power of the *State*, & that of the *Legislature*, on questions relating to the federal pact. On the supposition that the former is clearly the ultimate Judge of infractions, it does not follow that the latter is the legitimate organ, especially as a convention was the organ by which the compact was made." Madison explained that he thought this a weighty reason for employing general expressions in the Resolutions that would allow other states the freedom to choose whatever method they wished to express substantial agreement with Virginia, and "would shield the Genl. Assembly agst. the charge of usurpation in the very act of protesting the usurpations of Congress." [43]

Although Jefferson did not specifically declare in the Kentucky Resolutions that the state legislatures were the proper agents of the states to declare federal law unconstitutional, the tenor of his language was suited to that view. Certainly the other states placed this interpretation upon the Resolutions in their replies. Madison, on the other hand, accepted the theory that the Union was based upon a compact among the states, but he did not believe that the state legislature was empowered to declare federal laws "null, void, and of no effect." Nor did he believe that an individual state was the ultimate judge of both the violation and the mode of redress for other states. But these niceties of difference between the political philosophies of the two leaders were not too important for the principal Republican speakers on the Resolutions in the Virginia Assembly— James Barbour and John Taylor. These political souls were

[43] Madison to Jefferson, December 29, 1798. Draft. Madison Papers, L.C.

more concerned with proving the unconstitutionality of the measures by ample quotations from common law, "natural law," or the Constitution.

4

By the spring of 1799 the replies of the various states had been received in Virginia. On the whole, they were not favorable. The people and their legislatures had not yet sufficiently recovered from the "delusion of X.Y.Z.," was Jefferson's way of putting it. The Republican leadership in Virginia sensed at once the danger in letting the matter drop, and determined to renew the arguments of 1798 with even greater vigor. Jefferson particularly would not consider dropping a principle that he judged to be at the heart of democracy—the freedom to express thought without hindrance and to criticize political opponents even if the opposition happened to be the "government." In the past the ideology of the Republican Party had paid special attention to principles involving civil liberties, and its leaders had no intention now of forsaking that ideology. As the Federalists in Virginia bent every effort to discredit the Republicans, charging them with plotting "disunion," Jefferson and his associates determined to stand firm. And firmness was really needed, for the Federalists began an alarming campaign to charge the Republicans with a conspiracy to use violence. John Nicholas, younger brother of Wilson Cary Nicholas, repudiated his former Republican faith, alleging that the legislature had gathered a store of arms in Richmond as the first step in their plan to destroy the government. Completely unfounded as this charge was, it enjoyed wide currency. Not quite so unfounded was the charge that the Resolutions tended to disunion.

In early March 1799 Madison's decision not to accept any political office was shaken by an eloquent letter from John Taylor. Taylor was apprehensive for the fate of the Republican protest, and he had just learned that Patrick Henry, Jefferson's bitter enemy, had been persuaded by the Federalists to offer himself as a candidate for the assembly. Only Madison was strong enough to counteract Henry's influence in the legislature, Taylor correctly argued. He warned: "Consider that Virginia is the hope of republicans throughout the union, and that if Mr. Henry prevails in removing her resistance to monarchical measures, the whole body will be dispirited and fall a sudden and easy prey to the enemies of liberty." And even more telling for Madison was his patriotic appeal: "If you will not save yourself or your friend—yet save your country." Closing with a final political flourish, Taylor prophesied: "The public sentiment of Virginia is at a crisis—at the next assembly it will take a permanent form which will fix the fate of America." [44] Not even the calm spirit of Madison could remain impervious to these compelling arguments and such high political style. Moreover, the need for continuing the struggle was undeniable. Madison probably wanted the chance further to clarify and limit the doctrines expounded the year before, at the same time that he could refute the Federalist charges of the intervening months. He therefore proceeded to win a place for himself in the House of Delegates, from which position he could continue the fight against the Alien and Sedition Laws openly and lawfully.

Political tempers had risen in the year following the first Virginia and Kentucky Resolutions. A report came from Staunton, Virginia, that early in April 1799 the Virginia Resolutions of 1798 were torn to pieces and "trampled

[44] Taylor to Madison, Caroline, March 4, 1799. Rives Papers, L.C.

. . . underfoot" by the full court of Greenbrier County. General Davie of North Carolina, a prominent Federalist, despaired of Virginia after talking to visitors who had recently passed through that unruly state. He reported talk of "seceding from the Union," but hoped that such remarks would end in "nothing more than the miserable howlings of a baffled and sinking faction." His flattering hopes were doomed to disappointment.

In August, Jefferson set in motion the machinery to "push to extremities" the attack that was launched on a smaller scale in the Resolutions of the preceding year. From Monticello he took the first step in the organization of this dangerous campaign. Naturally Madison was the first one he turned to. On August 23, 1799 Jefferson wrote his friend an unusually important letter that has not previously been taken into account.[45] This letter is so crucial to an understanding of Jefferson's philosophy and mood in the year that closed the eighteenth century that it is quoted almost entire.

I inclose you a letter I received from W. C. Nicholas three days ago. It is so advantageous that Virginia & Kentucky should pursue the same tract on this occasion, & a difference of plan would give such advantage to the Consolidationers that I would immediately see you at your own house, but that we have a stranger lying ill here, whose state has been very critical, & who would suffer in spirits at least if not substantially by my absence. I shall not answer Mr. N's letter till Thursday next. Perhaps you could take a ride about that time, so as to have a meeting here with him on Sunday sennight, the day preceding

[45] I found the original of this letter in the W. C. Rives Papers, L.C. Only a mutilated and fragmentary press copy had been printed in Jefferson's *Writings* (Ford), VII, 287–8. The correct version was first printed, at my suggestion, in the *Library of Congress Information Bulletin*, August 4–11, 1947. It was printed again in my joint article with Ammon, loc. cit., p. 165.

our court. I dare say he will not go before court, and if you could drop him a line by post he would certainly meet you, and let us consider a little together what is to be done. Not that I should prepare anything, but the opportunity is certainly a valuable one of producing a concert of action. I will in the mean time give you my ideas to reflect on. That the principles already advanced by Virginia & Kentucky are not to be yielded in silence, I presume we all agree. I should propose a declaration or Resolution by their legislatures on this plan. 1st. Answer the reasonings of such of the states as have ventured into the field of reason, & that of the Committee of Congress. Here they have given us all the advantage we could wish. Take some notice of those states who have either not answered at all, or answered without reasoning. 2. Make a firm protestation against the principle & the precedent; and a reservation of the rights resulting to us from these palpable violations of the constitutional compact by the Federal government, and the approbation or acquiescence of the several co-states; so that we may hereafter do, what we might now rightfully do, whenever repetitions of these and other violations shall make it evident that the Federal government, disregarding the limitations of the federal compact, mean to exercise powers over us to which we have never assented. 3. Express in affectionate & conciliatory language our warm attachment to union with our sister-states, and to the instrument & principles by which we are united; that we are willing to sacrifice to this every thing except those rights of self government the securing of which was the object of that compact; that not at all disposed to make every measure of error or wrong a cause of scission, we are willing to view with indulgence to wait with patience till those passions & delusions shall have passed over which the federal government have artfully & successfully excited to cover it's own abuses & to conceal it's designs; fully confident that the good sense of the American people and their attachment to those very rights which we are now vindicating will, before it shall be too late, rally with us round the true principles of our federal compact. But determined, were we to be disappointed in this, to sever ourselves from that union we so much value, rather than give up the rights of self government which we have reserved, & in which alone we see liberty, safety & happiness.

These things I sketch hastily, only as topics to be enlarged on, and wishing you to consider on them or what else is best to be done. At any rate let me hear from you by the post or before it if you can. Adieu affectionately.

This letter reveals better than any other document the specific roles of Madison and Jefferson in initiating a renewal of the doctrines of 1798.Obviously, it was again Jefferson who took the first step leading to the reaffirmation of the principles defended in the Resolutions. Although he had requested Madison to confer with him and Nicholas, the latter could not come, and Madison alone hastened to a conference with his friend at Monticello. Madison himself is the authority for the fact that he made the visit, since he endorsed a copy of Jefferson's letter at the bottom with the words: "The visit invited took the place of an answer to the letter." [46]

Also this letter throws light on the degree of differentiation between Jefferson's and Madison's thinking on the vexed question of how best to cope with the insufferable Alien and Sedition Acts. Although Jefferson admitted that he sketched his ideas hastily, only for Madison to develop further, he had had more than a year in which to mature his thoughts. He was therefore fully prepared to realize the implications of what he wrote. Indeed, he had already elaborated some of those implications when he rejected Taylor's suggestion of disunion. It is noteworthy that by the summer of 1799 Jefferson had changed his views to the point where

[46] This is the Nicholas P. Trist copy of part of Jefferson's letter to Madison of August 23, 1799. It is in the library of the University of Virginia, and was called to my attention through the library's courtesy.

he was willing to abandon the studied ambiguity of his Resolutions of the year before. He was entering the fray with last-stand ammunition; he was now prepared to consider a doctrine that would contain the direct threat of disunion! In the perspective of Jefferson's massive correspondence over the years, this is one of the most extreme statements that he ever made. The context of the fateful remark reveals how far he was willing to go in fighting "arbitrary" government. He was prepared to answer the dilemma: preserve civil liberties or cleave to the Union that proscribes them, by choosing the former. Thus, Jefferson placed no *absolute* value upon "Union." Compared to the *extreme* evil of the ruthless suppression of liberty, it appeared to him that the destruction of the compact that bound the states together was the *lesser* evil. This line of thought is in accord with his earlier judgment that only an Adam and Eve left upon the earth, but left free, would be better than a host of men enslaved.

After Jefferson succeeded in enlisting Madison in his new campaign, his next step was to send another "sketch" of his ideas on the course Kentucky should pursue to the ever helpful Wilson Cary Nicholas for transmission to Kentucky. The significance of this letter could not be appreciated before, since the missing link was Jefferson's earlier letter to Madison of August 23. Now that the two letters can be read in relation to each other, it becomes clear that Madison's visit to Monticello was not in vain, and that as he "developed" Jefferson's ideas, they emerged as a more guarded and moderate doctrine. The extent to which Madison was able to soften Jefferson's views is shown by the fact that less than two weeks later Jefferson in writing to Nicholas added one vital qualification, and omitted one crucial point from his letter of August 23. In all other respects, the language is practically identical.

The qualification concerns Jefferson's proposal that the new set of resolutions should include a reservation of the "rights resulting to us from the palpable violations of the constitutional compact by the Federal government." Under Madison's influence, Jefferson confessed in his letter to Nicholas that here he would "recede readily, not only in deference to his [Madison's] judgment, but because as we should never think of separation but for repeated and enormous violations, so these, when they occur, will be the cause enough of themselves." There is little doubt that this represents part of Madison's discussion with Jefferson a few days earlier. It reflects the kind of realistic political intelligence that characterized Madison; and it shows his usual preference to avoid setting up a high and hard ground from which retreat is impossible as circumstances change. The crucial sentence that Jefferson eliminated was the extreme one referred to above—"But determined, were we to be disappointed in this, to sever ourselves from that union we so much value, rather than give up the rights of self government which we have reserved, & in which alone we see liberty, safety & happiness." The fact that Madison was able to convince Jefferson that he should eliminate this dangerous sentence from his sketch of ideas to Nicholas, less than two weeks after Jefferson had written it into his letter to Madison, is dramatic proof that he alone sobered the excited exaggerations of his friend. Had Madison failed to argue as sensibly as he did, there would have been substantial truth in the contention that the Virginia and Kentucky Resolutions contained in embryo the later doctrines of nullification and secession.

The softened Madisonian version of Jefferson's general plan for the second Kentucky Resolutions was eventually transmitted, by Wilson Cary Nicholas, to John Breckinridge, who once again secured the passage of the Resolutions by Kentucky. Although the direct author of the Kentucky Resolutions of 1799 is not known, they reflected both the energy of Jefferson's campaign to thwart the reactionary legislation of the federal government, and the prudent effect of Madison's advice.

Far briefer than the set of 1798, these Resolutions began with an outspoken preamble, denouncing the insinuations that Kentucky and Virginia had passed beyond the constitutional bounds for state legislatures, insinuations that had been made in the answers of the "sister states." They declared the commonwealth of Kentucky had been "anxious only to escape the fangs of despotism" and defied those who might expect Kentucky to "shrink from the principles" enunciated in 1798. After a brief declaration of Kentucky's "attachment to the Union," the Resolutions concluded by registering a "solemn protest" against the obnoxious laws and by affirming the right of the several states that were parties to the compact to oppose in a "constitutional manner" all future violations of the Constitution.[47]

The Kentucky Resolutions of 1799 have always been noted for their introduction of the dread word "nullification." That it was included in 1799 raises the question whether Breckinridge was responsible for the revision of Jefferson's draft of 1798. If he was, he removed the clause "a nullification of the act is the rightful remedy" only to re-

[47] The text of the Kentucky Resolutions of 1799 is given in E. D. Warfield: *Kentucky Resolutions of 1798* (New York, 1887), pp. 123–6.

place it in 1799. There seems to be reason to believe that Breckinridge was not the author of the second set of Kentucky Resolutions.

5

Jefferson was eager to take an active part in preparing Virginia's second set of Resolutions too, in order to make sure that she would renew the firm stand of the preceding year. Accordingly, he proposed a meeting with Madison, and prepared to set out for Madison's home, Montpelier, when James Monroe chanced to visit Jefferson and dissuaded him. As Monroe properly pointed out, such a meeting would be the subject of embarrassing comment, at the very least. Thomas Jefferson, Vice-President of the United States, and James Madison, the conspicuous delegate to the Virginia General Assembly, would be known to have met at the very time when both were trying to avoid the spotlight. Thus Jefferson's wish could not materialize. The composition of the Virginia Report of 1800 fell entirely upon Madison.

Cut off from visiting, Jefferson developed his views of the current political necessities to Madison in writing, and defined the "line of conduct" that the Republicans ought to follow for the presidential campaign and in the ensuing years. He wrote:

Our objects, according to my ideas, should be these. 1. peace even with Great Britain. 2. a sincere cultivation of the Union. 3. the disbanding of the army on principles of economy and safety. 4. protestations against violations of the true principles of our constitution, merely to save them, and prevent precedent and acquiescence from being pleaded against them; but nothing to be said or done which shall look or lead to force, and give any pretext for keeping up the army. If we find the monarchical party really split into pure Monocrats & Anglo-monocrats, we should leave to them alone to manage all those points of difference which they may chuse to take between themselves, only arbitrating between them by our votes, but doing nothing which may hoop them together.[48]

The coming presidential election was beginning to displace the powerful focus on the obnoxious laws that had abridged civil liberties. This letter, however, makes it unnecessary to *conjecture* any longer whether the Resolutions were an integral part of the Republican national campaign. They were here unambiguously characterized as one of the fundamental directives for the Republican Party's platform in federal affairs. The tone of this letter is noticeably milder, beginning with its emphasis on "sincere cultivation of the Union." Very likely this testifies, in part, to the steady exertion of Madison's influence in the three intervening months. Outward affairs had changed too, the prospects of restoring peaceful relations with France having visibly improved. It had thus become emotionally possible for Jefferson to key down his proposals to the mere recommendation of protest, for the sake of the record, and to block future "unconstitutional" laws. As for the explicit denial of everything "looking" or "leading" to force, both Jefferson and Madison had held this view consistently throughout all the excitement.

Madison was now faced with carrying the fight for his Report of 1800 without Jefferson's consultation or aid. This time he could openly sponsor his work in the legislature. As chairman of the committee to compose a reply to the criticisms expressed by the various states, Madison produced his

[48] Jefferson to Madison, Monticello, November 26, 1799. Rives Papers, L.C.

lengthy Report. The Federalist opposition in the assembly possessed about the same strength as in the preceding session. Their attack centered on the "alleged inconsistency" between the Report and the Resolutions of a year earlier and upon the right of the legislature "to interfere in any manner with denunciations of the measures of the General Government." Although Madison saw no inconsistency between the two documents, he admitted that both sides had been "inaccurate and inconsistent" in the discussions of 1798.[49] This finally voiced his own divided feeling about the constitutionality of the proceedings recommended by the Kentucky and Virginia Resolutions of '98. The House of Delegates approved Madison's Report on January 7. The Senate concurred several days later.

During the discussion in the legislature on the Report, Madison kept in constant communication with Jefferson, then in Philadelphia. The latter was impatiently awaiting an official copy of the Report so that he might have it printed for distribution as Republican propaganda. When it failed to arrive by the end of January, he prodded Governor Monroe: "The members of the different states are waiting to receive & forward a single copy to their states to be reprinted there. This would require half a dozen copies. But if you will send me one, we can have it reprinted here & sent out. Pray do it by the first post." [50] Finally the long-awaited copy arrived. Jefferson soon could inform Monroe that "a great

[49] Madison to Jefferson, Richmond, January 4, 1800. *Writings* (Congress), II, 154.

[50] Jefferson to Monroe, Philadelphia, February 6, 1800. *Writings* (Ford), VII, 424. Jefferson already possessed a copy of the Report, which Madison had sent him as soon as it was introduced, but he could not have the Report printed until he had a copy of it as it passed the legislature. Madison to Jefferson, Richmond, January 4, 1800. *Writings* (Congress), II, 153.

impression made here of the Resolutions has been sold off, and dispersed into the other states." [51]

Madison's Report, which Jefferson apparently considered highly useful for solidifying Republican sentiment in the second heroic year of fighting the reactionary legislation of Congress, reaffirmed the basic arguments of the preceding year. In a point-by-point exegesis of the Virginia Resolutions of '98, Madison denounced the centralizing measures of the federal government—by which he meant not only the Alien and Sedition Laws, but others, such as the carriage tax and the Bank Law. Reverting to his own interpretation of the Constitution which he had formulated during the debates on the establishment of the Bank of the United States, Madison restated his belief that republican government would be subverted if it construed the "necessary and proper" clause in the Constitution as a "grant of new powers to Congress." [52]

The Report included a notable defense of the basic human rights guaranteed by the first ten amendments to the Constitution. The right of free communication, without which intellectual freedom would perish, Madison regarded as fundamental to republican government. But to adhere to the principle of free communication certainly involved "the right of freely examining public characters and measures . . . the only effectual guardian of every other right." When managerial governments tampered with guaranteed liberties, they violated the injunction that these essential rights were neither theirs to give nor theirs to take away.[53]

To repudiate the charges that the Virginia Resolutions tended toward disunion and that the state possessed the

[51] Jefferson to Monroe, March 26, 1800. Jefferson Papers, L.C.
[52] *Report of 1800*, Madison: *Writings* (Congress), IV, 540.
[53] Ibid., IV, 551.

right to invalidate a law of Congress, Madison gave a new interpretation to the function of the Resolutions of '98 and '99. He declared that unguarded appeals to the rights of the states were as great a danger to a stable union as the deplorable tendency of the federal government to incorporate the separate and "balancing" powers into one omnivorous administrative center. The latter tendency would "transform the republican system of the United States to a monarchy." The former, however, could reduce the Union to a lamentable condition, worse than had prevailed under the Articles of Confederation (and Madison, it should be remembered, had been foremost in repudiating the weak government under the Articles).

At the close of the Report, Madison explicitly defined what he conceived to be the intent of the Virginia Resolutions. They were designed, he said, to be merely the expression of opinion. As such, they were "unaccompanied with any other effect than what they may produce on opinion by exciting reflection." Since the Resolutions were in the realm of opinion and belief, Madison insisted that they differed radically from judicial decisions, for the latter were "carried into immediate effect by force." Powerful as declarations of opinion, the Resolutions of '98 and '99 certainly possessed no intrinsic finality. Therefore, Madison concluded, Virginia had not transgressed her constitutional position in declaring the Alien and Sedition Laws to be unconstitutional. She had acted with perfect propriety in suggesting to the other states "their concurrence in a like declaration." [54]

In the terms of this far-sighted Report of 1800, Madison hardly deserved to be accused, as he was in Robert Hayne's interrogatory letter thirty years later, of writing

[54] Ibid., IV, 523, 553.

into his "admirable report" an argument for nullification.[55] In fact, Madison's Report was a careful and mature reiteration of the principles of republican liberty and self-government. It clarified the fact that state governments are intermediate between the people and the "General Government," and that they should be relied upon to prevent certain totalitarian imbalances from developing in any center of government authority. Madison's last testament, "Advice to my Country," avowed it as his deepest conviction "That the Union of the States be cherished and perpetuated." [56] The cumulative effect of Madison's Report, which is a genuine contribution to American political literature, bears out this last testament and shows that even in the heated resistance to the Federalist attack on civil liberties Madison labored for the same ideal.

6

By the spring of 1800 Jefferson was able to survey the whole campaign he had unleashed against the Alien and Sedition Acts. While it had got off to a cool start in 1798, he was now well content with its success. To Philip, Wilson Cary Nicholas's younger brother, Jefferson wrote that the time was soon approaching when "we must have 'a Declaration of the principles of the constitution' in nature of a Declaration of rights, in all the points in which it has been violated. The people in the middle states are almost rallied to Virginia already; & the eastern states are recommencing the vibration which had been checked by X.Y.Z." [57] By

[55] Robert Hayne to Madison, Charleston, July 22, 1830. Rives Papers, L.C.

[56] Madison: *Writings* (Congress), IV, 439.

[57] Jefferson to Philip Norborne Nicholas, Philadelphia, April 7, 1800. *Writings* (Ford), VII, 439.

this assertion Jefferson showed that he attributed to the example of Virginia, the recovery of Republican influence in the middle states, and the encouragement of that recovery in the Eastern ones.

To emphasize his continuing faith in the moral influence and effectiveness of open declarations of principles, Jefferson endorsed Nicholas's fresh suggestion for resorting in the future to an official declaration of rights. Thus some twenty years after the Declaration of Independence Jefferson still shunned "power politics" for the more humane realism that made place for political ideals, principles, and declarations of rights. By doing so, he revealed not only a faith wholly in keeping with the sincerity of his defense of fundamental liberties, but a wiser conception of the function of public opinion and long-range considerations of public right. As he had so truly said, in the midst of the oppressive atmosphere created by the Alien and Sedition Laws, he had never expected to see the day when, "breathing nothing but sentiments of love to our country & its freedom & happiness," men would have to whisper their political beliefs and keep secret their friendliest correspondence "as if we were hatching its [our country's] destruction!" [58]

From the foregoing account of Jefferson's and Madison's two-year campaign to protect the Republic from the police methods of "arbitrary" government, a number of important conclusions emerge. Prime among these is the fact that the slogans employed—"states' rights" particularly —in the Kentucky and Virginia Resolutions of 1798 and 1799 do not suffice to reveal the operational reality and significance of those interesting protests. The Resolutions

[58] Jefferson to Elbridge Gerry, Philadelphia, January 26, 1799. Ibid., VII, 336.

were measures of "solemn protest" meant to limit the scope of illiberal laws passed by an American Congress in a spirit incompatible with the Constitution, and especially with the Bill of Rights amendments. However interesting these famous Resolutions may be for the "states' rights" theory they appeal to, they were intended primarily as a defense of civil liberties. It must be remembered that this defense was liberal and forward-looking, not conservative or literalistic.

Despite previous mistakes in the attribution of authorship, it is now clear that Jefferson and Madison were the sole major authors of the Resolutions, although yeoman service was performed in supporting, sponsoring, and introducing slight changes in text by John Breckinridge of Kentucky, John Taylor and Wilson Cary Nicholas of Virginia. Their contributions to the content of the documents were, in perspective, distinctly small. Taylor's letters, previous to the composition of the Resolutions, however, doubtless helped to crystallize Jefferson's ideas.

In the course of these proceedings the closest collaboration between Jefferson and Madison is revealed. Closely studied, it presents an instructive pattern of individual difference within the framework of general agreement. Clearly, the origination of the Resolutions was Jefferson's, as were the more impetuous expressions of theory and sentiment. Madison is shown to have reined in his spirited friend in his regular consulting with Jefferson. The outward proof of Madison's greater caution is to be found in the comparison of Jefferson's Kentucky Resolutions with Madison's more guarded Virginia Resolutions and Report. It is interesting that Madison not only succeeded in toning down Jefferson's reckless impatience, but that Jefferson was both willing and able to take advice that he might not at first have liked from the bosom friend from whom he had "no secrets."

One is tempted to speculate whether it was merely a matter of personality that accounted for the divergences between Jefferson and Madison on the question of how far to push the protesting Resolutions. Madison himself once said of Jefferson, some years after his death, that "Allowances . . . ought to be made for a habit in Mr. Jefferson as in others of great genius of expressing in strong and round terms, impressions of the moment." [59] This is a fair statement, and helpful in explaining Jefferson's more extreme position. But Jefferson also had more objective reason to regard the Alien and Sedition Laws as directed personally against him than did Madison or anyone else in the United States. For Jefferson had been so close a runner-up in the past presidential election that the Federalists throughout the unhappy administration of lonely John Adams nourished secret fears of the outcome of the next election. As the Alien and Sedition Acts were put through Congress (not at Adams's instigation), Jefferson at once assessed their true design to be political muzzling and terrorism, meant to frighten and punish the outspoken propagandists of the Republican Party. For Jefferson this was tantamount to an illegal and underhanded choking off of his own presidential campaign. In larger terms, he detested the resort to instruments of repression that thwarted popular choice.

While Madison shared Jefferson's views, he was personally in a better position to take a long perspective on the issues. Politically, he was primarily concerned for the safety of the Union, for which he had so brilliantly labored through the drafting and ratification of the Constitution. He thought that such safety required the arrest of an evil doctrine, its dialectic, and related procedures—for all these

[59] Madison to N[icholas] P. Trist, Montpelier, May ——, 1832. *Writings* (Hunt), IX, 479.

he saw embodied in the ill-conceived congressional encroachments on the liberties of the citizens of this country.
But he also thought that that same safety made it urgent
not to sanction a counter-dialectic of "states' rights" that
would be resorted to as absolute sovereignty in federal
versus state conflicts, once the election was over.

There is little doubt that the Virginia and Kentucky
Resolutions served as efficient rallying devices for Republicans from Vermont to Georgia. As campaign documents,
indeed, they are of unusual significance, for at the first
dangerous period in the history of the Republic they overtly
condemned the suppression of public opinion in any form
and provided powerful precedent against future attempts to
destroy the sound status of civil liberties in the United
States. All who appeal in the contemporary world to "states'
rights" in a narrow and reactionary sense, as Jeffersonian or
Madisonian followers, are in fact not so. All who invoke
principles whose language they found in these powerful
protests of 1798 and 1799, but who use those principles to
thwart civil liberties and to restrict human and political
freedom, are arraying themselves in the supposed ranks of
Jefferson and Madison while burying the substance and
spirit of the famous Resolutions penned by these two great
Virginia Republicans.

Chapter Eight

THE REPUBLICAN ASCENDANCY

> *"It has been asserted that the Republicans have abandoned their Cause, and gone over to the policy of their opponents. . . . But they overlook the overbearing & vindictive spirit, the apocryphal doctrines, & rash projects, which stamped on federalism its distinctive character; and which are so much in contrast with the unassuming & unvarying spirit which has marked the Republican Ascendancy."*
> —MADISON to WILLIAM EUSTIS, May 22, 1823

JEFFERSON AND MADISON reaped the bitter-sweet reward of their powerful defense of the rights of citizens in a democracy to think, speak, and write as they saw fit. The Republicans won the election of 1800. The victory came only after Jefferson had been put through the wringer of an untrammeled Federalist press as a "Jacobin," "mad Tom," an "apostle of the race-track and the cock-pit." But at last the era of Republican leadership, which would last twenty-four years and launch the nation on a new continental scale—an era that Madison proudly termed "the Republican Ascendancy"—was about to begin. The principles that distinguished the "Ascendancy" were formulated by Jefferson and Madison in its early years. While the purely political events and issues of this period have their own fascination, and remain today a subject of violent controversy, it is the theory that guided Jefferson and Madison that concerns us here. The character of Republican objectives and intentions is the subject explored in this chapter.

Before Jefferson could begin his administration, a unique hazing was in store for him. There was a freak tie between Jefferson, the Republican's clear and undisputed choice for president, and Aaron Burr, who was meant to be the vice-presidential candidate. This tie would not have happened had the improved voting procedure of the twelfth amendment which distinguishes presidential from vice-presidential votes then been in effect. The inadequate election procedure permitted a grotesque parody of "the people's choice" to be staged by the lame-duck Federalists still in Congress. A period of terrible suspense and personal mortification ensued for Jefferson—perhaps an appropriate close to an era that he had described to Madison as marked by "maniac proceedings." [1] One thing was clear throughout the devious course of Federalist connivings to oust Jefferson and replace him by Burr, or to arrange an interregnum with John Marshall acting as temporary president, or to allow Jefferson his victory provided that he committed himself to bargain on terms with his opponents: Jefferson repudiated with vigor every suggestion of a political deal. He rejoiced in the "present democratical spirit in America" and declared unequivocally to all who approached him with "terms and promises" that he would not "receive the government on capitulation" or go into it with his hands tied. [2]

As if to heighten the unbecoming farce, John Adams, who had been in a shattered state of bad temper at the impending close of his administration, spent his last hours

[1] Jefferson to Madison, Monticello, November 9, 1800. Jefferson Papers, L.C.

[2] Jefferson to Monroe, Washington, February 15, 1801. *Writings* (Ford), VII, 490–1.

as President vengefully appointing as many Federalists to the judiciary as he could, in order to leave a legacy of "sound" men to watchdog the Republican administration. For these "midnight appointments" Jefferson never forgave Adams. They came to be good friends again, years later, when they were both lively sages in retirement, and they discussed with animation ideas and memories—but Jefferson once let Mrs. Adams see the depth of his feeling about her husband's conduct on leaving the Presidency. It was not a revelation to repeat.

Jefferson had anticipated trouble, knowing the character of John Adams to be eccentric under duress. As early as November 1800 Jefferson had written to Madison apprehensively: "I think it possible that Mr. Adams may put some foolish things into his speech on the possibility of its being his valedictory one; and that this may give the Senate an opportunity again of shewing their own malice. I propose therefore to give time for the speech & answer to be over before I arrive there." [3] But he could not arrive late enough to escape the impact of Adams's hurried departure from Washington, in order to avoid the inauguration ball and all ceremonies for his successor. Adams's ungracious behavior was not lost upon intelligent men. The perceptive Elbridge Gerry disapprovingly wrote: "Mr Adams' conduct at your inauguration has wounded his real, and been severely censured by his pretended friends. Excuse me from any remarks on the subject: your silence shews you do not expect them." [4]

The triumph of the Republican cause, however, was not really spoiled by the Federalists' legacy of problems.

[3] Jefferson to Madison, Monticello, November 9, 1800. Jefferson Papers, L.C.
[4] Elbridge Gerry to Jefferson, Cambridge, May 4, 1801. Jefferson Papers, L.C.

Before Jefferson had even taken office, old friends were saluting his new administration. John Dickinson, transported with enthusiasm, wrote: "Perhaps we are the selected People upon Earth, from whom large portions of mankind are to learn, that Liberty is really a transcendent blessing, as capable by its enlightened energies of calmly dissipating its internal enemies, as of triumphantly repelling its foreign foes." [5]

Jefferson himself was convinced that a new order had begun. He termed the accession to power of 1800 a "pacific revolution," meaning that the Federalist "*monarchie masquée*" had given way to a government that respected the people and placed confidence in their abilities for self-government. The Union had been designed for republicanism, he maintained; it had not done well in deserting republican principles and harking back to the "times of Vandalism when ignorance put everything into the hands of power & priestcraft," and "bigotry in Politics & Religion" were made the standard of patriotic conduct.[6] In the perspective of later years Jefferson gave his final judgment on the Republican rise to power. "The revolution of 1800," he declared, "was as real a revolution in the principles of our government as that of 1776 was in its form; not effected, indeed, by the sword, as that, but by the rational and peaceable instrument of reform, the suffrage of the people." [7]

At the very outset Jefferson announced that it would be the role of his administration to put the ship of state

[5] John Dickinson to Jefferson, Wilmington, February 21, 1801. Jefferson Papers, L.C.

[6] Jefferson to Dr. Joseph Priestley, Washington, March 21, 1801. *Writings* (Ford), VIII, 21.

[7] Jefferson to Judge Spencer Roane, Poplar Forest, September 6, 1819. Ibid., X, 140.

on "her republican track," and he warned that this was a crisis that would require "all the skill, the firmness & the zeal of her ablest & best friends." [8] With the restoration of a solid republican government, Jefferson hoped that "a standing monument & example for the aim & imitation of the people of other countries" could be established. The example he wished America to show was "that a free government is of all others the most energetic; that the inquiry which has been excited among the mass of mankind by our revolution & its consequences, will ameliorate the condition of man over a great portion of the globe." The republican experiment could not countenance a doctrine that considered "philosophy and republicanism terms of reproach, to persuade us that man cannot be governed but by the rod." Jefferson vowed that he would have the happiness of "living & dying in the contrary hope." [9]

On the occasion of the Inaugural Address the new President gave official expression to the political philosophy that he wished to make effective for the American Republic. He called it a "sacred principle" that the will of the majority should prevail. But that will, to be rightful, must be reasonable: "the minority possess their equal rights, which equal laws must protect, & to violate would be oppression." [10] But while Jefferson's insistence upon preserving the rights of the minorities by "equal laws" was democratic, it was critical of those democratic theories that allow any kind of majority will to be right. By introducing the term "rightful," Jefferson was admitting that the fundamental law and the fundamental principles of any nation

[8] Jefferson to Robert R. Livingston, Washington, December 14, 1800. Ibid., VII, 464.
[9] Jefferson to John Dickinson, Washington, March 6, 1801. Ibid., VIII, 8.
[10] Jefferson's Inaugural Address, March 4, 1801. Ibid., VIII, 2.

need constant interpretation. They never simply speak for themselves. A "rightful majority will," taken operationally, would mean the kind judged to be consistent with the spirit of the Constitution and the principles of republican liberty upon which the United States had been founded. The "*lex majoris partis*," essential as it was to a republic, should never proceed to deny minorities their basic rights, named in the Bill of Rights. In short, Jefferson thought it possible to transcend the dichotomy of majority will or minority rights. A disciplined democracy would embody *both* ideals.

The most shocking statement in the address, from the point of view of Jefferson's critics, was his powerful plea for unity. "We are all republicans: we are all federalists," the new President proclaimed. By disposition and the habit of a *philosophe*, Jefferson truly would not be pleased with any government that failed to inculcate in society that "harmony and affection . . . without which Liberty and even Life itself, are but dreary things." [11] The call for unity was a sincere indication of Jefferson's desire to create an atmosphere conducive to "social love" and that expansive intellectual activity which he preferred above any social grace.

Realistically, the strategy of this appeal was altogether sensible. Jefferson had appraised the extent to which the Federalist Party had lost support by its recent shameful history—in a campaign year!—of internecine warfare between "boss" Hamilton and ex-President John Adams. Moreover, moderate Federalists had deplored the assault on the liberties of their fellow citizens that their party in Congress had engineered. In these circumstances Jefferson knew he was invoking more than a principle, and using more than rhetoric, when he urged a new unity of Re-

[11] Ibid.

publicans and Federalists. Although the Federalist Party retained enough strength to harass and embarrass the Republican administrations of Jefferson and Madison, the Republican Ascendancy that began in 1800 marked the permanent defeat of the opposition.

Despite the diplomatic tone of his Inaugural Address, Jefferson had no intention of abiding by the dictatorial rulings made under the Alien and Sedition Acts. The new President had not forgotten the dangers and abuses to which some of his most respected friends had been subjected in the brief "reign of witches," which he was now ready to dispel. The foreign visitors and residents, the Republican editors and writers who had suffered imprisonment or fines, could at last be avenged. Those who were still in jail for "seditious" writing, Jefferson pardoned. Those who were yet to be sentenced, he freed of charges. Those who had paid fines had them restored. Apart from the broad liberal justification that Jefferson had for these actions, he argued that as chief executive of the United States the manifest unconstitutionality of the Alien and Sedition Laws empowered him to dismiss the cases that had been judged or were pending under those laws. One of the pleasantest fruits of victory for Jefferson was to be able to write to learned friends like Dr. Joseph Priestley, apologizing for the mean spirit his country had worn in the last administration and hailing his friend as "the great apostle of science and honesty." [12]

Now, on the verge of taking over the federal government, Jefferson was confronted by the issue of how much federal authority to endorse as against authority for the states. While he conceded that this question in the abstract

[12] Jefferson to Dr. Joseph Priestley, Washington, March 21, 1801. Ibid., VIII, 21–3.

easily admitted of "metaphysical subtleties" of little practical importance, he wished to state the general principle that he considered part of the Republican "creed." He therefore avowed as major objectives *both* "The support of the State governments in all their rights, as the most competent administrations for our domestic concerns, and the surest bulwarks against anti-republican tendencies" *and* "The preservation of the General government, in its whole constitutional vigor, as the sheet anchor of our peace at home & safety abroad." [13] The nature of the "federal compact" in Jefferson's estimate implied that both of these jurisdictions of power were necessary. A government largely or purely *national* would overturn the limited system of checks and balances that particularly characterized a federal republic. And a government of unlimited powers, in Jefferson's political philosophy, was the worst of political evils.

Less than a year before his death, Jefferson reiterated his moral repugnance for government that assumed unto itself all power, saying that the second greatest calamity that could befall the United States was the break-up of the Union; but the greatest of all political calamities would be "submission to a government of unlimited powers." [14]

At the time of entering upon the Presidency, Jefferson seemed to feel he could afford a bold generalization about constitutional powers. He tended to identify the power of the federal government roughly with that of foreign relations, while "domestic regulations & institutions" he thought belonged to every state in itself.[15] A good govern-

[13] Ibid., VIII, 4.

[14] Jefferson's draft of a "Declaration and Protest of the Commonwealth of Virginia on the principles of the Constitution of the US. . . ." Ibid., X, 351, n.

[15] Jefferson to Caesar Rodney, Washington, December 21, 1800. Ibid., VII, 473.

ment, then, would be one that would not intrude upon private enterprise and state jurisdiction. The Gordian knot that Jefferson would later have to cut, with considerable anguish to himself, was this: when new and critical situations arose, was it best to adhere to the letter of the Constitution, or to rely broadly upon its "vigor"?

2

In this atmosphere of Republican reasonableness and the appeal for unity, the new President turned to the selection of his Cabinet and other federal appointments. Although the old independent, John Adams, had breathed fire in many of his public addresses and cultivated enemies at a faster rate than friends, he had retained a Cabinet that was not of his creation, gave him no loyalty, and looked to a "private citizen," Hamilton, as its real chief. Jefferson was determined to work in quite the opposite way: to preach harmony and possibly by that preaching create an environment of better compromise between both parties; but to choose a cabinet that would have unquestioned loyalty to him and to his principles. The failure to achieve such a cabinet had to a large measure also riddled Washington's administration, as Jefferson, the pivot of the opposition there, probably recalled without too much effort. Jefferson's principle, as he explicitly avowed, was "that those of the Cabinet Council of the President should be of his bosom confidence." [16]

Madison, the man from whom Jefferson had no secrets, was a perfect choice for the all-important Secretaryship of State. Jefferson knew he needed Madison at his

[16] Jefferson to the Secretary of the Treasury (Samuel Dexter), Washington, February 20, 1801. Ibid., VII, 498.

side. He dashed off a note to Orange even before knowing the outcome of the election, but when he anticipated that February would present "storms of a new character." Should the election have a "particular issue," he plainly hinted, he would want Madison on hand a day or two, at least, before the 4th of March. "I know that your appearance on the scene before the departure of Congress would assuage the minority, and inspire in the majority confidence and joy unbounded, which they would spread far & wide on their journey home." [17]

This time Jefferson's direct appeal did not work. It was balked by Madison's unstable health and the illness of Madison's father. Madison also disagreed that his presence was necessary on the scene, and rather thought it unwise to appear before he was officially expected. In Jefferson's eagerness to induce Madison to hurry to Washington, he used an amusingly illogical argument, advising the sober Madison that "a change of climate, even from a better to a worse, and a change in the habits and mode of life, might have a favorable effect on your system." [18] The death of Madison's father, at the end of February, interfered further with Jefferson's persuasions, and he was forced to wait until May before he could count on Madison's co-operation in launching the Republican adminstration.

In selecting his Secretary of State, Jefferson was only acknowledging openly what he had known and depended upon for the past decade: Madison's invaluable co-operation in translating Republican ideals into political actualities. The two men needed each other to achieve the victory of their joint political philosophy. It is ironic that many

[17] Jefferson to Madison, Washington, December 19, 1800. Ibid., VII, 471.

[18] Jefferson to Madison [Washington], February 1, 1801. Ibid., VII, 485.

Americans know only that Jefferson later "gave" the Presidency to James Madison, forgetting that Madison worked mightily for the Republican cause from its very inception and had unfailingly supported or surpassed his dearest friend in the general management of the party. The Secretaryship of State, the first post in Jefferson's administration, fell to Madison because of his merit and because of their common past. At a later date the succession of Madison, who became heartily detested by narrow Republicans, supposedly for being a "federalist" Republican, would be disputed by John Randolph and the Virginia "Quids," who pushed Monroe forward as an opposing candidate. But the succession was never a question with Jefferson, who knew that the only other Republican of similar stature with himself in the United States was James Madison.

Albert Gallatin, whose spirited critiques of Hamiltonian economic doctrine in Congress and in the Republican press had delighted Jefferson and Madison as early as 1796,[19] was the second invaluable acquisition in Jefferson's circle of "bosom" advisers. Henry Adams aptly described the new Secretary of the Treasury with the Secretary of State and the President as the "democratic triumvirate,"[20] who managed the nation's affairs throughout Jefferson's eight years as President—he might have added through sixteen in all, counting Madison's two terms, when Gallatin retained the Treasury post and Jefferson, although in retirement in Virginia, was still a potent influence on the Republican Party. The lesser Cabinet positions went, in the order of importance: to Levi Lincoln, the staunch

[19] Jefferson to Madison [Monticello], March 27, 1796. Ibid., VII, 68–9.

[20] Henry Adams: *History of the United States* (9 vols. New York: Albert & Charles Boni; 1930), I, 190.

Republican of 1776 (as Gallatin described him), an excellent legal mind, the post of Attorney General; to General Henry Dearborn, that of Secretary of War; and, after considerable difficulty in finding the right man, to Robert Smith, the Secretaryship of the Navy.

Next Jefferson had to declare himself on the inevitable political question of patronage. For the most part, his policy was temperate and scrupulous. Since the country had manifested its overwhelming confidence in the Republican Party, it was right, Jefferson believed, that loyal Republicans whose merit was beyond question should be rewarded. On the other hand, Jefferson had no wish to expel from office moderate Federalists, whom he neatly defined as "republicans who would prefer a somewhat stronger executive." It was the extreme or "kingly" variety of Federalist for whom Jefferson reserved his punishment —"the Hamiltonians, the Essex-men, the revolutionary tories." In good Machiavellian style, Jefferson declared that such officials, if they remained in government, would not be "free" to employ their talents for opposition actively and openly. He meant to free them.[21]

As for nepotism, almost immediately upon taking office Jefferson had entirely ruled it out. He considered that John Adams had injured himself by resorting to it, while Washington had done himself honor. He was relieved when he received a letter from a kinsman, George Jefferson, who voluntarily declined a federal office to which neighbors and friends wished to recommend him, and Jefferson instantly wrote to him to express appreciation. "It is true," he added, "that this places the relations of the President in a worse situation than if he were a stranger,

[21] Jefferson to C. Parker, November 3, 1806. Jefferson Papers, L.C.

but the public good, which cannot be affected if its confidence be lost, requires this sacrifice." [22]

After two months in office, Jefferson wrote to his friend du Pont de Nemours, the French *philosophe* and physiocrat, that he had found the country entirely in the enemies' hands when he took office, and that out of many thousands of officers in the United States he removed only nine men for political principles and twelve for "delinquincies chiefly pecuniary. . . . Yet, the whole herd have squealed out, as if all their throats were cut," he protested.[23] These estimates, however, were far from a final report. By the end of two and a half years of office, Jefferson was writing to the discontented William Duane, the Republican editor (who later charged him with having become a Federalist), that of the 316 offices in the United States subject to the President's appointment and removal, only 130 were now held by Federalists. He claimed that this influx of Republicans to almost two thirds of the appointive offices had been effected "by means so moderate and just as cannot fail to be approved in future." [24]

3

By virtue of the change of administrators at the dawn of a new American century, the first great adversary of democracy had been subdued: the tyranny implicit in managerial government. The maxim with which Jefferson lived as a guide was inspiring: "I have sworn upon the altar of god, eternal hostility against every form of tyranny over the

[22] Jefferson to George Jefferson, Washington, March 27, 1801. *Writings* (Ford), VIII, 38.

[23] Jefferson to du Pont de Nemours, Washington, January 18, 1802. Ibid., VIII, 126, n.

[24] Jefferson to William Duane, Monticello, July 24, 1803. Ibid., VIII, 258.

mind of man." [25] But tyranny, Jefferson soon thought, was protean, for it shifted its form in the first decade of the new century. This time tyranny had lodged itself in a tower of respectability and more than common wisdom. Its agency was one man, the newly appointed Chief Justice, John Marshall, who administered the oath of office to Thomas Jefferson, the President-elect. As the two men faced each other, the greatest and most cosmopolitan Republican in America, and the formidable Federalist, leader of the minority opposition to the Virginia Resolutions and perhaps the greatest jurist of his century in the United States, they could not possibly have ignored the promise of eventual conflict.

Jefferson, who could outdo an opponent but who recoiled from hostility, sensed unhappily that the exhausting battles he had fought with Hamilton and Federalist leaders were not over, and that new ones were likely to mar the years of his power. John Adams had left a potent Federalist legacy: the judiciary, led by Chief Justice Marshall, was ready to challenge and obstruct the two elected branches of the government, the executive and the legislative. The will of a few men would be pitted against the majority of voting Americans. Jefferson knew this early in the Republican Ascendancy, but he stated it with classic finality a generation later when he flayed the judiciary as "the subtle corps of sappers and miners constantly working under ground to undermine the foundations of our confederated fabric." [26] Previously, in the first decade of government under the Constitution Jefferson had feared the enlargement of power that Hamilton had advocated for the execu-

[25] Jefferson to Dr. Benjamin Rush, Monticello, September 23, 1800. Ibid., VII, 460.
[26] Jefferson to Thomas Ritchie, Monticello, December 25, 1820. Ibid. X, 170.

tive, for the Treasury, and for the federal government in general. Jefferson had countered Hamiltonian centralization with a brilliant defense of the balanced and limited structure of the confederated Union. Now, in the heyday of the Republican Party's power, Jefferson feared the dangers to democracy from a judiciary independent of the vote and of the public opinion of the nation—"which from the citadel of the law can turn its guns on those they were meant to defend." [27]

The first step was made by Jefferson, who was determined to free himself of the new tyranny confronting him, the "midnight appointments" of federal judges and the crushing power that Marshall wished to wield over the Republican administration. Accordingly, Jefferson ordered Madison, as Secretary of State, not to deliver the signed commissions for five justices of the peace for the District of Columbia that John Marshall, as Adams's Secretary of State, in his eleventh-hour haste, had forgotten to send out. Among these appointments was one for William Marbury, whose chief significance in history consists in the contribution of his name to a famous Supreme Court case, *Marbury v. Madison.*

The decision on this case established, by an unexpected route (an obiter dictum on the repeal of a clause in the Judiciary Act of 1789), the supremacy of the Supreme Court in reviewing the constitutionality of congressional legislation. It thus proclaimed not only the power of judicial veto, but the additional power of deciding, in a conflict of two laws, "on the operation of each." To circumvent a head-on clash between Marshall and the Republicans about Marbury, Marshall employed the dodge that Marbury had

[27] Jefferson to John W. Eppes, Washington, May 28, 1807. Ibid., IX, 68.

applied in the wrong court. The Court's earlier request that Madison should show cause for not having turned over the commission to Marbury had been ignored. A show-down was then staved off by Congress's repeal of the Judiciary Act, under which the Supreme Court held session. The Court did not meet until more than a year later—in February 1803.

Jefferson's and Madison's repudiation of the political theory Marshall had written into *Marbury v. Madison* rested upon two principal grounds. The first was circumstantial. Marshall had presumed to judge a profound question concerning the intention of the framers of the Constitution without having access to the records of the Constitutional Convention—Madison's reliable notes of the "Debates" were being kept secret until the time when their publication could no longer harm the participants of the Convention. The second ground was an essential conflict over the political philosophy implicit in Marshall's more than legal decision.

The strongest early statement of Jefferson's views on judicial review were put into a trenchant paragraph on the Sedition Act in a preliminary draft of his First Annual Message, but deleted from the final version. Two possible explanations for the deletion occur. Jefferson had submitted his draft to Madison for "serious revisal" (but suggesting that he held "grammatical rigor in contempt" wherever its avoidance could achieve condensation).[28] He had also submitted it to Gallatin, whose detailed reply queried the passage on the Sedition Act, doubting its propriety in the eyes of Congress, and demurring: "Are we sure of a Senatorial majority originally opposed to that law?"[29] In any case,

[28] Jefferson to Madison, November 12, 1801. Ibid., VIII, 108, n.
[29] Gallatin's "Notes on President's Message," November 1801. Ibid., VIII, 117, n.

Jefferson's argument held that the Sedition Act was in palpable and unqualified contradiction to the Constitution. He stated:

Our country has thought proper to distribute the powers of its government among three equal and independent authorities constituting each a check upon one or both of the others in all attempts to impair its constitution. To make each an effectual check it must have a right in cases which arise within the line of its proper function, where equally with the others, it acts in the last resort and without appeal, to decide on the validity of an act according to its own judgment and uncontrolled by the opinions of any other departments.[30]

These principles Jefferson reaffirmed at the time of the Burr trial when the President pointedly announced that he desired *Marbury* v. *Madison* not to be cited as authority, because it was not law. "The doctrines of that case were given extra-judicially and against law, and . . . their reverse will be the rule of action with the Executive," he warned.[31] Again his theory referred to three great branches of government "co-ordinate and independent of each other." Conflict might indeed arise between the branches, depending upon varying constructions of the same act, Jefferson admitted; but "less mischief," he thought, would result than if any one branch had control over the others.

It should not be overlooked that Jefferson's philosophy of the "earth belongs to the living" conceived the "will of the majority" honored by democratic theory not as the *primordial* majority will, but as the current or continuing majority will. Jefferson's confidence in the men who fashioned the Constitution had been high. Yet he had

[30] [November 1801], Jefferson Papers, L.C. (Misdated March 25, 1801.)
[31] Jefferson to George Hay, Washington, June 2, 1807. *Writings* (Ford), IX, 53, n.–4, n.

warned that the Constitution must not be regarded as permanent. It might be "the wisest ever yet presented to men," [32] but Jefferson had contempt for those who "look at constitutions with sanctimonious reverence and deem them like the ark of the covenant, too sacred to be touched." [33] If, then, this great instrument itself had to be reviewed by the people whom it was meant to serve and not to master, how could a handful of legal experts pretend that their ruling superseded the rights of the living majority? Only on the arrogant Federalist theory that men were too ignorant and indolent to govern themselves and that the impartial executive or judge could better regulate the political universe for them.

Admittedly, Jefferson's denial of judicial review, on the democratic theory that the elective branches of the government have at least equal rights with the non-elective corps of judges to decide on the "constitutionality" of federal legislation was not based on legal grounds.[34] It was based rather on political beliefs and moral values. Jefferson had no inclination whatsoever to leave determinations of policy to judges who were "effectually independent of the nation." [35] On the Jeffersonian rule that whatever power in any government is independent is absolute,[36] the judges, who could not be removed by the majority voice, were the most suspect source of decision in a democratic government. Even with honest men as judges, Jefferson feared

[32] Jefferson to David Humphreys, Paris, March 18, 1789. Ibid., V, 89.
[33] Jefferson to Samuel Kercheval, Monticello, July 12, 1816. Ibid., X, 42.
[34] The reader should consult Henry Steele Commager's discussion of this question in *Majority Rule and Minority Rights* (New York: Oxford University Press; 1943).
[35] Jefferson's Autobiography. *Writings* (Ford), I, 112.
[36] Jefferson to Spencer Roane, Monticello, September 6, 1819. Ibid., X, 141.

what he called the peculiar creed of the craft, that "it is the office of a good judge to enlarge his jurisdiction." Jefferson's position was firm: each of the three departments of the federal government possessed an equal right to decide for itself its constitutional duty. If there were to be any part of a democratic society to be trusted with independence, it could be "trusted nowhere but with the people in mass." The judiciary, left free to pursue its own tendencies and work its own art, can treat the Constitution as "a mere thing of wax . . . which they may twist and shape in any form they please." [37]

Politically, Madison was in sympathy with Jefferson's fight against Chief Justice Marshall's practice of mingling with the Court's proper judgment comments and reasonings of a scope beyond its authority.[38] He conceded that "the Judiciary career" had been perverted from its correct constitutional path into "a rostrum for partizan harangues." He pointed out, however, that although the Court by extra-judicial reasonings had designed to enlarge the general authority at the expense of the local, and to amplify its own jurisdiction, "the abuse of a trust does not disprove its existence." [39]

Two powerful limitations on judicial review Madison imposed, in accord with his philosophy of politics. The co-ordinate nature of the three great branches of the government, being essential to the balanced order of the Union, could not be jeopardized by assigning the Court the power to decide controversies in which it would be a contestant, or an interested party. Madison did not express this view as strongly as did Jefferson, but he had used this argument

[37] Ibid.

[38] Madison to Spencer Roane, Montpelier, May 6, 1821. *Writings* (Hunt), IX, 56.

[39] Madison to Jefferson, Montpelier, June 27, 1823. Ibid., IX, 143.

in protesting Hamilton's banking proposals, and his repeated declarations against the "consolidation" of powers support it. Against the theoretical right of the three departments to expound the Constitution, however, Madison admitted that the "Judicial department most familiarizes itself to the public attention as the expositor, by the order of its functions in relation to the other departments; and attracts most the public confidence by the composition of the tribunal." [40]

An even greater importance Madison gave to the ultimate right of the people of the states, in cases of profound crisis, to judge conflicts involving federal versus state authority. Although he did not hold with Jefferson's idealistic proposal that the Constitution be remade by every successive generation, Madison emphatically believed that the parties to the constitutional compact—not the state governments, but the states in their sovereign capacity, or the people in the states—retained the right to interpret the fundamental compact. This was, theoretically at least, a distinct limit on the power of the judiciary.

In practice, Jefferson and Madison agreed perfectly, opposing with one instinct the putative despotism emanating from what Madison termed the "judicial oligarchy." Jefferson personally would bear the full force of the enmity of the Chief Justice as he pronounced the supremacy of the Supreme Court during the Burr trial. In that eventful trial Marshall's wish that the President be subpoenaed to testify, and the overt attacks on the conduct of the executive made by the Chief Justice and by Luther Martin, were alarming proofs of the prescience of Jefferson's and Madison's fears for the safety of the co-ordinate branches of the government under the onslaught of a partisan judiciary.

[40] Madison to Mr. ———, 1834. *Writings* (Congress), IV, 349.

Marshall's last act in the weird treason trial was to be a
defiant gesture at the President—the guilty Burr was to be
acquitted on a deliberately tricky formulation of treason,
providing the defendant the necessary loophole.[41] Had
Burr's subsequent conspiratorial attempts succeeded—to
raise money in England and France in order to set on foot
another expedition, to capture Southern territory in the
United States, or in Mexico—the Chief Justice might have
been royally embarrassed by the lengths to which he had
carried the contest of strength between himself and the
President.

4

The Republican administration was still young and
relatively serene when news reached Washington that Spain
had ceded the Louisiana Territory to Napoleonic France,
one of the two greatest powers of the early nineteenth-
century world. In alarm, Jefferson wrote to the American
Minister in Paris, Robert Livingston: "It completely re-
verses all the political relations of the U. S. and will form a
new epoch in our political course." [42] He carefully noted that
France, of all nations, had been America's natural *friend*.
Nothing could instantaneously change the character of this
communion of interests except possession of the one spot
on the globe that automatically rendered its possessor
America's *natural* enemy: New Orleans. For New Orleans
was slated soon to yield "more than half of our whole produce and contain more than half our inhabitants." In the
hands of "restless" France, a point of "eternal friction"

[41] Marshall's definition of treason is quoted in Henry Adams, op. cit.,
III, 443.
[42] Jefferson to the U. S. Minister to France, Washington, April 18,
1802. *Writings* (Ford), VII, 144.

with the United States would necessarily exist. Surely France must realize that, just as America did; and "the day . . . France takes possession of N. Orleans . . . seals the union of two nations who in conjunction can maintain exclusive possession of the ocean. From that moment we must marry ourselves to the British fleet and nation."

No political reversal could be more radical for Jefferson. After two decades of championing France and fending off the influence of the British monarchy, the threat of "holding the two continents of America in sequestration for the common purposes of the United British and American nations" [43] was a grim new note in Franco-American relations. Jefferson hastened to suggest that in peacetime France would not need Louisiana; while in time of war Louisiana would be valueless, because it could be intercepted so easily. Livingston would do well to remind the French government of these facts, and intimate that the best reconciliation of French and American interests would be to cede to America the "island" of New Orleans and the Floridas.

By the fall of 1802 Jefferson was no longer hesitant in confessing to Livingston his belief that France no longer had any remains of friendship for the United States and that "an unfriendly spirit prevails in the most important individuals of the government towards us." [44] The belief was not unfounded. Napoleon resented republican democracy. The fact that Jefferson had been an enthusiastic friend of French liberals and was still currently adored by the philosophers who composed the faculty of the *Institut National*, the leading academy of learning under Napoleon, only exacerbated Napoleon's resentment. Jefferson, in fact,

[43] Ibid., VII, 145.
[44] Jefferson to the U. S. Minister to France, Washington, October 10, 1802. Ibid., VIII, 173.

was more than friendly with French *idéologues* like Destutt de Tracy, the master mind of the *Institut*, and Cabanis, the moral philosopher and anatomist whose *Rapports du physique et du moral de l'homme* Jefferson once described as "the most profound of all human compositions." [45] Jefferson was an honorary member of the *Institut*. Napoleon, himself a member until 1803, then exercised the prerogative of a dictator and closed the class in social philosophy —the very class to which Jefferson had been elected. In a succinct generalization Jefferson later typed Napoleon's animus toward the United States: "Bonaparte hates our government because it is a living libel on his." [46]

The Western farmers who neighbored on the Mississippi were thrown into panic once the rumor reached them that Spain had secretly relinquished its Louisiana province to Napoleon. In the summer of 1802 a royal order from Spain to close the port of New Orleans to American shipping seemed to confirm their darkest fears. The clamor raised by Westerners ruffled Jefferson's moderate delaying and bargaining tactics. He decided shortly after to send a "Minister Extraordinary" to reinforce Minister Livingston. Jefferson had never been wholly confident of Livingston's skill in dealing with Talleyrand or with Talleyrand's chief, the enigmatic and arbitrary dictator of Europe. He determined, therefore, to call upon James Monroe, a perennial favorite with the Western farmers, and once a marked favorite in France.

[45] Jefferson to Thomas Cooper, Monticello, July 10, 1812. *Writings* (Memorial), XIII, 177. See Koch, *The Philosophy of Thomas Jefferson* (New York: Columbia University Press; 1943), Chapter vii, "Jefferson and Ideology," pp. 54–64; Chapter viii, "The Doctrine of Ideology," pp. 65–82; and Chapter ix, "Cabanis and the Issue of Materialism," pp. 83–8.

[46] Jefferson to William Duane, Monticello, November 13, 1810. *Writings* (Ford), IX, 287.

Monroe was forthwith dispatched to Paris. He was sent to solve the immediate crisis, not to purchase a vast empire. Neither President Jefferson nor his Secretary of State Madison were aggressive expansionists in desire, intention, or plan. They were striving to preserve peace and protect the economic needs of an important part of the American Republic. Nevertheless, Jefferson inclined to think that the future destinies of the American Republic would depend on the success of Monroe's mission. The object was moderately stated: the purchase of New Orleans and the Floridas. Discretionary powers were given Monroe, however, in view of the fluidity of the circumstances.

Two weeks before Jefferson decided to dispatch Monroe, an extraordinary Christmas present arrived at the White House—a present "of a thought on Louisiana" from the brilliant and indefatigable "idea man," Thomas Paine. Paine stated the question succintly. "Spain has ceded Louisiana to France and France has excluded the Americans from New Orleans and the Navigation of the Mississippi— the people of the Western territory have complained of it to their government, and the government is of consequence involved and interested in the affair. The question then is, What is the best step to be taken first." Paine's review of "the next step" was uncanny. One possibility he described as a "memorial and remonstrance against an infraction of a right," but almost instantly dismissed this as ineffectual. The other possibility, of which he obviously approved, was to begin "by accommodation, still keeping the right in view, but not making it a ground work. Suppose then the government begin by making a proposal to France to repurchase the cession made to her by Spain of Louisiana, provided it be *with the consent of the people of Louisiana or a majority thereof.*" He argued that "By beginning on this ground anything can be said without carrying the appearance of a threat—the growing power of the western territory can be stated as matter of information, and also the impossibility of France to prevent it." Paine further pointed out that a "monied proposal" would be interesting to France as "the French treasury is not only empty but the government has consumed by anticipation a great part of the next year's revenue." [47] Although Jefferson and Paine had cooled considerably in their friendship at this time, the unusual Christmas present added its weight to the scale of Jefferson's deliberations about Louisiana.

One other friendship entered into the question of Louisiana in a fashion not generally known. Jefferson's close friend, the French philosopher, economist, and educator du Pont de Nemours, had long been a warm friend of America, where his own family had already settled. Jefferson had taken it upon himself to entrust du Pont with a secret and weighty mission: to make known to influential French citizens and government officials the American point of view and interest in the Louisiana situation. At the time when Jefferson confided this delicate mission to du Pont, the latter was high in the graces of the French government; and as Jefferson's third letter on the subject avowed, he was trying to turn his private friendship with du Pont "to the good of our respective countries." For America wanted to buy from France merely a sandy and unproductive pocket of land, from New Orleans to East Florida, which "peace alone . . . makes . . . an object with us, and which ought to make the cession of it desirable to France." [48] Jefferson was careful to keep secret his

[47] Paine to Jefferson [endorsed as received December 25, 1802]. Jefferson Papers, L.C.

[48] Jefferson to du Pont de Nemours, Washington, February 1, 1803. *Writings* (Ford), VIII, 206–7.

appeal to du Pont de Nemours, sharing it only with his bosom friend, the Secretary of State. When Madison mentioned the President's letter to du Pont in writing out Monroe's instructions on Louisiana, Jefferson objected. "As that correspondence will make no part of the public record, perhaps it is as well it should not be spoken of in them." [49]

Of his ministers Jefferson demanded "candid and honorable" behavior. He worried about "the game" Livingston had boasted he was playing with the French. Jefferson indicated that he would be unwilling to accept any advantage that would be obtained by other than honorable means; and added that "no other means can probably succeed there." This remark testified to a sensitive American's estimate of his country's diplomatic inexperience. An American contending by strategem against those exercised in it from their cradle would be undoubtedly outwitted by them. In such a field and for such an actor nothing but "plain direct honesty can be either honourable or advantageous," Jefferson wrote. [50]

Shortly after Monroe's departure on his new mission to France the American government was informed that Spain had corrected her blunder of excluding America from the right of deposit in New Orleans. This news cut the ground from under the groups favoring war, and doubly relieved Jefferson and Madison, whose taste for "alliance with England" was small. They hastened, therefore, to send fresh proof of the moderateness of their ambitions regarding Louisiana, writing to Monroe that while it was certain that the hopes of the Western people were "strongly fixed on the Mississippi for the future boundary," patience could

---

[49] Jefferson to Madison, February 22, 1803. W. C. Rives Papers, L.C.

[50] Jefferson to Madison, Monticello, March 19, 1803. W. C. Rives Papers, L.C.

be counted on in obtaining the desired improvements.[51]

In the midst of these modest intentions Napoleon's decision to rid himself of colonial preoccupations in North America hit the harassed American diplomats like a whirlwind. Napoleon's "reasons" were obscure, but prominent among them was the failure of the French expedition to Santo Domingo, and the paramount plan for war with England (for which money was needed in the treasury) in order to establish mastery over the European continent.[52] Had Napoleon's plan to subjugate England been successful, his alienation of the Louisiana province could have been justified by dictating to the United States terms of trade agreeable to France. His sudden decision to sell the whole of Louisiana—a territory of more than a million square miles, for a total sum of fifteen million dollars—overwhelmed Livingston, who had been bargaining discouragedly for months for a tiny fraction of that area, land east of the Mississippi and the Floridas.

In the middle of July 1803 Jefferson sent a memorandum to Madison requesting his Secretary of State to write to "Messrs. Livingston & Monroe expressly approving their obtaining Louisiana, and the sum agreed to be given for it," and further instructing Monroe "to endeavor to purchase both or either Florida at the prices before settled, or at any rate to establish a plenary right to the use of all rivers which, arising within the Spanish territories, pass thro' ours." [53]

Initially, Jefferson was determined to obtain constitutional authorization for his magnificent chance to purchase national expansion at a unique bargain price. He wished to

[51] Madison to Monroe, Washington, April 20, 1803. *Writings* (Hunt), VII, 47, n.

[52] Henry Adams, op. cit., II, 25–50, discusses this question.

[53] Jefferson to Madison, July 17, 1803. W. C. Rives Papers, L.C.

submit the annexation of Louisiana to the approval of the nation and obtain express consent in the form of a constitutional amendment.[54] The President was warned, however, that Napoleon, who had suddenly come to his momentous decision, might as suddenly withdraw his offer. Clearly, the most vital issue in the young Republic's history was at stake. Elsewhere Jefferson had already declared his belief that "the law of self-preservation overrules the laws of obligations," and had naturally conceded that the judgment of what was self-destructive for a nation depended upon its own judgment that the danger was "imminent" and the degree "great." [55] It would not be strange if securing the guarantee for peaceable homes and safe channels for the disposal of produce for a large part of the population of the United States and forestalling an aggressive European power from digging in on the North American continent looked like just such an occasion of self-preservation. And, as we have seen, Jefferson considered the needs of the living, with their "natural right" to labor the earth and to control the governments under which they would live, superior to even the best written constitution.

Had there been time and no sizable external danger in consulting the people beforehand on the annexation, Jefferson would not have gambled with cherished principles. Forced to act quickly, however, he was genuinely distressed that he had departed from his normal principles about the Constitution. In view of the circumstances, however, he certainly had not, as Henry Adams charged, made "blank paper" of it, nor "waste paper" of the Resolutions that Madison and he had formulated five years earlier.[56] After

[54] Jefferson to John Dickinson, Monticello, August 9, 1803. *Writings* (Ford), VIII, 262.

[55] See Koch, op. cit., pp. 144–5.

[56] Adams, op. cit., II, 94.

all, the citizens of the United States were still members of a free, elective democratic republic. They could vote the Republican administration and Jefferson's measures out of office when they chose. Furthermore, there was little popular discontent: the opposition to Jefferson's immensely successful Louisiana decision centered in the New England states, and was carried on only by the most extreme Federalists, the moderates having joined the Republicans in approbation of the treaty.

When Jefferson had retired from the Presidency, he wrote what should be considered the classic justification of his decision regarding Louisiana.[57] Jefferson's correspondent had asked whether circumstances sometimes occur that make it a duty in officers of high trust to exercise authorities beyond the law. Jefferson declared this question "easy of solution in principle, but sometimes embarrassing in practice." He continued:

A strict observance of the written laws is doubtless one of the high duties of a good citizen, but it is not the highest. The laws of necessity, of self-preservation, of saving our country when in danger, are of higher obligation. To lose our country by a scrupulous adherence to written law, would be to lose the law itself, with life, liberty, property and all those who are enjoying them with us; thus absurdly sacrificing the end to the means.

Jefferson offered several illustrations from the history of the Revolutionary War, showing that the unwritten laws of necessity, and of public safety, surpass the written laws (of property) in situations of extreme distress. He then turned to a hypothetical case, the imagined purchase of the Floridas, but the real case, the actual purchase of Louisiana, plainly forces its way through the "hypothetical" argument:

[57] Jefferson to John B. Colvin, Monticello, September 20, 1810. *Writings* (Ford), IX, 279–82.

Further to exemplify the principle, I will state an hypothetical case. Suppose it had been made known to the Executive of the Union . . . that we might have the Floridas for a reasonable sum, that that sum had not indeed been so appropriated by law, but that Congress were to meet within three weeks, and might appropriate it on the first or second day of their session. Ought he, for so great an advantage to his country, to have risked himself by transcending the law and making the purchase? The public advantage offered, in this supposed case, was indeed immense; but a reverence for law, and the probability that the advantage might still be *legally* accomplished by a delay of only three weeks, were powerful reasons against hazarding the act. But suppose it foreseen that a John Randolph would find means to protract the proceeding on it by Congress, until the ensuing spring, by which time new circumstances would change the mind of the other part. Ought the Executive, in that case, and with that foreknowledge, to have secured the good to his country, and to have trusted to their justice for the transgression of the law? I think he ought, and that the act would have been approved.

Jefferson added another illustration to his list, and was then prepared to generalize his moral principles:

All these constituted a law of necessity and self-preservation, and rendered the *salus populi* supreme over the written law. The officer who is called to act on this superior ground, does indeed risk himself on the justice of the controlling powers of the constitution, and his station makes it his duty to incur that risk. But those controlling powers, and his fellow citizens generally, are bound to judge according to the circumstances under which he acted.

Jefferson here specifically excepted those who overleap the law for trifling reasons, and in ordinary circumstances; for then the breaking of the law is of greater evil than strict adherence to its "imperfect provisions." But in the dangerous circumstances he had been discussing it was otherwise:

It is incumbent on those only who accept of great charges, to risk themselves on great occasions, when the safety of the nation, or some of its very high interests are at stake. An officer is bound to obey orders; yet he would be a bad one who should do it in cases for which they were not intended, and which involved the most important consequences. The line of discrimination between cases may be difficult; but the good officer is bound to draw it at his own peril, and throw himself on the justice of his country and the rectitude of his motives.

In this remarkable review of his moral scruples about the Louisiana Purchase, Jefferson showed that he had not denied his principles of limited government, in the old Republican slogan of a "government by laws and not by men." Yet he was impressed with the truth that no charters, laws, constitutions, or commandments can be devised that provide for every situation or prove adequate to every fundamental conflict arising to confront the safety of a people. In the last analysis, then, he was thrown back upon the character of the leaders in a democracy, as in every form of government. The rules of democratic society are more protective and more limiting on those in power than the rules of any other governmental form. They are not, however, the mechanical nor can they be the magical solution of all grave issues. The responsible leader must, then, depend upon his own character, his own known reputation to act for the good, and *precede* the Congress or anticipate the "popular will," accepting a rebuff if he has wrongly read the nation's needs and intentions.

Therefore, the intentions of the men in power are relevant to the general significance of the Louisiana Purchase. Jefferson knew himself and his Cabinet to be free of dictatorial ambitions. He had the welfare of the nation so closely in view that it would not be long before impetuous Virginia Republicans would accuse their onetime idol of having become "federalized" along with Madison, deserting, it would be charged, "the old Republicans." Unquestionably, the sacred privileges of democracy had been protected under Jefferson's ægis. As a token of them, there was complete freedom of the press, not barring scurrilous Federalist attacks on the Republican President. And while Jefferson had been forced in a world of aggressive empires to accept the road of national expansionism, he was determined to use that avenue to advance the "amelioration" and social happiness of free society as far as it would go.[58]

Thus "the empire of circumstances," to use Talleyrand's phrase, had intruded upon the philosopher statesmen who were guiding the Republican administration in the United States. Jefferson at the height of his Presidency was confronted with fateful issues and decisions that were clearly not of his own design. His choices were severely limited by the combination of events, the *faits accomplis* of other hands. It was in the press of emergency, therefore, that he and Madison had cast the new line of national expansionism. Privately perturbed about the political morality of the Purchase, Jefferson became wildly popular for it. In his scrupulous conscience he could not be easy about deeds that were stamped by nationalism and that undeniably enlarged executive authority. It was to Jefferson's and Madison's eternal credit that they converted the unsolicited "empire of circumstances" into a political philosophy that retained the essential ideals of their earlier belief in the "cause of liberty." Accepting the realities of national survival and growth, but eschewing empire as such, Jefferson deliberated a new political conception: an "empire for liberty." This conception is still packed with momentous meaning for our future.

[58] Jefferson's First Annual Message, December 8, 1801. Ibid., VIII, 124.

The "empire for liberty" was first developed as a key idea by Jefferson in the fall of 1803, when he wrote to Andrew Jackson of the immense importance of the new acquisition. Jefferson specifically stated that he valued Louisiana because it effectually removed America from "the intrigues of foreign nations to a distance from which they can no longer produce disturbance between the Indians and us." He secondly stressed Louisiana as opening an asylum for the Indians, and "to our posterity it opens a noble prospect of provision for ages." He promised exultantly that "The world will here see such an extent of country under a free and moderate government as it has never yet seen." [59]

This favorite theme of an "empire for liberty" Jefferson now developed to other Republican friends. At the end of 1803 he repeated it in a letter to DeWitt Clinton, sketching what he hoped to accomplish before he retired, and ending: "In the hour of death we shall have the consolation to see established in the land of our fathers the most wonderful work of wisdom and disinterested patriotism that has ever yet appeared on the globe." [60] About two years later Jefferson congratulated the administrators of the territory of Indiana on their arrival at the threshold of self-government. On this occasion, he developed his theme more explicitly. "The addition of a country so extensive, so fertile, as Louisiana, to the great republican family of this hemisphere, while it substitutes for our neighbors, brethren and children in the place of strangers, has secured the blessings of civil and religious freedom to millions yet unborn. By enlarging the empire of liberty, we multiply its auxiliaries, & provide new sources of renovation, should its principles,

[59] Jefferson to Andrew Jackson, Monticello, September 19, 1803. Jefferson Papers, L.C.

[60] Jefferson to DeWitt Clinton, Washington, December 31, 1803. Jefferson Papers, L.C.

at any time, degenerate, in those portions of our country which gave them birth." [61]

The best statement of all, however, came at the end of Jefferson's second term as President, when the President's mantle had been placed on Madison's shoulders. Writing to this great friend, Jefferson confided the bright prospect he saw ahead for the United States. Once the question of the Floridas was satisfactorily settled, he believed, the world would see a spectacle of a great democratic country that had not betrayed its definitive liberal and humane principles. The new extent of the American nation would reveal to the world "such an empire for liberty as she has never surveyed since the creation; and I am persuaded no constitution was ever before so well calculated as ours for extensive empire and self-government." [62]

Jefferson had plainly decided that real national power was necessary, if only to protect peaceful nations from the aggressive actions of unscrupulous great powers. But if empire there must be, let it be "empire for liberty." This slogan reveals a development in Jefferson's thought. It is directed to a different problem from that of the Declaration of Independence, but it does not cancel that philosophy nor subvert Jefferson's prior beliefs that were designed to maximize freedom. Without accounting for this stage in the growth of Jeffersonian realism, one distorts the complex and practical aspects of Jefferson's philosophy. Eighteenth-century Jeffersonian "idealism" is only part of his philosophical horizon; his nineteenth-century compromise, precipitated by the Louisiana Purchase, comes to terms with the "empire of circumstances," emerges triumphantly with the

[61] To the President and legislative council, the Speaker and House of Representatives of the territory of Indiana, December 28, 1805. Jefferson Papers, L.C.

[62] Jefferson to Madison, April 27, 1809. W. C. Rives Papers, L.C.

Republican vision of an "empire for liberty," and retains the vitality of Jeffersonian ideals under the rude impact of a world of power relationships.

5

On the ace political question of how an "empire for liberty" can best deal with a world, not of routine power politics, but of brutal and rampant dictatorship, Jefferson had some experimental ideas. The first approach Jefferson envisaged was a kind of isolation. This was a natural reaction to the spread of the American nation over the North American continent, in an age that could afford to consider the separation of this continent from Europe by a broad ocean a considerable protection. Jefferson's hopes on this score were not destined to last for many years.

With a more universal insight than isolationism Jefferson urged justice upon nations if they would have the firm friendship of other countries. Of Great Britain, unable to win allies in the great battle with Napoleonic France, Jefferson wrote that she was a living example "that no nation however powerful, any more than an individual, can be unjust with impunity. Sooner or later public opinion, an instrument merely moral in the beginning, will find occasion physically to inflict its sentences on the unjust. Nothing else could have kept the other nations of Europe from relieving her under her present crisis. The lesson is useful to the weak as well as the strong." [63]

Absolute pacifism Jefferson plainly considered a futile panacea. He informed Thomas Cooper that "The love of

[63] Jefferson to the Secretary of State, Monticello, April 23, 1804. *Writings* (Ford), VIII, 300.

peace which we sincerely feel and profess, has begun to produce an opinion in Europe that our government is entirely in Quaker principles, & will turn the left cheek when the right has been smitten. This opinion must be corrected when just occasion arises, or we shall become the plunder of all nations." [64] The resolution to stay clear, if possible, of European war was therefore not part of a sentimental or pseudo-religious national humility. In fact, Jefferson had shown himself capable not only of vigorous national pride but of energetic and stern measures against the Barbary powers, the Mediterranean blackmail nations of that day. The successes of the small American navy—a haphazard fleet of oddly assorted frigates, brigs, and schooners—proved the validity of Jefferson's surmise that "douceurs" in some cases needed the backing of force.

Even with friendly powers Jefferson and Madison were both ceaselessly careful to be spared entangling friendships, showing a stubborn American concern for independence and the reputation that accompanies it. Jefferson had cultivated the youthful Emperor Alexander of Russia, on the advice of European friends and Jefferson's trusted diplomatic observer Joel Barlow, the Republican poet and writer. The Emperor Alexander had a reputation for liberal political philosophy, and a general enthusiasm for benevolent government, knowledge, and science very much to Jefferson's taste. An interesting correspondence sprang up between them, with Jefferson in the role of elder philosopher and guide. Nevertheless, when Madison heard that the Russian Emperor had interceded on behalf of the United States in an argument with the Turkish government,

[64] Jefferson to Judge Cooper, Washington, February 18, 1806. Jefferson Papers, L.C.

he wrote Jefferson that "I wish however that with this ob-liging temper, there may not be blended some little view of drawing the U. S. into the politics of Russia." [65] Jeffer-son agreed. However much he was willing to sacrifice to preserve peace, he was never prepared to sacrifice America's effective independence.

Repeatedly Jefferson had pledged his Republican ad-ministration to peace, which he ardently prized. Through the tangled and precarious early years of the renewed Na-poleonic wars until the great battle for supremacy between France and England, Jefferson strove to keep the country free of militarism and neutral. The Republican philosophy of peace and domestic economy was severely impaired, how-ever, by Great Britain's blockade of the European continent in 1806. To this trial Jefferson responded with the Non-importation Act, closing American ports to certain British goods. He expected the consequent economic re-strictions to induce better treatment of American ships on the seas. Soon disappointed in this, and faced with more galling restrictions on American trade by Britain and France, Jefferson devised a truly hard and stoic policy to stave off war—the Embargo Act, passed by Congress at the close of 1807. By the difficult course of this law, which hurt the South and West as well as New England, Jefferson earned little gratitude from the nation he had tried to pro-tect from greater havoc. Summing up his disappointment in looking at the failure of his other pacific policies, Jeffer-son reflected that at any other period the "even-handed justice we have observed towards all nations . . . would have preserved our peace, and secured the unqualified con-fidence of all other nations in our faith and probity. But

[65] Madison to Jefferson, September 22, 1804. Jefferson Papers, L.C.

the hurricane which is now blasting the world, physical and moral, has prostrated all the mounds of reason as well as right. . . . And when is this state of things to end?" [66]

Jefferson saw that the death of Bonaparte would remove "the first and chiefest apostle of the desolation of men and morals, and might withdraw the scourge of the land." But he knew that a permanent solution, of peace on land and on the sea, was harder to realize than the death of Napoleon, or the death of George III. A system of tyranny, such as the one Napoleon had yoked upon France and other nations, was not so ephemeral as its leaders. "The principle that force is right" was the root of international evil. Only the pursuit of that which is right could undo the effects of this principle. Meanwhile those who pursued the right might have to endure reproach and put up with charges of "imbecility." In a practical way, however, Jefferson was positive that there was one thing worse than a world divided between two dictators. A world under *one* dictator was the most awful eventuality of all. Surveying the Europe of his time, Jefferson was convinced: "One man bestriding the continent of Europe like a Colossus, and another roaming unbridled on the ocean" was an evil spectacle. "But even this is better than that one should rule both elements. Our wish ought to be that he who has armies may not have the dominion of the sea, and that he who has dominion of the sea may be one who has no armies." [67]

As Jefferson's second term drew to a close, and he was submerged by multitudes of petitions from citizens and groups calling for the repeal of the Embargo, he saw that

[66] Jefferson to Caesar A. Rodney, Monticello, February 10, 1810. *Writings* (Ford), IX, 271–2.

[67] Jefferson to Thomas Lomax, Washington, January 11, 1806. Jefferson Papers, L.C.

the stoic plan he had devised to fend off war had failed. As he quite simply explained, when he was already two days an ex-President, the basic reason why the Embargo had to be discontinued was that it cost America more than war! [68] Having arrived at this conclusion, Jefferson already realized the imminence of war. Meanwhile the temporary strategy was to lengthen "the term of our prosperity, liberating our revenues and increasing our power." He himself might not have repealed the Embargo, despite the intense opposition it had induced throughout the country; but there were only two honorable alternatives, as Jefferson saw it: embargo or war. A third alternative, entertained by some, he rejected as dishonorable: submission and tribute.[69] He was unwilling to bind the incoming administration with decisions that they would be forced to implement. With this in mind, he purposely waited upon congressional initiative for policy-making in the last months of his Presidency. After Congress repealed the Embargo, to be effective on March 4, the day the new administration would begin, Jefferson wrote to William Short: "Our embargo has worked hard. It has in fact federalized three of the New England States. . . . We have substituted for it a non-intercourse with France and England and their dependencies and a trade to all other places. It is probable the belligerents will take our vessels under their edicts, in which case we shall probably declare war against them." [70] Utterly weary of the "dry and dreary waste of politics" Jefferson was looking forward to private friendships and the rich fields of nature,

[68] Jefferson to General Armstrong, March 6, 1809. Jefferson Collection, New York Public Library.

[69] Jefferson to Lieutenant Governor Levi Lincoln, Washington, November 13, 1808. *Writings* (Ford), IX, 227.

[70] Jefferson to William Short, Washington, March 8, 1809. *Writings* (Ford), IX, 249–50.

"where alone I should have served as a volunteer, if left to my natural inclinations & partialities." [71]

6

At last it was time for Madison, Jefferson's partner in so many years of arduous labor, to take the helm. But serious difficulties were to face the new chief of the Republican Ascendancy. And the measures taken to overcome these difficulties were to lead to charges that the Republicans had abandoned their program and had, indeed, become Federalists in practice. These charges were made by the "Old Republicans" in Virginia, by the extreme Federalists throughout the country, and by the overwhelming majority of American historians since then. If true, they would appear to qualify seriously the whole Republican ideology as nothing more than ideology, a weapon that may be useful to secure power, but not a set of ideals to advance the cause of real democracy. For this reason a review of some crucial measures in the Madison administration may disclose the operational reality of the Republican principles developed by both Jefferson and Madison.

The first real signs of criticism appeared even before Madison's election. His unpopularity with the "Old Republicans" of Virginia, who formed themselves into an organization known as the Essex Junto, had been growing by leaps and bounds. They regarded Madison as a traitor to "federalism" because of his mild decision, as Secretary of State, to displace as few Federalists from office as possible and because the Embargo, which he helped Jefferson to develop, worked hardships upon the Southern planters, when

[71] Jefferson to Dr. Caspar Wistar, Washington, June 21, 1807. Ibid., IX, 85.

trade with Britain and the Continent had been cut off. John Randolph, the brilliant but disgruntled Republican who had led the opposition to Jefferson in his second administration, did his best through innuendo, persuasion, and intrigue to oppose Madison's candidacy for the Presidency and supported James Monroe. Monroe was keenly disappointed by Jefferson's support of Madison and lent himself to the opposition plans in a somewhat bewildered and vacillating fashion, feeling little pleasure in traveling a political road apart from Jefferson.

Once Monroe's half-hearted attempt to oppose Madison's candidacy had failed, Jefferson tried to heal the breach in "the bosom" of the Republican family. Jefferson, who never rested content with a broken friendship, and who felt in the case of Monroe the concern of an accustomed older master for his protégé, was not disposed to forget Monroe's capacities for firm Republicanism and earnest leadership. To mend the shattered friendship Jefferson made the first move. Less than one month after Madison's inauguration as President, Jefferson appealed to his friend in an enlightening but little-known letter. He described a recent meeting with Monroe and prepared Madison for a personal and political reunion. "I learn from several that he has quite separated himself from the junto which had gotten possession of him, & is sensible that they had used him for purposes not respecting himself always. He & J. R. [John Randolph] now avoid seeing one another, mutually dissatisfied. . . . On the whole I have no doubt that his strong & candid mind will bring him to a cordial return to his old friends." [72]

Jefferson's wishes bore fruit in 1811, when Madison,

[72] Jefferson to Madison, Monticello, March 30, 1809. W. C. Rives Papers, L.C.

having reason to dismiss Robert Smith, appointed Monroe to his place as Secretary of State. Jefferson heard the news with delight: "I do sincerely rejoice that Monroe is added to your councils. He will need only to perceive that you are without reserve towards him, to meet it with the cordiality of earlier times. He will feel himself to be again at home in our bosoms, and happy in a separation from those who led him astray. I learn that John Randolph is now open-mouthed against him. . . ."[73]

Madison's difficulties as President, however, were not solved by acquiring the support of an experienced diplomat as Secretary of State. The Embargo policy had originally had Madison's backing. He had contributed a long dissertation on the British theories and practice concerning neutral trade.[74] With the failure of the Embargo, Madison found himself forced into the position of Commander in Chief in a half-hearted and unheroic war. The War of 1812 was "won" by the United States—but only after an ignominious and incendiary invasion of Washington by the British. Worse still, America's major objective in entering the war, the demand that impressments be abandoned, conspicuously failed to appear in the terms of peace. And in its train the war brought with it grave consequences, including the administration measures, which were roundly condemned by former Republicans as Federalist. Throughout the mortifications Madison had to endure in this unhappy period, Jefferson gave him consistent and unwavering support and comfort.

The charges that Madison had turned Federalist were

[73] Jefferson to Madison, Monticello, April 7, 1811. W. C. Rives Papers, L.C.

[74] *Examination of the British Doctrine Which Subjects to Capture a Neutral Trade, Not Open in Time of Peace.* Washington, 1806. Madison: *Writings* (Hunt), VII, 204–395.

plausible—but specious. The Republicans and Madison had originally been for peace; Madison led the country in a war. The Republicans and Madison had preached the reduction of the national debt; after the war it was greater than ever before in the nation's history. The Republicans and Madison had battled mightily against the United States Bank, protesting its unconstitutionality; Madison approved the bill for the Second United States Bank sponsored by a Republican Congress. The Republicans and Madison had opposed protectionist tariffs for American manufacturers; Madison in 1816 approved a protective tariff bill of a high protectionist sort. The Republicans and Madison had originally argued forcefully against the power of Congress to appropriate public moneys outside the enumerated powers in the Constitution; Madison in 1815, following Jefferson's proposal of 1806, recommended to Congress that it consider the establishment of roads and canals throughout the United States, preferring this work to be undertaken by the federal government rather than the states because it could better provide the means and more systematically accomplish its undertaking. Madison, like Jefferson, considered a constitutional amendment proper to remedy "any defect of constitutional authority which may be encountered." [75]

Thus the policy of the Republican Ascendency had changed to suit a complex of events different from those existing when the Republican Party originally opposed Federalist measures. The timing of political measures is an essential component in a realistic appraisal of their significance. The Republican ideology had set its course to establish a nation dedicated to liberty and courting peace.

[75] I am indebted for some of this material to an unpublished study of the "Appropriation of Public Moneys Outside Enumerated Powers" by Lucius Wilmerding of the Institute for Advanced Study at Princeton.

The greatness of Jefferson and Madison as political leaders lay in their devotion to these ideals and in their ability to put political values in inspiring terms and yet in practicable forms. They were not great men in the purely managerial sense. Nor were they great in the pursuit, study, or execution of war. These shortcomings of the Republican leaders do not justify the accusation that they "forsook" their principles in the sixteen-year period of their Republican administrations.

Jefferson and Madison had shown the genuineness of their ideal of simplicity, honesty, and economy by effecting economies in the first years of the Republican Ascendancy and by practically extinguishing the national debt. But the Embargo inflicted heavy losses upon the nation's agriculture, industry, and commerce, and the War of 1812 yoked a huge debt of over 127 millions upon the exhausted nation.[76]

In the case of the Bank of the United States, the reversal of earlier views was considered the lesser evil. The government had only two alternatives in honoring the tremendous financial obligations incurred by them on account of the war: private banking, on whatever terms the Northern owners of capital would choose; or a second national bank under Republican political supervision.[77]

In the case of the tariff protecting American manufacturers, Jefferson and Madison had witnessed the collapse of the import trade in manufactured goods during the Embargo and even more rudely during the War of 1812. In the wartime emergency it had been necessary to depend upon new American industries for essential machine goods. Directly after the war those concerned with safeguarding

[76] Charles A. Beard and Mary Beard: *The Rise of American Civilization*, (2 vols. in one. New York: The Macmillan Company; 1937), I, 430.
[77] Ibid.

national welfare could not legislate out of existence industries that already had served the country in wartime. Nor
could these young industries stand the competition of old
and thriving European firms. Madison, therefore, had to
modify his official agricultural preferences and accept the
Revenue Act of 1816 to ensure continued American independence of Europe in an industrial sense, and to help protect the home market that had been cultivated by the
American citizens who had put their investments and several years' labor into the new enterprises.

As for Jefferson's break with his earlier views on the
appropriation of public moneys outside the enumerated
powers, timing was again essential. In 1806 Jefferson contemplated an American treasury with surplus funds derived
from the sale of public lands. Albert Gallatin, Secretary of
the Treasury under Madison as well as under Jefferson, advocated a national network of river, harbor, and canal in-
stallations and improvements which both Republican Presidents approved. When Madison recommended to Congress
that roads and canals be established throughout the United
States by the federal government, he was trying to sur-
mount the problems created by the overwhelming territorial growth of the United States since the opening of the
nineteenth century. The American "Empire" for which
many sacrifices had already been made could not be con-
solidated without these internal improvements,[78] and the
haphazard and uneven contributions of the various states
and territories, if left to their own resources and management, would obviously have fallen short of national needs
for good transportation and communication. Madison was

[78] See Madison's Seventh Annual Message. *Writings* (Hunt), VIII,
342.

firm, however, in maintaining that a constitutional amendment was necessary to secure this power.

In one other interesting instance both Jefferson and Madison recommended an enlargement of the functions of the federal government, but believed that an amendment to the Constitution would be necessary to sanction this power because it had not been enumerated in the Constitution. First Jefferson and then Madison proposed to Congress that a national university be created. Jefferson argued, in his Sixth Annual Message, that "Education is here placed among the articles of public care, not that it would be proposed to take its ordinary branches out of the hands of private enterprise, which manages so much better all the concerns to which it is equal: but a public institution can alone supply those sciences which, though rarely called for, are yet necessary to complete the circle, all the parts of which contribute to the improvement of the country, and some of them to its preservation." [79] Madison then proposed, in his Second Annual Message to Congress, "a seminary of learning instituted by the National Legislature within the limits of their exclusive jurisdiction, the expense of which might be defrayed . . . out of the vacant grounds which have accrued to the nation within those limits." [80] Madison justified this request by the general principle that "a well-instructed people alone can be permanently a free people." He thought of the proposed university as a "temple of science" that would elevate American culture at home and abroad and "strengthen the foundations . . . of our free and happy system of government."

[79] Sixth Annual Message, December 2, 1806. *Writings* (Ford), VIII, 494.

[80] Second Annual Message, December 5, 1810. *Writings* (Hunt), VIII, 127.

On the whole, then, it appears that the fundamental reasons for changes in Republican policy were changed times and circumstances, largely outside the control of the American Presidents. Both Jefferson and Madison knew a further reason—one that is ordinarily omitted from conventional accounts of history. They knew with the assurance of self-knowledge that they were political leaders who had no hunger for capturing the state or enlarging their constitutional powers. They never had grounds to believe that the ambitious, monarch-minded Federalists whom they had opposed were imbued with similarly liberal or democratic ideals. Once the infant American nation had become set in the habit and character of a true republic, and the mass of citizens had begun to learn the fundamentals of their political rights and powers, the Republican leaders saw that the enlargement of federal powers was no longer the same threat. Thus through the first sixteen years of the nineteenth century Jefferson and Madison had made some compromises, as all those who govern must. But who could deny that they had maintained a high spirit of enlightened public policy and devotion to the fundamental democratic values of the American Experiment?

The French economist Jean Baptiste Say had sent a personal tribute to Madison in 1814 from Paris—a tribute that was singularly arresting in a comparison it drew between Europe and America. In old Europe, Monsieur Say wrote, there are enlightened men who advocate a liberal system of government, but they are few and *"bien timide."* In America they govern the nation. In Europe, he continued, we know sometimes how to say what should be done. You, in America, know how to do it. The time may come, Say prophesied, when the enlightened thinkers of

Europe may have to come to America for asylum.[81] He felt confident that if that dark day of political oppression arrived for the European continent, the country that had benefited by tolerant national leaders such as Jefferson and Madison would not desert its profession of democratic hospitality to those who were persecuted for the freedom of the human mind. The "empire for liberty" would show its reliable nature in that future crisis.

In the perspective of old age, Madison sagely confronted the charges that had been leveled against the Republican Ascendancy and gave a thoughtful reply that must be submitted to the judgment of the reader. He wrote:

It has been asserted that the Republicans have abandoned their Cause, and gone over to the policy of their opponents. Here the effort . . . fails. It is true that under a great change of foreign circumstances, and with a doubled population, & more than doubled resources, the Republican party has been reconciled to certain measures & arrangements which may be as proper now as they were premature and suspicious when urged by the Champions of federalism. But they overlook the overbearing & vindictive spirit, the aprocryphal doctrines, & rash projects, which stamped on federalism its distinctive character; and which are so much in contrast with the unassuming & unavenging spirit which has marked the Republican Ascendancy.

There has been in fact a deep distinction between the two parties. . . . The distinction has its origin in the confidence of the former [Republican], in the capacity of mankind for self Government, and in a distrust of it by the other or by its leaders; and is the key to many of the phenomena presented by our Political History.[82]

[81] Say to Madison, Paris, June 16, 1814. W. C. Rives Papers, L.C.
[82] Madison to William Eustis, Montpelier, May 22, 1823. *Writings* (Hunt), IX, 135–6.

Chapter Nine

TAKE CARE OF ME WHEN DEAD

*"If ever the earth has beheld a system of administra-
tion conducted with a single and steadfast eye to the
general interest and happiness of those committed to
it, one which, protected by truth, can never know
reproach, it is that to which our lives have been
devoted. To myself you have been a pillar of support
through life. Take care of me when dead, and be
assured that I shall leave with you my last affections."*
—JEFFERSON to MADISON, Monticello,
February 17, 1826

ONCE MADISON WAS FREED from the burdens of office, Jefferson was the first to greet him as a long-absent voyager,
home at last. "I sincerely congratulate you," Jefferson wrote
feelingly, "on your release from incessant labors, corroding
anxieties, active enemies & interested friends, &, on your return to your books & farm to tranquility & independence.
A day of these is worth ages of the former. But all this you
know." [1] To John Adams, with whom Jefferson had established a fresh *entente cordiale* after Benjamin Rush, the
friend of both, had interceded to restore the ancient friendship, Jefferson confidently asserted that he entertained no
apprehensions "for the happiness of our brother Madison
in a state of retirement. Such a mind as his, fraught with
information and with matter for reflection, can never know
ennui. Besides, there will always be work enough cut out for
him to continue his active usefulness to his country." [2]

Already Jefferson had plans on foot to draw Madison,

[1] Jefferson to Madison, April 15, 1817. W. C. Rives Papers, L.C.
[2] Jefferson to John Adams, Monticello, May 5, 1817. *Writings* (Memorial), XV, 109.

as well as the new President, James Monroe, into an important educational project—the founding of a university that
would establish, Jefferson hoped, science and intellectual
freedom beyond the level of any other American institution. "The good Old Dominion, the blessed mother of us
all," he wrote to fellow Virginians, "will then raise her head
with pride among the nations, will present to them that
splendor of genius which she has ever possessed, but has
too long suffered to rest uncultivated and unknown, and
will become a centre of ralliance to the States whose youth
she has instructed, and, as it were, adopted." [3]

The peculiar fascination that the dream of a university
exercised over Jefferson was due not only to his long-cher-
ished love of knowledge and the social arts, but to his conviction that freedom and enlightenment were essential to
each other. Consequently, the university he wished to father would be dedicated to "the free range of mind." Madison shared this belief, and gave it pithy expression when he
wrote, approving a system of general education in Kentucky: "What spectacle can be more edifying or more sea-
sonable, than . . . Liberty & Learning, each leaning on the
other for their mutual and surest support?" [4] Thus when
Jefferson drew Madison into the nine-year cycle of preparatory work to create the University of Virginia, and asked
him to take over its direction after his death, the two friends
were embarking upon the last great work of their lives, their
last significant partnership.

Official histories of the University of Virginia [5] throw

[3] "Thoughts on Lotteries," February 1826. *Writings* (Ford), X, 371.

[4] Madison to W. T. Barry. Montpelier, August 4, 1822. *Writings*
(Hunt), IX, 108.

[5] N. F. Cabell, ed.: *Early History of the University of Virginia, as
Contained in the Letters of Thomas Jefferson and Joseph C. Cabell* (Richmond, 1856). This work contains the best source material on the early
years of the university.

light on the uphill campaign, in which all the "art of management" the veteran Republican leaders had learned, all
the tact and discretion and perserverence that they could
muster, were needed to cajole sufficient appropriations from
a reluctant legislature. But Jefferson was determined, this
time, to see the fruition of his plan for improving the educational standards of the rising American nation, a plan
that had evolved from early attempts like his "Bill for the
More General Diffusion of Knowledge," presented to the
Virginia Assembly in 1779. Unlike those who regarded education as a luxury, or the ornament of the rich, Jefferson
and Madison viewed it as the right of all to have access to
elementary education, and the right of the talented youth
from any class to the higher education they merited.[6] It
was, of course, the field of higher education, its curriculum,
and the spirit that should dominate it that the two philosopher statesmen found most congenial to their interests.

Jefferson had prepared himself for his role as educational leader, not only by the studious habits of a lifetime,
but by taking a few talented pupils under his wing, in an
informal way, opening to them the resources of his unsur-
passed library, guiding their plans for reading, lecturing on
special subjects of interest,[7] and infusing his own broad and
sound philosophy of learning and life. In general, Jefferson's
approach to education was sharply critical of the kind of
"specialization" that precedes a general philosophical orien-
tation in the realm of ideas. He vigorously stated his ideal
of a philosophical approach to any chosen field in a letter
to a promising student. "Nothing can be sounder than

[6] Madison to W. T. Barry. [Montpelier], August 4, 1822. *Writings*
(Hunt), IX, 106.

[7] Some lecture notes were taken by William Cabell Rives, one of
Jefferson's most talented students, and can now be found in the W. C.
Rives Papers, L.C.

your view of the importance of laying a broad foundation in other branches of knowledge whereon to raise the super-structure of any particular science which one would chuse to profess with credit & usefulness. The lamentable disregard of this, since the revolution has filled our country with Blackstone lawyers, Sangrado physicians, a ranting clergy, & a lounging gentry, who render neither honor nor service to mankind, and when their country has occasion for scientific services, it looks for them in vain over its wide extended surface." [8]

2

While the University of Virginia was the child of Jefferson's labor, Madison contributed far more to its creation than has been recognized. There was hardly a step Jefferson took without consultation with Madison. Measures and plans were discussed by the old friends in advance of presentation to the other members of the board. They shared the vicissitudes and strain of personally recruiting the faculty. They plotted together on ways and means of influencing members of the legislature to obtain appropriations for the first-rate construction called for by Jefferson's blueprint —a benign sort of plotting that unfortunately never brought large enough appropriations to ease the corroding worries of the two public-spirited friends.

Jefferson first enlisted Madison's aid in the battle over the location of the proposed university.[9] Jefferson, who would supervise every detail of its physical construction, naturally wanted it within easy reach of Monticello. The

[8] Jefferson to W. C. Rives, Monticello, September 18, 1811. W. C. Rives Papers, L.C.

[9] Jefferson to Madison, Monticello, April 13, 1817. W. C. Rives Papers, L.C.

counterclaims of Staunton, Williamsburg, and other sites were quickly overcome. Then in the fall of 1817 Jefferson borrowed from Madison a copy of Palladio's treatise on architecture and kept it for a year. Nobody else in that part of the country, Jefferson told Madison,[10] would have a copy of it. The buildings, already begun, were to benefit from Jefferson's use of this architectural treatise, with its descriptions of neoclassic colonnaded houses, its conception of a villa as a whole, organized throughout, in plan and elevation, according to rules that integrated it with the landscape. Jefferson later had reason to be satisfied with the "academic village" he designed. It is still, in grounds and architecture, one of the most beautiful colleges in the United States.

Madison was soon also introduced to the problem of recruiting the faculty. The expert Dr. Thomas Cooper would have set up a first-rate department of medicine and chemistry for the new university, but Jefferson had heard that Cooper had received more attractive offers to remain in Philadelphia at a greater salary than could be guaranteed by the new university. Madison urged Jefferson to try to assure the munificent sum of $1,500 salary as bait to Cooper "in order not to be hard on him and the college." Unfortunately, Madison's and Jefferson's interest in luring Cooper to the University of Virginia backfired. Cooper was a latitudinarian Christian, far too liberal and unorthodox for the conventional tastes of other members of the Board of Visitors than Jefferson and Madison, not to mention the legislature. A lengthy negotiation to attract Cooper to Charlottesville consequently turned into an embarrassed effort to relinquish "our claim on him." [11]

[10] Jefferson to Madison, Monticello, November 15, 1817. Madison Papers, L.C.

[11] Jefferson to Madison, Monticello, January 2, 1818. Madison Papers, L.C.

Jefferson's next move was to devise a plan to enlist the help of Dugald Stewart, the Scottish "common-sense" philosopher whom Jefferson had known in Paris, and whose work Jefferson ranked with the highest of the "experimental" philosophers—the only kind of philosopher that Jefferson considered valuable.[12] Jefferson also enlisted other academic acquaintances in England, Scotland, and on the Continent. Madison's first response to these proposals was interesting. He suggested that he had heard that one English scholar Jefferson meant to appeal to was "unfriendly to the U. S." and that Stewart's aid would be preferable, "if as I presume his political feelings be not at variance with his philosophical dispositions." [13] As early as this, in the complicated maneuver of finding a high-grade group of professors for the university, Jefferson and Madison touched the highly charged periphery where political convictions impinge on professional competence.

By the beginning of 1818 Jefferson had prepared a letter for the Virginia legislators, outlining the progress on the plans for the university, and disclosing his intention to seek for professors abroad, in order to secure a faculty of genuine intellectual distinction. He sent the letter, as he so often had done before, to Madison for perusal and criticism. Madison thought it "well adapted to its object." He evidently disliked the idea of seeking professors abroad, thinking it might "excite prejudices with some who entertain them against the countries furnishing the professors." [14]

Jefferson also asked Madison to read and revise his important "Rockfish report," in preparation for the meet-

---

[12] Jefferson to Madison, Monticello, November 15, 1817. Madison Papers, L.C.

[13] Madison to Jefferson, Montpelier, November 29, 1817. Madison Papers, L.C.

[14] Madison to Jefferson, Montpelier, January 1, 1818. Madison Papers, L.C.

ing of the educators and legislators at Rockfish Gap. The report, which outlined the basic schools within the contemplated university, was not, Jefferson said, the kind he would propose "to an assembly of philosophers, who would require nothing but the table of professorships." He had endeavored to adapt it to the Virginia House of Delegates, he said, and had deliberately tried to catch "the floating body of doubtful and wavering men" by throwing in leading ideas on the uses of education "in the hope that some of these might catch on some crotchet in their mind, and bring them over to us." Jefferson also apologized for having had to include sections on the general system of primary and secondary schools preliminary to the university. Madison was asked to revise the report in the light of these limiting circumstances. Jefferson expected to consult with Madison and Judge Spencer Roane a few days before setting out for the Gap together. On his own initiative, Jefferson refused an invitation for Madison and himself to spend time at neighboring Staunton with a friend, who offered his house as their quarters—knowing that Madison would agree with him that it was important to "avoid not only the reality but the suspicion of intrigue; and be urged to short work by less comfortable entertainment." [15]

Occasionally, meetings between Jefferson and Madison, and possibly one or two of the visitors, would suddenly become necessary. Jefferson would then invite Madison to Monticello; but conscious that he must not allow his age to impose on his colleague, he would propose alternating "journeyings." At the age of seventy-six, directly after an illness that left him "in a state of increased debility"—although debility for Thomas Jefferson was normally pretty good health for any average man—a meeting was "im-

[15] Jefferson to Madison, [Monticello], June 28, 1818. Madison Papers, L.C.

mediately necessary," and Jefferson wrote to Madison that he was bringing his neighbor General Cocke to Montpelier the following week. It was midwinter and the roads were impassable for a carriage, Jefferson added. Therefore he would come on horseback, taking two days.

The following year Jefferson was being congratulated on a "proud epoch" in the history of Virginia: the passage of his bill for the establishment of "an University at the Central College" by the Virginia House of Delegates. The bill had encountered "active and persevering opposition" on the floor, and intrigue and cabal out of doors.[16] Almost upon receiving this letter, Jefferson hastened to drive further his advantage for the beloved university. He asked Cabell, then a member of the assembly, whether it would cause any ill effect to request the legislature to turn over to the university unused funds "offered to the pauper schools and not accepted by them." He carefully recited that a review of the university funds showed that only two pavilions and their dormitories could be added to the two already constructed; that this provided for but four of the ten professorships proposed; that there was no chance of purchasing "a chemical apparatus, an astronomical apparatus with its observatory, a building for a library with its library, etc." [17]

So hard did Jefferson work on the university project, personally supervising the construction, ordering the materials, revising his fund-raising plans, and keeping accounts, as well as continuing with faculty procurement, that his health suffered. In October 1819 he wrote to Madison specifically to reassure his friend that a recent illness was over:

[16] W. C. Rives to Jefferson, Richmond, January 20, 1819. Jefferson Papers, L.C.

[17] Jefferson to W. C. Rives, Monticello, January 28, 1819. Jefferson Papers, L.C.

"I thought it due to your friendship to free it from the uncertainty of floating rumors." [18] Madison's reply thanked Jefferson for his kindness in relieving him from anxiety, but counseled: "I must entreat that your health may be more a primary object than you have hitherto allowed it to be. Your constitution has been well tested, and you owe it to many considerations to bestow on it the care which its remaining strength justly merits." [19] Madison's advice would have been well taken, for Jefferson continued to suffer from a variety of ailments attendant upon old age—rheumatism, stiffening of his legs and wrists, a general slowing of physical pace.

Jefferson did not spare himself from the exacting and exciting last job to which he had given himself, because he held that education was the greatest of all human causes as it was the indispensable road to liberty. When the exhausted Cabell, worn down by repeated battles in the legislature in behalf of the university, voiced his discouragement to Jefferson and intimated that he wished to withdraw from political life, the aged statesman recalled his young aide to his patriotic duty. He asked what service can we ever render our country equal to promoting education. "What object of our lives can we propose so important? What interest of our own which ought not to be postponed to this? Health, time, labor, on what in the single life which nature has given us, can these be better bestowed than on this immortal boon to our country? The exertions and the mortifications are temporary; the benefit eternal." He then added, referring to his own labors, as he almost never did: "If any member of our college of visitors could justifiably withdraw from this sa-

[18] Jefferson to Madison, Monticello, October 18, 1819. W. C. Rives Papers, L.C.

[19] Madison to Jefferson, Montpelier, October 23, 1819. Madison Papers, L.C.

cred duty, it would be myself, who . . . have neither vigor of body nor mind left to keep the field; but I will die in the last ditch. . . ." [20]

The more the buildings took shape and piecemeal grants for the university were made by the legislature, the more confident did Jefferson become about obtaining all the desired facilities. By the fall of 1821 he began discussing with Madison the cost of the excellent library he wished to provide for the university. He revealed his general philosophy: to make the total plan and construction of the university as complete as possible, and as excellent. "The world will never bear to see the doors of such an establishment locked up." [21] This kind of gambling courage, necessary in good causes as well as selfish ones, carried through Jefferson's ideal of a university, despite the repeated obstacles he had to meet and overcome. His policy was firm: "Our course is a plain one, to pursue what is best, and the public will come right and approve us in the end." This he wrote when objections arose in the legislature over the library building, which was to be a rotunda on the model of the Parthenon, and which Jefferson insisted should be dominant in the campus group. He was sure that "the establishment is now at that stage at which it will force itself on." [22] And he doggedly returned to plans for gaining more ground.

3

Undeniably, there was a specifically Virginia pride involved in the grueling fight to establish a first-rate university

[20] Jefferson to J. C. Cabell, Monticello, January 31, 1821. *Writings* (Memorial), XV, 312.

[21] Jefferson to Madison, Monticello, October 30, 1821. Madison Papers, L.C.

[22] Jefferson to Madison, Monticello, April 7, 1822. Madison Papers, L.C.

in the South. That Jefferson and Madison, the two most intellectual statesmen of the South (and, with John Adams, the best in the entire nation), should promote an educational institution that would place the South on equal terms with the North as a center of culture and learning was entirely fitting. Jefferson urged his ever-helpful friends Joseph Cabell and W. C. Rives, who represented him and Madison on the firing-line of the Virginia legislature, to have "courage and patience" in keeping the standards of the University of Virginia the highest. It would not do to "become suitors to Yale and Harvard for their secondary characters, to become our first," Jefferson wrote, on the vexed problem of securing a good faculty. That was why Jefferson was counting on "foreign aid," in order to develop a self-reliant and altogether new center of learning in America.[23]

On grounds of expediency, Jefferson was willing to wait with plans for pushing the primary and intermediate schools, for fear that the request for funds for these would injure the progress of the university. Free elementary schools, for every small township, or what Jefferson called "wards," and intermediate "colleges or academies" that would offer scholarships for impoverished but talented students from every ward, were related parts in a total system of education. But "I believe we had better do one thing at a time; the University first. . . ."[24]

By 1823, when Jefferson had become an octogenarian, it was essential that he conserve his time for his majestic educational enterprise. Savage demands were being made upon both ex-Presidents for replies to letters from friends, acquaintances, and unknown thousands of citizens seeking

[23] Jefferson to W. C. Rives, Monticello, December 29, 1822. W. C. Rives Papers, L.C.
[24] Jefferson to W. C. Rives, Monticello, January 28, 1823. W. C. Rives Papers, L.C.

intellectual, moral, or political advice. At the beginning of 1823 Jefferson asked Madison to reply to a friend who had asked for Jefferson's views on the forthcoming presidential election. "It is impossible for me to write to him with two crippled hands. I abandon writing but from the most urgent necessities; and above all things I should not meddle in a Presidential election, nor even express a sentiment on the subject of the Candidates." [25] The "most urgent necessities" were a small circle of old friends, Madison foremost among them; and the university. Nor could Jefferson and Madison remain immune to queries that affected the fundamental political principles of their own lives. These letters the two aged statesmen felt impelled to scrutinize with their usual keen critical intelligence. They supplied answers breathing the ripe wisdom of long experience.

In the fall of 1823 Jefferson thought it time to dispatch an agent to Great Britain to procure the indispensable professors—with the exception of a law professor, whom Jefferson and Madison agreed would have to be a native American. Francis Walker Gilmer, himself a talented legal scholar, received this unique commission to the "republic of letters" in England and Scotland. Dugald Stewart, Samuel Parr, an eminent Oxford professor of classics, Richard Rush, then American Minister in London, and other friends of Jefferson had been enlisted to aid Gilmer on his important mission. The University of Virginia had not only authorized Gilmer to select professors; it had promised to be "bound by his selections." [26] But Gilmer's mission was not altogether happy. Stewart proved to be too aged and infirm to be able to help. The fall of 1824 brought a letter from Mad-

[25] Jefferson to Madison, Monticello, February 24, 1823. Madison Papers, L.C.

[26] "A true copy of Rector Thomas Jefferson's authorization . . .," April 26, 1824. Madison Papers, L.C.

ison to Jefferson commenting on a recent report of Gilmer's of dismaying increases in the expense of his trip, and discouraging results in England. Scotland and Germany still remained to be canvassed. To Germany, Madison objected: "an alien language, and less affinity of manners are grounds of unfavorable comparison. It would seem that we must at last be obliged to resort to the domestic fund for filling most of the chairs. Foreigners of the first rate only would be relished by the public." [27]

The issue became even graver in the following months when Gilmer informed Jefferson that British salaries were too high for American competition. It looked as though Gilmer would return without any professors; and Jefferson was alarmed at the turn of events. He wrote to Madison that rather than have the legislature and the public consider Gilmer's mission a failure, "we had better bring the best he can get. They will be preferable to secondaries of our own country; because the stature of these is known, whereas those he would bring would be unknown, and would be readily imagined to be of the high grade we have hitherto calculated on." [28] The crisis in events had pressed hard on Jefferson. Madison's response was calm and resourceful. He recommended Gilmer's going on to Ireland, and thought that if he could return with three or four professors, of modern languages, ancient languages, mathematics, and astronomy, by April of 1825, the university could open. "I am sensible of the disadvantage and mortification of taking secondary characters," he wrote, "whether native or foreign; but I am not sure that the objections to the former are stronger than to the latter, especially if the former should be of good dis-

[27] Madison to Jefferson, September 17, 1824. Madison Papers, L.C.
[28] Jefferson to Madison, October 6, 1824. Madison Papers, L.C.

positions better ascertained; and the two be *secondary* in the same degree of secondaries." [29]

Thus Madison thought it necessary to "prepare for the worst" and make inquiries in every direction in America. He repeated a belief he had already expressed earlier, that there were enough medical men of good standing in this country to find a competent professor here.[30] Jefferson, however, did not share Madison's confidence that American resources in medical science had "risen towards a level with those of Europe." He persisted in calling American medical men "Sangrados" and crisply informed Madison that the university could afford to open without a "Medical Professor" at all. "Better nothing than bad. It is the school we are least prepared for." [31]

At last Jefferson was able to write that the academic problem was temporarily solved. "Gilmer is arrived in New York sick of a fever which he had thro the whole voyage of 35 days. . . . He has engaged 5 Professors to wit: George Long, Antient Languages; George Blätterman, Modern Languages; Thomas H. Key, Mathematics; Charles Bonnycastle, Natural Philosophy; Robley Dunglison, Anatomy. . . . The last wishes to add chemistry to his lectures, which we may well agree to as we are not well prepared for anatomy. . . . We shall advertise the Dormitories as soon as they arrive. The Hotels are all engaged. There were numerous applications for them." [32]

With a nucleus of foreign professors safely secured, a

[29] Madison to Jefferson, Montpelier, October 9, 1824. Madison Papers, L.C.

[30] Ibid.

[31] Jefferson to Madison, Monticello, October 11, 1824. Madison Papers, L.C.

[32] Jefferson to Madison, Monticello, November 20, 1824. Madison Papers, L.C.

fresh problem arose—the choice of an appropriate professor of ethics. Jefferson considered ethics an indispensable part of general education, but hated to have it emerge in the distorted forms of authoritarian morality to which the clergy normally confined it. He was determined not to allow a clergyman to take over the teaching of moral philosophy, and preferred to see a well-educated and brilliant layman in charge of this controversial subject. He argued: "it is a branch of science of little difficulty to any ingenious man. Locke, Stewart, Brown, Tracy, for the general science of mind furnish materials abundant, and that of Ethics is still more trite. I should think any person with a general education rendering them otherwise worthy of a place among his scientific brethren might soon qualify himself." [33] He suggested a young man formerly a student at William and Mary, who had been later educated at Edinburgh, and was considered one of the most distinguished American students ever there. The significance of this candidate proposed by Jefferson is that Jefferson put his faith in the Scottish school of common-sense empiricist philosophy in preference to the more metaphysical variety of philosophy then fashionable at Oxford and Cambridge.

In negotiating for native talent, Jefferson and Madison encountered an obstacle that has plagued American education ever since: "the difficulty in our country of withdrawing talents from rival pursuits into the service of Education." [34] A long chase for a native professor of law, of ethics, and of literature brought home this truth with uncomfortable insistence to the eager founders of the University of Virginia. It also inadvertently forced to a head the issue of

[33] Jefferson to Madison, Monticello, November 30, 1824. Madison Papers, L.C.

[34] Madison to Jefferson, Montpelier, January 15, 1825. Madison Papers, L.C.

academic freedom and correctness of political principles in an institution that Madison had thought of as a future "nursery of Republican patriots as well as genuine scholars." [35]

The search for an adequate law professor, after Gilmer declined the professorship, generated delicate questions of how far tolerance should go concerning the political beliefs of the prospective faculty. At first Jefferson only confessed his fears that they might hire "a mere Gothic lawyer who has no idea beyond his Coke Littleton, who could not associate in conversation with his Colleagues, nor utter a single Academical idea to an enquiring stranger." [36] Jefferson, as he revealed in this value judgment, abhorred the tribe of narrow, pedantic scholars and expected philosophical awareness and breadth of interest as well as European conversational ease from the hand-picked professors. In recommending a candidate, Madison described him as a "convert to the constitutionality of canals. In other respects he adhered, I *believe*, to the Virginia Creed of which he had been a warm advocate. What his political sentiments are at present I know not." [37] The issue was now out in the open. Jefferson, one of the few surviving "Argonauts" of 1776, and Madison, the dominating spirit of the Constitution, were unwilling to allow the entry of political doctrines contradictory to the cherished freedoms of democratic society and Republican ideology. The United States was already witnessing, in a quiet, educational context, the paradox of restrict-

[35] Madison to Samuel H. Smith, Montpelier, November 4, 1826. *Writings* (Hunt), IX, 259.

[36] Jefferson to Madison, Monticello, January 23, 1825. W. C. Rives Papers, L.C.

[37] Madison to Jefferson, Montpelier, February 17, 1825. Madison Papers, L.C. This letter is printed in the Congress Edition of Madison's *Writings*, but so unscrupulously edited, with omissions from the text not indicated, that the original must be consulted.

ing freedom in order to preserve the most fundamental freedom of all—a democratic society.

In an effort to come to grips with this vital problem, Jefferson wrote the following important note to Madison, raising the distressing question of prescribed texts in the field of government:

In most public seminaries a text-book is prescribed to the several schools as the Norma docendi in them; and this is frequently done by the Trustees. I should not propose this generally in our University because I believe none of us are so much at the heights of science, in the several branches, as to undertake this. And therefore that it will be best left to the Professors, until occasion of interference shall be given. But there is one branch in which I think we are the best judges, and the branch itself is of that interesting character to our state, and to the U. S. as to make it a duty in us to lay down the principles which are to be taught. It is that of government. Even . . . Mr. Gilmer . . . was believed by some . . . to be too much infected with the principles of the Richmond laywers, who are rank Federalists, as formerly denominated, and now Consolidationists. I do not believe this myself. . . . But now that he is withdrawn . . . a possibility has arisen that a Richmond lawyer or some one of that school may be proposed. I think it a duty to guard against danger by a previous prescription of the texts to be adopted. I inclose you a resolution which I think of proposing at our next meeting for your consideration, with a prayer that you will correct it freely, and make it what you think it ought to be.[38]

Madison's reaction to Jefferson's proposed list of prescribed texts in government was once again alive with subtle differences in approach between the bold and positive nature of Jefferson's imagination and the sober and sound quality of Madison's critical powers of analysis. Madison ap-

[38] Jefferson to Madison, Monticello, February 1, 1825. W. C. Rives Papers, L.C.

preciated the importance of ensuring that "the true doctrine of liberty, as exemplified in our Political System, should be inculcated on those who are to sustain and may administer it." [39] He realized that some informal screening of scholars to teach law and political theory would be inescapable if they wished to preserve the democratic faith. But he immediately considered the drawbacks when it came to prescribed texts. Algernon Sidney and John Locke, the basic sources for English republican theory, inspire a love of freedom, he granted; yet they cannot prevent unwholesome interpretations of American republican constitutions. The Declaration of Independence, "tho' rich in fundamental principles," similarly cannot guard against unsound constructions. *The Federalist*, although probably the most authentic exposition of the federal Constitution, "did not foresee all the misconstructions which have occurred." Nor did it present a unified interpretation: "neither of the great rival Parties have acquiesced in all its comments." Modestly Madison conceded that it might be employed as "a school book" on a less ambitious expectation about its usefulness. The Virginia and Kentucky Resolutions and Madison's Report on the Virginia Resolutions, Madison thought dangerous to prescribe, since not all members of even one party had agreed upon their doctrines. "Are we sure that to our brethren of the Board it is so [satisfactory]?" [40]

The general principle that Madison was working toward was that orthodoxy in political principles was almost as difficult to ensure in books as orthodoxy in religion was to establish in churches. He granted that "the public right" was very different in the two demands for orthodoxy, but asked whether framing a political creed did not present the

[39] Madison to Jefferson, Montpelier, February 8, 1825. *Writings* (Hunt), IX, 218.
[40] Ibid., IX 219-20.

difficulty of being stated in such general terms that it meant little, or in such particular terms that it would "divide & exclude where meant to unite and fortify." The best compromise, he thought, was "to avoid the two extremes, by referring to selected Standards without requiring an unqualified conformity to them, which indeed might not in every instance be possible." He had accordingly modified Jefferson's resolution "to relax the absoluteness of its injunction" and he had added Washington's Inaugural Speech and Farewell Address to help balance the more partisan list of texts Jefferson had proposed. In concluding, Madison put his trust once again in character—just as he and Jefferson had had to do in political crisis. "An Able & Orthodox Professor, whose course of instruction will be an example to his successors," was the most effective safeguard against "heretical intrusions into the School of Politics." [41]

This problem, the apparent collision between the ideals of liberty and freedom, on the one hand, and standardization and repression, on the other, remains an acute problem for democratic societies. It is highly significant that Jefferson, himself the greatest figure in the liberal tradition of American democracy, should have recommended that in the basic realm of political theory tolerance could not be confused with unwitting innocence. The essential limits on freedom, Jefferson saw, included uncompromising opposition to systems of thought that would, if made effective, undermine that freedom. The epic difficulty of achieving and preserving "human rights" in America was well understood by its early protagonists. Only the most romantic or sentimental liberals would be willing to jeopardize such gains by welcoming the very doctrines that proclaimed the end of human liberty. Madison's wish, then, to choose an orthodox

[41] Ibid., IX, 220.

professor, and count on the example he would provide to successive generations, was only a difference in method and technique, not a disagreement over the objective of ensuring the preservation of "the distinctive principles" of the United States.

In the late spring of 1824 Jefferson had begun to work on a book catalogue for the library of the university, devoting four hours a day to it for the period of two months and the entire day for several additional months. He told Madison he had undertaken to make out the catalogue because he had in his possession "a collection of excellent catalogues, and knowing no one capable, to whom we could refer the task. It has been laborious far beyond my expectation . . . and not yet in sight of the end. It will enable us to judge what the object will cost." [42]

Jefferson's fascination with books had never deserted him. He had sold his first great library to the United States, to form the nucleus of the library of Congress, after the British had burned the national library in 1814. Jefferson had instantly begun to collect another library for himself after the last shipment of books had gone to Washington. This library was willed to the University of Virginia, but it was necessary for the family to sell most of it at auction instead, to pay part of the debt on Jefferson's estate. In any event, it was inconceivable that Jefferson would assign this task, always partly a labor of love, to anyone else. He did ask Madison for a list of books on divinity, which Madison dutifully supplied. "The good moral writers, Christian as well as Pagan I have set down; but there are writers of celebrity in religious metaphysics . . . whom you can suggest," Jefferson had written. [43] By September, Jefferson's wearying task

[42] Jefferson to Madison, Monticello, August 8, 1824. Madison Papers, L.C.
[43] Ibid.

was finished—a catalogue of more than six thousand items, "complete except the alphabet," estimated to cost just under $25,000.[44]

Fortunately, the University was opening. Students were coming by the Richmond and Fredericksburg stages as far as they could, and hiring horses when those got stuck in the unpassable roads. Books had not yet arrived for the young men, but the electric atmosphere of a new educational world was beginning to be felt.[45] A law professor, John Tayloe Lomax, recommended by Madison's friend Judge Barbour, was appointed, after determining that he had "extended his studies beyond the ordinary municipal law, to the law of nations and to the more philosophical view of the general subjects." [46] The "bantling of forty years' growth and nursing" was about to take its place in the world.

4

The following year found Jefferson convinced that he would soon "remove beyond the reach of attentions to the University, or beyond the bourne of life itself"; and he wrote to Madison committing the university to his care in that event, and professing ardently the joy and satisfaction he had received from this friendship of half a century.

Bewilderingly heavy financial difficulties had arisen for Jefferson to disturb his last months with agonizing worries about the fate of his family's resources. He petitioned to

[44] William H. Peden, ed.: *1828 Catalogue of the Library of the University of Virginia* (Charlottesville: Printed for the Alderman Library, University of Virginia; 1945), p. II.

[45] Jefferson to Madison, Monticello, March 22, 1825. Madison Papers, L.C.

[46] Madison to Jefferson, Montpelier, August 4, 1825. Madison Papers, L.C.

sell his lands at public lottery, retaining only Monticello itself. The purpose of the lottery was to obtain better prices than the depreciated land value at the time would have netted in an ordinary sale—a purpose, unfortunately, that was not realized. These troubles he confided to Madison, who was himself in hard-pressed circumstances and who foresaw a similar end for his own estate. Jefferson did not like to afflict others with his troubles, and indeed he had been singularly adequate to all of life's burdens in his long career. But, he confessed, "pains are lessened by communication with a friend."

It was on this occasion that Jefferson stated, once in his life, the luminous truth that had been the source of so much consolation to him throughout his active life and in the retirement that, despite its many afflictions, had been made rich and happy. "The friendship which has subsisted between us, now half a century," Thomas Jefferson wrote to James Madison, "and the harmony of our political principles and pursuits, have been sources of constant happiness to me through that long period." He then committed the university to Madison's care and resumed:

It has also been a great solace to me to believe that you are engaged in vindicating to posterity the course we have pursued for preserving to them, in all their purity, the blessings of self-government, which we had assisted too in acquiring for them. If ever the earth has beheld a system of administration conducted with a single and steadfast eye to the general interest and happiness of those committed to it, one which, protected by truth, can never know reproach, it is that to which our lives have been devoted. To myself you have been a pillar of support through life. Take care of me when dead, and be assured that I shall leave with you my last affections.[47]

[47] Jefferson to Madison, Monticello, February 17, 1826. *Writings* (Ford), X, 377–8.

With the courtesy and delicacy that had distinguished their long friendship, Madison soon replied: "You do not overrate the interest I feel in the University, as the Temple thro which alone lies the road to that of liberty. But you entirely do my aptitude to be your successor in watching over its prosperity. It would be the pretension of a mere worshipper 'remplacer' the Tutelary Genius of the Sanctuary. The best hope is, in the continuance of your cares, till they can be replaced by the stability and self-growth of the Institution." [48] Madison's reserve had generally prevented him from protesting the friendship that his every action proved. Now he sensed the quality of leave-taking in Jefferson's affectionate communication, and he responded:

You cannot look back to the long period of our private friendship & political harmony, with more affecting recollections than I do. If they are a source of pleasure to you, what ought they not to be to me? We cannot be deprived of the happy consciousness of the pure devotion to the public good with which we discharged the trusts committed to us. And I indulge a confidence that sufficient evidence will find its way to another generation, to ensure, after we are gone, whatever of justice may be withheld whilst we are here. The political horizon is already yielding in your case at least, the surest auguries of it. Wishing & hoping that you may yet live to increase the debt which our Country owes you, and to witness the increasing gratitude, which alone can pay it, I offer you the fullest return of affectionate assurances.[49]

Two months later Jefferson, still in communication with his friend on the subject of the university, reported that his health was "greatly better" than the year before, and were he permitted to give himself to the most agreeable

[48] Madison to Jefferson, Montpelier, February 24, 1826. *Writings* (Hunt), IX, 244–5.
[49] Ibid., IX, 245–6.

occupation, reading, "I should probably wear on in tolerable ease and tranquility. I must still however rest on the hitherto illusive hope that the discretion of those who have no claims upon me, will at length advert to the circumstances of my age and ill health, and feel the duty of sparing both. The correspondence of my bosom-friends is still very dear, and welcome, and consolatory. Yours among the most, being ever, and the most affectionately yours." [50]

Madison was more than sympathetic. He scolded, as the best of friends do: "The epistolary taxation with which you are still persecuted is a cruelty not to be borne." He knew it would never cease of itself, and the "discretion" of strangers was a flimsy reed to clutch at. "Why not adopt a formula, to be copied by one of the family, acknowledging the communication, and referring to the general rule, imposed by necessity, of limiting the answer to that, and an expression of thanks. Nothing short of some positive check will relieve you from the afflicting burden. . . ." [51]

It was late in the day for Jefferson to go against the grain, changing the habits of his long and good life. At the end of the following month he was gravely ill. On the 1st of July, Madison had a note from Dr. Dunglison referring to the danger of Jefferson's condition. And on the 4th of July, on the fiftieth anniversary of the Declaration of Independence, Thomas Jefferson died.

5

The generous spirit that had animated Jefferson's work and life was kept alive by Madison in his role of spiritual

[50] Jefferson to Madison, Monticello, May 3, 1826. W. C. Rives Papers, L.C.

[51] Madison to Jefferson, Montpelier, May 6, 1826. Madison Papers, L.C.

guardian of his friend's reputation. The care of the University of Virginia, which had been placed in his hands, was conscientiously accepted. At the sacrifice of health and the precious time that remained, Madison took on the thankless duties for eight years after Jefferson's death. Though he could hardly afford it, he gave the university pecuniary aid, and provided, in a codicil to his will, a bequest of needed books that his library could supply. He could not allow himself proper credit, tendered by friends, for his work as rector of the university, so anxious was he to have the world remember Jefferson as its creator and creative genius. In summing up the work his dearest friend had put into it, Madison himself became eloquent. "The University of Virginia, as a temple dedicated to science and liberty, was, after his retirement from the political sphere, the object nearest his heart, and so continued to the close of his life. His devotion to it was intense, and his exertions unceasing. It bears the stamp of his genius, and will be a noble monument of his fame." [52]

More personal services to the memory of Jefferson were too numerous to be described. To great and good friends Madison wrote long letters describing the tragic circumstances of Jefferson's death in the midst of severe financial embarrassments—the poor reward for a life spent in public service and for generosity to friends whose requests for loans Jefferson could never refuse. To Lafayette, Jefferson's trusted friend, Madison communicated some of the pain he felt over the trials Jefferson had endured before his death. When Madison suggested that Jefferson's works were being prepared for publication in America and might be simultaneously published in France, Lafayette responded at once

[52] Madison to Samuel H. Smith, Montpelier, November 4, 1826. *Writings* (Hunt), IX, 259.

that he would arrange a translation of the work and its publication in the country Jefferson had adopted as second love
after his native land.[53] For the first volumes of Jefferson's
writings that Thomas Jefferson Randolph, favorite grand-
child of Thomas Jefferson, prepared for publication, Madison wrote a fine preface. The intention at the time was to
publish Jefferson's "Memoir" (the *Autobiography* and
Anas) separately. When plans were changed, Madison
agreed to write an additional preface to suit the enlarged
publication.[54]

Meanwhile biographers and historians from all over the
country were soliciting Madison for authentic information
about Jefferson. They wanted light on Republican principles, suggestions of what Jefferson would believe "now,"
anecdotes, and personal reminiscences. To the historians
Madison's replies were sophisticated and methodological.
He referred them to groups of Jefferson's documents, more
authentic even than his own friendly reconstruction ever
could be. To the biographers Madison supplied information
only when he was persuaded that it would be made use of
intelligently, and he did not undertake to create for the eyes
of the public the quality of friendship that blossoms in privacy. To a friend who sought aid in preparing an address on
Jefferson and specifically inquired about the philosopher
statesman's habits of study, Madison wrote an informative
answer, referring to Jefferson's rule of "never letting the sun
rise before him." He added that Jefferson's "relish for Books
never forsook him. . . . He was certainly one of the most
learned men of the age," but lest the essential quality of his
more than bookish friend would be missed, Madison added

[53] Madison Papers, L.C. No date. [August 1826?]
[54] Madison to Thomas Jefferson Randolph, Montpelier, December
22, 1828. Madison Papers, L.C.

that "the Genius of Philosophy ever walked hand in hand with him." [55]

To Henry Gilpin, who sent his book on the *Life of Thomas Jefferson* to Madison for correction, Madison noted some factual errors. Two of these concerned the personal appearance of his friend. Madison protested that Jefferson's hair had not been "*red*, but between *yellow and red.*" He was equally protective about the size of his friend's nose: it had been "rather under, certainly not above, common size." [56] Gilpin thanked Madison for his corrections and promised to use his suggestions when revising the biography for republication.[57]

In truth, however, Madison had no very great patience with those who were curious about the details of personality and private life. Both he and Jefferson had given their lives to public causes of the most earnest and fateful kind. What they wished posterity to be concerned with lay in the voluminous collection of thoughtful letters they had written, in what Jefferson had called "the freshness of fact." A few days after Jefferson's death Madison had written to Nicholas P. Trist, Jefferson's son-in-law and executor, a brief letter of condolence, very simply saying that he hoped that Jefferson's death would "not be permitted to impair any of the beneficial measures which were in progress or in project. It cannot be unknown that the anxieties of the deceased were for others, not for himself." [58] Jefferson himself had written

[55] Madison to Samuel Harrison Smith, Montpelier, November 4, 1826. *Writings* (Hunt), IX, 260–1.

[56] Madison to Henry D. Gilpin, Montpelier, October 25, 1827. *Writings* (Congress), III, 594.

[57] H. D. Gilpin to James Madison, January 4, 1828. Madison Papers, L.C.

[58] Madison to N. P. Trist, Montpelier, July 6, 1826. *Writings* (Hunt), IX, 248.

some years earlier that to Madison's "consummate powers were united a pure and spotless virtue, which calumny in vain attempted to sully." Neither one had been wrong.[59]

Beautifully obedient to the charge: "take care of me when dead," Madison soon found his last political work cut out for him. The South Carolina argument for nullification had developed after Jefferson's death. To protect the name and memory of his great friend from the political misuse of the nullifiers, Madison himself, aged and troubled with rheumatic hands for which writing was a painful chore, wrote or dictated innumerable letters expounding the true principles of Virginia Republicanism. Although Jefferson had written with emotional fervor at the time of the Kentucky Resolutions, Madison maintained that his friend had never given sanction to the heresy that a single state, remaining within the protection of the Union, could by its solo legislative decision, nullify the laws of the federal government. The new nullification doctrine, Madison pointed out, implied that a single state "may arrest the operation of a law of the United States, and institute a process which is to terminate in the ascendancy of a minority over a large majority, in a Republican System, the characteristic rule of which is that the major will is the ruling will." [60] This "newfangled theory," he scathingly observed, had been wrongly fathered on Mr. Jefferson, the apostle of republicanism, whose own words declared that " 'acquiescence in the decision of the majority is the vital principle of it.' " Admitting that the Kentucky Resolutions had stated that "when powers are assumed which have not been delegated, a nullification of the act is the rightful remedy: that every state has a

---

[59] "Autobiography." *Writings* (Ford), I, 57.
[60] *Notes on Nullification.* 1835–6. *Writings* (Hunt), IX, 588–9.

natural right in cases not within the compact . . . to nullify," Madison called attention to the significant point that the remedial right of nullification here appealed to was expressly a *natural* right. Thus it was not a right derived from the Constitution, "but from abuses or usurpations, releasing the parties to it from their obligation." [61]

Madison also defended Jefferson from the extreme states' rights Republicans who quoted him to sanction their opposition to a federal tariff. Madison thought the tariff constitutional, and explained the meaning of Jefferson's denunciation, in 1825, of the assumption of power by the general government "indefinitely . . . over Agriculture and Manufactures." Madison suggested that this passage, written carelessly and in a confidential letter, did not discriminate, as Jefferson would otherwise have done, "between an assumption of power and an abuse of power; relying on the term 'indefinitely' to indicate an excess of the latter, and to imply an admission of a definite or reasonable use of the power to regulate trade for the encouragement of manufacturing and agricultural products." [62] Madison then cited convincing evidences that Jefferson, by the tenor of his past recommendations, accepted a power in Congress to encourage manufactures by commercial regulations.

The exegesis of political policies and doctrines, Madison clearly understood, was a slippery and endlessly repeatable game. In the crushing new world that was beginning in America the objectives and standards of a less industrial age required considerable "interpretation" to retain practicability. When political devotees turned to Madison on economic matters for guidance, he did not mince words. "That Virginia must soon become manufacturing as well as agri-

[61] Ibid.

[62] Madison to Joseph C. Cabell, Montpelier, December 5, 1828. *Writings* (Hunt), IX, 326, n.

cultural, and be divided into these two great interests, is obvious & certain," he wrote.[63] No longer an agricultural "Paradise," even the Old Dominion would witness the same great classes of agricultural and industrial workers that had formed in every advanced society in Europe.

But the vital directive principles of the Republican faith of Jefferson and Madison would breast the tide, not only of Jacksonian democracy, but of the more developed capitalistic democracy of a later day. These vital principles, however, would have more to do with the broad philosophy and spirit of Republicanism than with any particular economic organization of society. The security of the Union, the inflexible dependence upon "majority government," the sovereignty of the people with their natural right to self-preservation, the safeguarding of cherished civil liberties like the freedom of the press and freedom of religion—all these were unchanging ideals for political democracy. Holding fast to these values of republican government, Madison saw that the root principle of them all, the will of the majority, could not automatically remove the conflict of interests within society. Indeed, such conflicts were natural to society, and "if the will of the majority cannot be trusted where there are diversified and conflicting interests, it can be trusted nowhere, because such interests exist everywhere." [64] But the only appeal from a system of free government that worked out *some* compromise was to a refuge of authority that would subvert freedom completely. Having dispelled the myth of a perfect government, Madison summarized his political conclusions with a profoundly shrewd insight: "that no government of human device and

[63] Madison to ——. [Majority Governments] [1833]. *Writings* (Hunt), IX, 525.
[64] Ibid., IX, 528.

human administration can be perfect; that that which is the least imperfect is therefore the best government." [65]

To the very end Madison, like Jefferson, adhered to the cause of liberty. Jefferson's instructions for the inscription on his gravestone were that he be known as " 'author of the Declaration of American Independence, of the Statute of Virginia for religious freedom, and Father of the University of Virginia' because by these, as testimonials that I have lived, I wish most to be remembered." [66] All three achievements bore out Madison's claim that his great friend was above all a benefactor of humankind. Madison left a different form of testament. His last words of "Advice to my Country" were a warning, patriarchal in conception, prophetic in tone. His deepest wish was "that the Union of the States be cherished and perpetuated. Let the open enemy to it be regarded as a Pandora with her box opened; and the disguised one, as the serpent creeping with his deadly wiles into Paradise." [67] Here, in words "issuing from the tomb," one can glimpse the profound harmony that prevailed between the two friends. With nobility and a depth of passion, their last anxieties proved to be for "the happiness of our country & the hope of the world." [68]

[65] Ibid.

[66] Jefferson: *Writings* (Ford), X, 396.

[67] Undated original, in Madison's hand, in Madison Papers, L.C. (Vol. xc, between item 178 and 179); usually known in Dolly Madison's hand, and so reproduced in Hunt.

[68] Madison to ——, March 1836. *Writings* (Hunt), IX, 610.

POSTSCRIPT

LIKE ALL SUCCESSFUL lifelong partnerships, that of Jefferson and Madison seems like a perpetual miracle. Probably no other American then living but James Madison could have stood up to the battery of Jefferson's brilliant talents. Others would have become lieutenants, subordinate intellects taking commands and sensing out their leader's cues. Madison's was a deep and keen intelligence, perpetually growing in comprehension and critical power. He was thoroughly himself, thoroughly independent in all matters save when courtesy and friendship make strong people compliant.

Since Jefferson and Madison were philosopher statesmen, perhaps the best this nation has ever produced, their long careers demonstrate the real power of intellect and moral integrity in shaping the structure of a free society. Because of this, their habits of mind are at least as important as the outward acts of their official careers.

To generalize is probably to risk a personal impression for a grounded conclusion, but it is undeniably tempting. It would seem that Jefferson was normally bolder and more imaginative in the projection of hypotheses than Madison. He had the gift of clothing his ideas in the rhythms of a powerful and moving rhetoric, of which the most finished example is the Declaration of Independence; but all of his letters have something of a kindred distinction. The characteristic temper of Jefferson's thinking was experimental and pragmatic in the best sense—obedient to observation and ascertainable fact, but exploratory, fertile in drawing implications, and suggestive of fresh starting-points.

Madison's consistent quality was different. His mind was strongly logical, and as he allowed his logic to operate on concrete issues in politics and the theory of society, he developed an amazing control over points of information and masses of detail. It was possible for Madison's logic to cut deeper on certain kinds of issues than Jefferson's did. We have seen some of those issues in the course of this study. The tremendous fertility, the rich spirit of enthusiasm and organic confidence that permitted Jefferson to strike fire frequently with his first try, were hardly likely to come in couples. These were not markedly present in Madison.

Temperamentally Jefferson had distinct advantages over Madison. He possessed a superb ability to charm others —a response, perhaps, to the warmth of his own nature, although the warmth was rarely without reserve. Some indefinable quality of cosmopolitan accommodation made Jefferson at home with French noblemen, English diplomats, and humdrum kinsmen and neighbors all over Virginia.

Madison, too, formed enthusiastic connections with men who valued his leadership; but Madison never left America, whether because of the unreliability of his health, as he said, or because he was in and of Virginia and America so completely that the need for European experience did not exist in him. Party leaders, officials, and politicians throughout the United States turned to Madison for thoughtful directives and willingly initiated the plans he proposed. His extraordinary richness of information was appreciated. He could attend to issues of principle and yet discriminate among details in terms of relative importance. Private audiences enjoyed his abundant personal anecdotes, drawn from history as well as from his own experience, and varying in color depending upon the sex of his company. For, strange to say, Madison had a better sense of humor than Jefferson; he was often witty, and sometimes even permitted himself a baudy verbal incontinence that was utterly unlike Jefferson's own disposition. "The Great Little Madison," despite his capacity for being "fascinating," as one lady put it, was often impeded by genuine shyness, a shyness wholly absent from Jefferson's make-up. Because Madison tended to be reserved at large gatherings or in a self-consciously "brilliant" company, he was often judged to be unimportant, dry, even dull and insipid—an erroneous judgment that acquaintance with his life dispels.

Differences of judgment naturally arose between men who were independent thinkers. Madison as a member of Jefferson's Cabinet might differ with the President, and the President would take account of his difference; or Madison as President might take action not fully in line with what Jefferson had advised. Neither of the friends fell out over differences; they did not glower in the privacy of their chambers, resenting disagreements. Their communication was frank, quick, and manly. The one exception to this behavior, the difference discussed in connection with the *Federalist* papers, is worth noticing precisely because it is an exception.

Jefferson and Madison, then, were equal in understanding and complementary in their talents. That they complemented each other as political partners is one of the happy accidents of this democratic nation's past. Both men were staunch and far-seeing democrats in the most moral sense of the term. The one concentrated on individual rights, and on that fateful phase of opposition when the underdog minority becomes the legal ruling majority.

The other spent his political strength in effecting order and a reasonable atmosphere for civilized compromise in all the many-sided affairs of government.

Above their fateful achievements as political partners is the unique transcendence these statesmen effected of the meanly or purely political life. The breathtaking scope of Jefferson's cultural interests and Madison's steadily humane dispositions are demonstrations of a rounded democratic faith. The state is not all for these philosophical friends, any more than it is meant to be all in the sound democratic theory they bequeathed to the country they loved. One of the great freedoms that a good society confers upon its members is the freedom, after political obligations are met, to cultivate as one pleases the interests of the mind and the enjoyments of trained tastes.

The apotheosis of their existence above and beyond the political sphere, on the part of men who were called on to spend their lives in the very heart of it, was the friendship that developed for Jefferson and Madison. Theirs was indeed a "cordial and affectionate friendship," which, as Jefferson phrased it in his last will, "for nearly an half century has united us in the same principles and pursuits of what we have deemed for the greatest good of our country."

INDEX

Academic freedom, see Freedom
Academical village, TJ's, 264
Academy of Sciences, French, 81
Adams, Abigail (Smith), 214
Adams, Henry, 222, 239
Adams, John, 36, 84, 135, 138, 186, 225; administration of, 167–70, 174–6, 210; book on constitutions, 34; breaks with TJ, 91; Cabinet of, 175–6, 220; TJ on, 117–18, 167, 214; TJ's friendship with, 173–6, 260; leads anti-republicans, 124; JM on, 171–2, 176; midnight appointments, 213–14; nepotism of, 223; on Shays' Rebellion, 45; on titles, 101; philosopher statesman, 270; political theory of, 138–9; relations with Hamilton, 177, 217–18; Republican attack on, 182–3; special commissioner, 15
Adams, John Quincy, author of *Publicola* papers, 118
Address to the States, JM's, 8–9
Advice to my Country, JM's, 207, 290
Aggression, JM on, 158
Agrarianism, 131–3, 148, 161–2
Agriculture, TJ on, 131–3; JM on, 123, 131–3, 289
Albemarle County, Va., 182–3
Alexander I, of Russia, 248–9
Alien and Sedition Acts, 174, 177; TJ on, 184, 208, 218; repeal of, 188–9
Alienation of rights, 79
Amendments, constitutional, 42; JM on, 51–2, 56–60, 205–6, 256–7
"American," pseudonym of Hamilton, 119
Americanism: TJ's, 149; JM's, 292
Ames, Fisher, 138
Anas, TJ's, 138–9, 285
Anatomists, 234
Anglo-American relations, 136–7; see also Great Britain, influence on U. S. politics
Anglomany, 137, 156
Anglo-monocrats, 203
Anti-Republicans, 118, 122, 124; JM on, 125
Appeasement, TJ on, 149
Argonauts of 1776, 275

Aristocracies, 101–2; John Adams on, 138; TJ on, 166, 171; military, TJ on, 154
Armies: TJ on, 203; standing, 41
Art: Burke's theory of, 90; TJ on, 261
Articles of Confederation, see U. S. Articles of Confederation
Astronomy, 272–3
Atheism, 136, 143
Autobiography, TJ's, 285

Baltimore, TJ in, 7
Bank of England, 108
Bank of United States, 107, 111, 255; Hamilton's plan for, 108–9; TJ on, 109, 130; JM on, 109, 205, 254
Banks, national, 108
Barbé-Marbois, François, Marquis de, 24
Barbour, James, 193, 280
Barlow, Joel, 247
Beckeley, JM at, 162
Beckwith, Colonel, 114
Bennington, Vt., 115
Bill for Religious Freedom, see Virginia, Bill for Religious Freedom
Bill of Rights, see U. S. Bill of Rights; Virginia Bill of Rights
Bills of rights, 40, 74
Biographers, TJ's, JM aids, 285–6
Blackstone, Sir William, 263
Blätterman, George, 273
Blockade, 248
Bonaparte, see Napoleon I
Bonnycastle, Charles, 273
Books: TJ's, 17–18, 279–80; TJ's selection for JM, 15, 18–19; scientific, 19
Bounties, TJ and JM on, 133
Brant, Irving, biography of JM, viii
Breckinridge, John, and Kentucky Resolutions, 185, 187–8, 201, 209
Bridges, Paine's, 82
British agents, 114
British debts, 158–9
British politics, Paine on, 84
Brown, Thomas, 274
Buffon, George Louis Leclerc, Comte de, 68–9
Burgoyne, General John, 116

i

Index